Feminist Scholars on the Road to Tenure

Feminist Scholars on the Road to Tenure

The Personal Is Professional

KATE RICHMOND, ISIS H. SETTLES, STEPHANIE A. SHIELDS, AND ALEXANDRA I. ZELIN

EDITORS

SAN DIEGO

Bassim Hamadeh, CEO and Publisher
Amy Smith, Senior Project Editor
Celeste Paed, Associate Production Editor
Emely Villavicencio, Senior Graphic Designer
Kylie Bartolome, Licensing Coordinator
Natalie Piccotti, Director of Marketing
Kassie Graves, Senior Vice President, Editorial
Jamie Giganti, Director of Academic Publishing

Copyright © 2023 by Cognella, Inc. All rights reserved. No part of this publication may be reprinted, reproduced, transmitted, or utilized in any form or by any electronic, mechanical, or other means, now known or hereafter invented, including photocopying, microfilming, and recording, or in any information retrieval system without the written permission of Cognella, Inc. For inquiries regarding permissions, translations, foreign rights, audio rights, and any other forms of reproduction, please contact the Cognella Licensing Department at rights@cognella.com.

Trademark Notice: Product or corporate names may be trademarks or registered trademarks and are used only for identification and explanation without intent to infringe.

Cover image copyright © 2018 iStockphoto LP/boule13.

Printed in the United States of America.

To feminist academics, past, present, and future.

Brief Contents

Acknowledgments xv

CHAPTER 1   Guideposts to Achieving Tenure as a Feminist Scholar 1
     Kate Richmond, Isis H. Settles, Stephanie A. Shields, and Alexandra I. Zelin

CHAPTER 2   The Promise and Perils of Conducting Feminist Research ... 11
     Jioni A. Lewis and Marlene G. Williams

CHAPTER 3   The Tenure Clock: Understanding Your Tenure Process and Pacing 23
     Leah R. Warner

CHAPTER 4   Building Your Invisible College 37
     Ying Tang

CHAPTER 5   Publishing 101: Manuscript Preparation and Navigating the Editorial Process 51
     Jan Yoder

CHAPTER 6   Publishing 102: Navigating the Peer Review Process 66
     Sarah J. Gervais and Kathryn J. Holland

CHAPTER 7   Developing a Research Program at a Teaching (Nonresearch) Institution 81
     Alexandra I. Zelin and Sahana Mukherjee

CHAPTER 8   Building a Lab at a Research-Intensive Institution: A Feminist and Sustainable Approach to Productivity 94
     Jes L. Matsick and Natalie J. Sabik

CHAPTER 9   Securing Grants 112
     Danielle Dickens and Katie M. Edwards

CHAPTER 10   Intersectional and Antiracist Pedagogy: Teaching as the Soul's Work 125
     Kim A. Case and S. Brooke Vick

CHAPTER 11   Resetting Dysfunctional Education Ecologies: Dealing With Marginalization in the Classroom 140
     Kat Klement, Jill Fish, and Sarah Cronin

CHAPTER 12 *Movidas*, Rage, and Last Chances on the Road to
Achieving Tenure With Community-Based Research 156
   Desdamona Rios

CHAPTER 13 Value-Driven Service and the Right to Say No 169
   NiCole T. Buchanan and Martinque K. Jones

CHAPTER 14 Cultivating Communities: A Feminist Reframing
of Networking Academia 185
   Dionne Stephens

CHAPTER 15 Another Country: Thriving Through the Travels
and Travails of Interdisciplinary Scholarship 200
   Patrick R. Grzanka and Elizabeth R. Cole

CHAPTER 16 That Tenured Feeling of "What Now?":
Recalibration, Power, and Focus 214
   Asia Eaton and Kim A. Case

CHAPTER 17 Conclusion: Your Success Is a Feminist Project 225
   *Isis H. Settles, Stephanie A. Shields,
   and Kate Richmond*

Index 231
About the Editors 235
About the Contributors 237

Detailed Contents

Acknowledgments xv

CHAPTER 1 Guideposts to Achieving Tenure as a Feminist Scholar 1
Kate Richmond, Isis H. Settles, Stephanie A. Shields, and Alexandra I. Zelin
What Is a Feminist Academic? 3
The Institutes for Academic Feminist Psychologists and Development of This Book 3
Themes in the Feminist Path to Tenure 5
Final Thoughts 8
References 9

CHAPTER 2 The Promise and Perils of Conducting Feminist Research 11
Jioni A. Lewis and Marlene G. Williams
Critical Reflexivity Statements 12
   Jioni 12
   Marlene 12
Strategies on How to Conduct Feminist Research 13
   Develop Intersectional Feminist Research Questions 13
   Embrace Mixed Methods and Methodological Flexibility 14
   Situate the Research in a Structural and Multilevel Analysis 14
   Engage in Critical Reflexivity and Cultivate Feminist Research Ethics 15
   Commitment to Social Justice and Empowerment 15
How to Navigate the Challenges of Conducting Feminist Research 16
   Cultivate a Feminist Mentorship Network 16
   Build Your Sister Circle of Support 17
   Resist Sexism and Push Back Against Dominant Research Paradigms 18
   Protect Your Energy if Your Public Scholarship Is Targeted 20
Conclusion 21
References 21

CHAPTER 3 The Tenure Clock: Understanding Your Tenure Process and Pacing 23
Leah R. Warner
Strategies and Tactics 24
   Understanding the Institution's Tenure Process 24
   Research and Scholarship Requirements 26
   Teaching Requirements 27

    Service Requirements ... 28
        Putting It All Together: Pacing and Work–Life Balance ... 30
    Recommendations for Institutions ... 32
    Resources ... 34
    References ... 35

CHAPTER 4   Building Your Invisible College ... 37
    Ying Tang
    The Origin and Conceptualization of an Invisible College ... 38
    The Need to Build an Invisible College ... 38
    Approaches and Strategies in Building an Invisible College ... 39
    Maintaining an Invisible College ... 44
    Issues and Challenges in Building an Invisible College ... 45
    Conclusion ... 46
    References ... 47

CHAPTER 5   Publishing 101: Manuscript Preparation and Navigating the Editorial Process ... 51
    Jan Yoder
    Manuscript Preparation ... 52
        Tips for Successful Writing ... 52
        Targeting a Specific Journal ... 55
    Navigating the Editorial Process ... 55
        Understanding the Review Process ... 56
        Successfully Revising a Paper ... 60
        The Importance of Reviewing ... 62
    Publishing Is for All of Us ... 64
    References ... 65

CHAPTER 6   Publishing 102: Navigating the Peer Review Process ... 66
    Sarah J. Gervais and Kathryn J. Holland
    Step 1: Submitting a High-Quality Paper to the Right Outlet ... 67
    Step 2: Tracking Your Article After Submission ... 71
    Step 3: Interpreting Decision Letters ... 72
    Step 4: Dealing With Negative Emotions During Peer Review ... 73
    Step 5: Revising and Resubmitting Manuscripts ... 76
    Step 6: Keeping Your Manuscripts Moving Along the Pathway ... 77
    Conclusion ... 80
    Reference ... 80

CHAPTER 7   Developing a Research Program at a Teaching (Nonresearch) Institution ... 81
    Alexandra I. Zelin and Sahana Mukherjee
    Who We Are ... 81
    General Tenure Requirements at Teaching-Focused Schools ... 82
    What Is Sufficient Research? ... 83
    I Know My Requirements. Now What? ... 85
    Working With Students ... 87
    Building Your Research Lab/Team ... 88

Protecting Your Research Time 91
Our Parting Advice 92
References 93

CHAPTER 8   Building a Lab at a Research-Intensive Institution: A Feminist and Sustainable Approach to Productivity   94
Jes L. Matsick and Natalie J. Sabik

Developing a Vision for Your Research Program 95
Allowing Your Vision to Take Shape Within the Constraints
   of Your Institution 96
Getting Started 96
Mentoring Students Within Your Lab 98
   Establishing Boundaries 98
   Mentoring Processes 99
   Mentorship for Yourself 100
Promoting a Feminist Lab Environment 101
   Collegiality 102
   Collaboration 104
Sustainability 106
   How to Create a Plan for Sustainable Research 106
   How to Create Sustainable Life–Work Integration 109
Conclusion 110
Suggested Resources 110
References 111

CHAPTER 9   Securing Grants   112
Danielle Dickens and Katie M. Edwards

Why Feminists Should Secure Grants 112
Positionality 113
   Danielle Dickens 113
   Katie Edwards 113
How to Start: Writing Your First Grant 114
   Start Small and Then Grow 114
   Deciding on a Project 114
   Study Funded Grants 115
   Who Can Help? 115
What's in a Grant Proposal? Understanding the Components
   of a Grant 117
   Specific Aims or Project Summary 117
   Project Narrative 118
   Other Components and Considerations 118
   Budget 118
   Timeline: Planning and Organizing Writing 119
Writing a Strong Grant Proposal 120
   Know Your Audience: Grant Reviewers 120
   Know the Review Criteria 121
   Make It Easy to Read 122
   Get Feedback on Your Proposal 122
Managing Rejection and Staying Motivated 123

Managing Grants 124
Recommended Resources 124

**CHAPTER 10 Intersectional and Antiracist Pedagogy:
Teaching as the Soul's Work 125**
Kim A. Case and S. Brooke Vick

Teaching as the Soul's Work 125
What We Mean by "Feminist Scholar" 126
Our Intersectional Identities and Impact on Teaching 127
    Kim's Social Location 127
    Brooke's Social Location 128
Our Intersectional Pedagogy Journeys 128
Feminist Pedagogy Means Intersectional and Antiracist Pedagogy 130
Growing Your Intersectional Pedagogy Skills 130
Inclusive Practices Do Not Equal Intersectionality 132
Critical Pedagogies and Your Career Journey 132
Strengthening Your Case for Promotion and Tenure 134
    Addressing Student Dissatisfaction 136
    Intersectional Pedagogy Is Inclusive 136
Curating Your Community 137
References 138

**CHAPTER 11 Resetting Dysfunctional Education Ecologies:
Dealing With Marginalization in the Classroom 140**
Kat Klement, Jill Fish, and Sarah Cronin

Our Positionality 141
Coping With Dysfunctional Education Ecologies 141
    Embracing Our Identities 142
    The Burden of Extra Labor 144
    Being Perceived as an Expert 148
The Challenges We Face Outside of the Classroom
  and Strategies for Coping 149
    Being a Target 149
    Building Supportive Networks 150
Challenging Oppressive Structures in Academia 151
Conclusions 152
Resources 153
References 153

**CHAPTER 12 *Movidas*, Rage, and Last Chances on the Road
to Achieving Tenure With Community-Based
Research 156**
Desdamona Rios

Learning From Our Elders 157
Overcoming Structural Barriers: The Role of *Movidas* and Rage 157
Context 159
    When a "Last Chance" Becomes a First Chance 159
    Developing a Trusting Relationship 160
    (Re)Socialization From the Academy to the Community.
      And Back 162

(Im)Practical Outcomes	163
Social Support While on the Tenure Track	163
Classroom Without Borders	164
Back to *Movidas*	165
Final Reflections	167
References	167

CHAPTER 13   Value-Driven Service and the Right to Say No   169
NiCole T. Buchanan and Martinque K. Jones

Author's Values and Positionality to This Work	169
Service and the Raced-Gendered Context of the Ivory Tower	170
Risk of Not Enacting Your Values	171
Value Driven or Not: Narratives From Black Women Faculty	172
Marti's Story: "Congratulations, You've Been Elected to Serve on the Diversity Committee!"	172
NiCole's Story: "If I Don't Do It, Who Will? I Am the Only One Here …"	174
Six Tips for Prioritizing and Enacting Your Values	175
Tips and Tricks for Saying No	180
Resources	182
References	183

CHAPTER 14   Cultivating Communities: A Feminist Reframing of Networking Academia   185
Dionne Stephens

Reconceptualize Networking Meanings	187
Restructuring Networking Strategies	188
Reassess Your Target Spaces	190
Maintain the Momentum	195
Concluding Thoughts	196
References	197

CHAPTER 15   Another Country: Thriving Through the Travels and Travails of Interdisciplinary Scholarship   200
Patrick R. Grzanka and Elizabeth R. Cole

A Strengths-Based Approach to Interdisciplinary Careers	203
Preparing for an Interdisciplinary Job	204
Making the Interdisciplinary Job Work	206
On the Dividends of Interdisciplinary Travel	212
References	212

CHAPTER 16   That Tenured Feeling of "What Now?": Recalibration, Power, and Focus   214
Asia Eaton and Kim A. Case

Our Intersectional Social Locations	215
Celebrate and Relax	215
Lean Into Your Power	216
Your Justice Work as a Tenured Feminist Scholar	217
Which Justice? Whose Justice?	217

  Advocate and Amplify ... 217
   Curate Your Service ... 219
 Recalibrate and Refocus ... 220
 Our Wishes for You ... 222
 Resources ... 223
 References ... 223

CHAPTER 17   **Conclusion: Your Success Is a Feminist Project** ... 225
  Isis H. Settles, Stephanie A. Shields, and Kate Richmond
 Academic Life After Tenure ... 225
 How Is Life as Professor Different From Life as Associate Professor? ... 227
 How Is Working Toward Professor Different From Working Toward Tenure? ... 228
 Your Success Is a Feminist Project ... 229
 Not-So Final Words ... 230
 Reference ... 230

Index ... 231
About the Editors ... 235
About the Contributors ... 237

Acknowledgments

There is a famous proverb that says "it takes a village to raise a child." Well, it takes a village, and in our case, an invisible college (Chapter 4) to create, sustain, and advance the feminist project in higher education. Our original inspiration was the need for feminist support within the broad and often-fragmented landscape of our discipline of psychology. In psychology and other disciplines, we have seen feminist scholarship grow to be stronger and more productive with each passing decade. Yet, today we are at a crucial point in the further development of academic feminist scholarship. On the one hand, there are a substantial number of academic scholars who identify as feminist researchers, teachers, and practitioners. On the other, these individuals are often the only or one of very few at their institution. And the ground continually shifts in terms of how their work is received.

This book grew out of the work of what began as a task force of the 2011–2012 SPW president (Stephanie Shields) and then developed into the Committee on Academic Feminist Psychologists of APA Division 35 (Society for the Psychology of Women; SPW). We want to first thank SPW for their support of this important project. We are especially grateful to SPW's Publications Committee for encouraging us to produce the book, especially Peggy Signorella, 2017–2018 SPW president, who was an enthusiastic supporter from the get-go and who linked us with our publisher, Cognella.

We are deeply grateful to the many academic feminist psychologists with whom we have worked since 2011. Their efforts have culminated in this book. We first and foremost acknowledge the 120 participants in our (so far) three Institutes for Academic Feminist Psychology who showed us the usefulness a book like ours could have. We are also grateful to invited plenary speakers at each institute who covered the range of topics needed in a guide to tenure and who inspired us to think broadly about how to make the book contents as expansive and inclusive as we could. We also thank past and present members of the Committee on Academic Feminist Psychologists who worked to ensure the success of the institutes on which this book is based and encouraged us to publish a book version of the institute content. We also thank participants in conference panels we have organized who have helped to continue and deepen this important network.

CHAPTER 1

Guideposts to Achieving Tenure as a Feminist Scholar

- **Kate Richmond**
  Muhlenberg College

- **Isis H. Settles**
  University of Michigan

- **Stephanie A. Shields**
  Pennsylvania State University

- **Alexandra I. Zelin**[1]
  University of Tennessee at Chattanooga

We begin by telling you something that you probably already know: The long road to tenure for scholars who identify as feminist is challenging. Although diversity continues to increase among academics, the feminist goal of achieving equitable representation is far from being realized. The problem of the slow pace of progress combined with continuing inequities is particularly acute for scholars with multiple marginalized identities. Because mainstream academic disciplines continue to ignore and/or minimize feminist methodological and theoretical contributions (e.g., Settles et al., 2020), feminist academics are at risk of being marginalized or isolated. This isolation can make the time before tenure feel particularly overwhelming. After all, the beginning of your career is a time when your research and teaching direction, pace, professional style, and focus are evolving alongside decisions around personal relationships and family planning, and when pressures of evaluation by students and colleagues can have a disproportionate influence on your teaching, scholarship, and service, and, in turn, tenure.

---

1. Authors are listed in alphabetical order. Each contributed equally to the ideas and preparation of this chapter.

It is against this landscape, in the past several years, that grassroot groups (e.g., Academics for Black Survival and Wellness; #blackintheivory; Malisch et al., 2020) are calling for a review and revision of all aspects in higher education that reinforce oppressive systems. You may already be participating in such initiatives, and, even if not, your desire to see real change occur will pull you in. We are also keenly aware that you must continually weigh individualized goals (that are most often highly rewarded) with collective goals (that are often associated with invisible forms of labor) as you work toward tenure. This is no easy task.

Our goal for this book is to share the wisdom offered by feminist academics from across career stages who have learned effective strategies to approach the three demands of academic life—scholarship, teaching, and service—and how to succeed in meeting those demands in a socially just and personally enriching way. We address individual needs and institutional change using an intersectional framework and specifically focus on early career professionals (although the advice is likely beneficial for faculty at all career stages). We believe that your professional needs, and those of all feminist academics, are connected to larger changes that must occur within academia. In this way, *the professional is political.*

Everyone who has contributed to this book is doing so with the goal of helping you achieve tenure, flourish in your career, and work toward making the academic workplace, and society generally more equitable and just. That is, we all want to enable you to have your research, teaching, and service be, in the words of feminist foremother Naomi Weisstein (1993), "activist, challenging, badass feminist" scholarship (p. 244). Contributors weave autobiographical narratives into practical strategies to counter the "I am alone" feeling that you might have, especially pre-tenure. Our contributors' stories show the many forms resilience and resistance take as well as lessons learned along the way.

Even more important, though, our contributors offer you community and ideas about how you can intentionally develop and commit to your invisible college. The term *invisible college* was first coined in the 17th century to describe the sustained connections among a group of scientists, known as the Royal Society (Chapter 4, this volume). Members of this group were not institutionally or formally connected. Rather, their sustained informal patterns of communications promoted productivity, intellectual engagement, and psychological support. These networks emerged when there was a need to share psychological, financial, and intellectual resources. The collective power of sharing and trust building was core to the foundation of all the members' success. Although you may feel alone in your institution, we believe the reciprocal benefit of an invisible college can help you both achieve your professional goals *and* advance feminist goals of achieving equity.

What Is a Feminist Academic?

There are many definitions of feminism, and we choose to go with one that can be incorporated into the widest set of definitions. Put simply, we think of feminist academics as individuals who embrace the view that political, economic, personal, and social equality should not be limited by gender and bring that view to inform their professional activities and career goals. Within that definition, we specifically focus on feminism's efforts to promote equity and positive social change through action. As feminism has evolved over the past 2 centuries (though feminism has far, far deeper roots), it has increasingly acknowledged the interrelation of advancing all women's and girls' rights and the rights of all marginalized peoples as well as a commitment to using feminist agendas to promote broader social change. In the context of research, teaching, and service at the postsecondary level, feminist academic work strives to level unlevel playing fields, make visible unacknowledged structural systems of inequity, discover or recover research topics and pedagogical practices that open that space of learning and research to a wider audience, and foster positive social change in communities beyond the work environment. In psychology, significant recent publications show the breadth and depth of feminist research and teaching over the past 2 decades and how feminist psychologists can make a difference (e.g., Dess et al., 2018; Fenstermaker & Stewart, 2020; Flores-Niemann et al., 2012; Newton & Bookwalla, 2022; Roberts et al., 2016; Travis & White, 2017).

The Institutes for Academic Feminist Psychologists and Development of This Book

One of the vehicles that can support feminist scholars and create and maintain links between researchers as diverse as the feminisms they represent is community. The formation of community through the creation of an invisible college was the driving force behind the Institutes for Academic Feminist Psychologists (hereafter referred to as "the Institutes"). This book stems from the Institutes and reflects our desire to expand our invisible college of feminist scholars to include you. And although the Institutes were developed for feminist psychologists, as part of the Society for the Psychology of Women (American Psychological Association, Division 35), we believe all feminist academics can benefit from the shared wisdom of our invisible college.

The Institutes were born of the Task Force on Academic Feminist Psychologists appointed by Stephanie Shields, then president of the Society for the Psychology of Women, to promote and encourage mentoring and networking among early career academic feminist psychologists.[2] The 2-day meetings of the Institutes, held in 2012, 2016, and 2018, embraced the goals of feminist professional spaces. At all three meetings, participants were exposed to a wealth of academic and practical knowledge shared by keynote speakers, and in panel presentations and breakout sessions. Topics concerned best practices for scholarship, teaching, and service—and how to effectively balance them regardless of home institution—through the lens of academic feminism. Participants in the Institute meetings gained a solid sense of community, support, and empowerment that, later maintained through social media and future gatherings, would not have been possible without initial face-to-face interaction.

An explicit goal of the Institutes was to empower and support early career scholars in their pursuit of tenure in academia, fostering a network that enables them to collaborate with, support, and advocate for each other. We focused on supporting tenure because it is a central means for achieving increased job security, institutional power, academic freedom, and an effective voice in the academy. A strong community of tenured academic feminist psychologists enables the continuation of impactful feminist research, institutional change, and social justice work. The Institutes are one of the few spaces for early career feminists to gather in large numbers to network and strategize around career development, collaboration, and leadership within academic contexts. They fill a specific and critical niche in creating and consolidating feminist community. The community fostered at the meetings was intended to outlast the meetings themselves, to help create a new generation of academic feminist psychologists.

Because we saw the ways in which the Institutes contributed to the careers of those who participated, we wanted to share those insights with you through this book. Stephanie, Kate, and Isis organized the three Institutes that have occurred to date, and Alex participated in the third Institute, after which she reached out to get involved in planning future Institutes and collaborating in our larger mission to support academic feminists. As four feminist scholars who range in demographic status, rank, institution type, and area of scholarship,[3] we know from our varied academic and

---

2. Chaired by Isis Settles and Kate Richmond, and with the invaluable on-site organization by Division 35's then-secretary Kathryn Anderson, the first Institute was held in January 2012. The second Institute (organized by Nicola Curtin, Asia Eaton, Nicola Newton, Richmond, Settles, and Shields) was held in early March 2016, and the third Institute took place in May 2018 (organized by Ying Tang, Dionne Stephens, Eaton, Settles, Richmond, and Shields).
3. Alex is a recently tenured associate professor of psychology at the University of Tennessee at Chattanooga (a teaching-focused institution), where she studies women's workplace mistreatment. Kate is a clinician and professor of psychology and director of women and gender studies at Muhlenberg College (a liberal arts college) where she studies how social identity influences mental health outcomes. Isis is a professor of psychology and Afro-American and African studies at the University of Michigan (a research-intensive university) where she studies experiences of mistreatment among

life experiences that supporting future generations of feminist scholars is critically important to the strength of our institutions, the academy, and even society.

Themes in the Feminist Path to Tenure

With the larger goal of supporting early career feminists along the path to tenure, there were five themes that emerged from planning the Institutes and that inform organization of this book: (a) providing feminist scholars with an honest awareness of the field and the state of higher education; (b) using self-knowledge and reflexivity to shape career-related decisions; (c) developing community and collaboration; (d) incorporating a social justice perspective that includes the ability to envision a different academia; and (e) learning strategies and tools to support career advancement. We asked contributors to consider each of these themes as they planned their chapters and to consider sharing how they use each of these themes themselves in their own academic journey. We see these themes as core features of what it takes for feminist academics to successfully achieve tenure while meeting both their individualized personal and professional goals and our collective goals to create positive social change.

Providing feminist scholars with an honest awareness of the field and the state of higher education. To move through an academic career, to thrive and not just survive, you must have a clear understanding of how academia works. This includes an awareness of what constitutes "good" teaching, research, and service; how productivity and success are defined and measured; and the norms and expectations that may be widely held in your field. At the same time, the criteria for success in each of these areas are often unstated, and there are unwritten rules of how things are done. In this book, our contributors share the honest (and sometimes ugly) truth about making a career in academia.

As a feminist scholar, you are an "outsider within" (Collins, 1986, p. 14). You are part of the academic system by the nature of your role as a faculty member, but you sit with conditional acceptance and inclusion as a feminist scholar. Such a position provides you with the unique ability to see the status quo and question the policies, practices, and norms which, to many others, seem natural, logical, and right. Understanding the academic system and being part of it does not require you to accept it without question. Rather, through this lens of an outsider within, you can work toward change by

---

members of marginalized groups. Stephanie is an emeritx professor of psychology and women's, gender, and sexuality studies at Pennsylvania State University (a research-intensive university) where she studies gender and emotion, interventions to promote gender equity, and the history of the psychology of women and gender.

bringing feminist values and practices to the table. But first you need to have an honest awareness of how things are—*for now*.

In the upcoming chapters our contributors discuss how to succeed within these "conventional" aspects of academia when your research, teaching, and service are uniquely feminist. For example, Warner (Chapter 3) starts with placing our collective advice within the context of managing the ever-ticking tenure clock. Yoder (Chapter 5) and Gervais and Holland (Chapter 6) share their intimate knowledge of the publishing process to help you be successful in what is a critical step in the road to tenure and promotion. Zelin and Mukherjee (Chapter 7) share insights on how to successfully publish while also maintaining a high teaching load, and Dickens and Edwards (Chapter 9) reveal some of the hidden curriculum that influences obtaining research funding. Klement, Fish, and Cronin (Chapter 11) discuss how oppressive structures have led to marginalization within the classroom. After all, our goal is to help you navigate your way to tenure and beyond: Your success as a feminist teacher and scholar is itself a way to change academia!

Using self-knowledge and reflexivity to make career-related decisions. Feminist scholarship has long been characterized by an emphasis on reflexivity, that is, "taking stock" of one's own assumptions and how they have shaped one's research and practice, as well as shaped the field. But just as you can reflect on your position relative to your research participants, students, and the communities you study and teach about, you can engage in self-reflection about your career path. The awareness of your relative access, power, and privilege as they relate to your professional position can importantly combine with your personal and scholarly values to inform your career-related decisions. Self-reflection and reflexivity are not always prioritized in academic settings, although engaging in them can often provide self-insights into how to navigate one's careers. Contributors have included reflection questions for you to consider to enhance your own reflexivity. You will also see how authors engaged in self-reflection at key moments in their career and the way their own self-analyses shaped their way forward.

For example, Matsick and Sabik (Chapter 8) describe how feminist values can be implemented through the practices and norms you use in your research lab. Buchanan and Jones (Chapter 13) discuss how to make decisions about professional service in ways that are informed by one's own values and the change you want to see. Grzanka and Cole (Chapter 15) reflect on their professional journeys as interdisciplinary scholars with an understanding of their own values as well as the different values of the disciplines to which they are most connected. Finally, Eaton and Case (Chapter 16) consider how the achievement of tenure offers a new position from which to think about personal and professional goals, and greater freedom to pursue priorities. Then, with promotion to professor, you have an even greater opportunity to challenge institutional barriers and broader opportunities to realize your scholarly and pedagogical values.

Developing community and collaboration. Given our aim of creating an invisible college, it will be no surprise that we see the development of communities and collaborations as essential to your success as a feminist scholar. Members of our invisible college can push us to further our scholarship and teaching, share resources and expertise from their past experiences, and provide social and emotional support. Moreover, a feminist invisible college will be uniquely able to understand and be mindful of relational power dynamics, and to see the structural barriers and challenges of academia.

An additional role of your invisible college is to help you broadly disseminate your work, which also means that our research is more likely to become a part of important public conversations. As Rios discusses in Chapter 12, there are many different arenas and products of collaboration—community partnerships, research collaborations, joint symposia, and exchange of teaching ideas and materials. Stephens (Chapter 14) underscores that building networks and ensuring that one's work is well publicized serves feminist goals. Social and professional networks provide a platform to potentially promote other feminists' scholarship, along with having allies in the field who will amplify you and your career, both of which serve to increase awareness of your professional contributions as well as your feminist scholarship. Thus, feminist exchanges, importantly, can occur across disciplines and with colleagues outside of higher education.

Incorporating a social justice perspective that includes the ability to envision a different academia. As Yoder (Chapter 5) points out, the "so what?" question is imperative to the work we do. Academic feminists are a diverse group of scholars, but a unifying thread among us is our commitment to enacting feminist values in research, teaching, and service, including conducting scholarship in service of social change. Many of us do the work we do to apply our expertise to the pressing social issues of the day. If we do not work to make our findings public and do not develop the skills to do so, we run the risk of our scholarship withering on the vine. Even if we inform other social and behavioral scientists and feminist colleagues in women's, gender, and sexuality studies, we do not want our work to exist only in the narrow confines of academia. We must continue to develop means to ensure that we answer the "so what?" question so that people whose lives are affected (whether negatively or positively) by the issues we study can benefit from our answers.

In addition to broad social change, many feminist scholars seek to change the academy. In her 2014 Carolyn Wood Sherif address on transformational moments in the history of feminist psychology, Stephanie Shields (2015) observed that "transformation is about finding and using social spaces where we can be disruptive *and* constructive simultaneously" (p. 149; emphasis in original), that is, challenge the *status quo* while also creating inclusive and effective alternatives. For instance, Lewis and Williams (Chapter 2) discuss how they have incorporated intersectionality into their feminist research and why it is imperative to continued research progression within any field. Case and Vick (Chapter 10), give examples of ways that we can incorporate intersectionality into our own classrooms, regardless of our content, thereby demonstrating that recognition of identity is important. They also show how you might incorporate social change at multiple levels (e.g., academy, society) in your academic career and still get tenure.

Learning strategies and tools to support career advancement. It is not enough to know *what* to do to be successful as a feminist scholar, you also need to know *how* to do it. As your invisible college grows and expands, so will your access to the strategies and tools that others have used to their advantage. The feminist values of interconnection, cooperation, and equity exhort us to share our lessons learned and to improve circumstances for the future generations of feminist scholars. Thus, throughout this book our contributors emphasize the *how*—tips, tricks, tools, and strategies that will support your feminist research, teaching, and service. We recognize that you already have a wealth of skills to support your career; our aim is to add to your toolbox. And we only ask that you pay it forward to your colleagues and students.

Final Thoughts

We want to end by emphasizing that this book is meant to be the beginning. It is one resource in your toolbox. When you are ready to think about what comes after tenure, read our final chapter (Settles, Shields, and Richmond, Chapter 17) where we start the conversation about preparing for promotion to professor. We have drawn on the experiences and expertise of feminist colleagues, most of whom are further along than you in their professional journey. And, typically, when we think of mentoring, we do look to people who have already traveled the road we are on. As several of our contributors remind us (e.g., Stephens, Chapter 14; Tang, Chapter 4), our early career peers form a crucial part of our support system. We often think of sharing our travails with peers simply as a way to manage stress and gain important emotional support. But peers are the foundation of one's Invisible College, people who are figuring it out as they go along, just as you are. Another critical tool is face-to-face community building and providing instrumental and emotional support to scholars early in their careers, such as that offered by the Institutes.

As a last word we want to remind you of one more important set of mentors. Our history as feminists in academe is often overlooked as a source of mentoring. The struggles that you face—having one's work taken seriously, making a positive difference in the structures and processes within academe and in our larger communities, figuring out a way to have one's personal values inform how they meet professional demands, and more—have faced feminist scholars and scientists even before women were first admitted to graduate study in the United States in the 1880s.

Feminist psychology, for example, from its earliest versions has been a project concerned with social change (e.g., Johnston & Johnson, 2008; Rutherford et al., 2010). In addition, examination of history can inform our understanding of contemporary social and scientific problems and debates (e.g., Shields, 2007, 2016; see also Rutherford, 2013). You can learn from interviews with feminist activists through the Global Feminisms Project (https://sites.lsa.umich.edu/globalfeminisms/). And a great place to find mentors from the inception of psychology to the present is feministvoices.com, established and maintained by feminist historian of psychology, Alexandra Rutherford. It is a rich source for learning about feminist academic psychologists, from the 19th century to the present. If you believe knowledge is power, then knowledge of history is a powerful tool, indeed.

We wish you all the best on your pathway to tenure and beyond. And never forget that the feminists who came before you, those who are your colleagues now, and those following you, are with you every step of the way. Call on us!

Acknowledgment: We would like to acknowledge Nicola Curtin and Nicky Newton for their contributions to early thinking on ideas presented in this chapter.

References

Collins, P. H. (1986). Learning from the Outsider Within: The Sociological Significance of Black Feminist Thought. *Social Problems, 33*(6), S14–S32. https://doi.org/10.2307/800672

Dess, N. K., Marecek, J., & Bell, L. C. (Eds.). (2018). *Gender, sex, and sexualities: Psychological perspectives*. Oxford University Press.

Fenstermaker, S., & Stewart, A. J. (Eds.), (2020). *Gender, considered: Feminist reflections across the social sciences*. Macmillan/Palgrave.

Flores-Niemann, Y., Harris, A., González, C. & Gutiérrez y Muhs. G. (Eds.), (2012). *Presumed incompetent: The intersections of race and class for women in academia*. Utah State University Press.

Johnston, E., & Johnson, A. (2008). Searching for the second generation of American women psychologists. *History of Psychology, 11*(1), 40–72. https://doi.org/10.1037/1093-4510.11.1.40

Malisch, J. L., Harris, B. N., Sherrer, S. M., Lewis, K. A., Shepherd, S. L., Pumtiwitt, C., McCarthy, J. L. S., Karam, E. P, Moustaid-Moussa, N., McCrory, J., Calarco, L., Talley, A. E., Canas-Carrell, J. E., Ardon-Dryer, K., Weiser, D. A., Bernal, X. E., & Deitloff, J. (2020). Opinion: In the wake of COVID-19, academia needs new solutions to ensure gender equity. *Proceedings of the National Academy of Sciences, 117*(27), 15378–15381. https://doi.org/10.1073/pnas.2010636117

Newton, N., & J. Bookwalla, J. (Eds.). (2022). *Reflections from pioneering women in psychology.* Cambridge University Press.

Roberts, T. A., Curtin, N., Duncan, L. & Cortina, L. (Eds.). (2016). *Feminist perspectives on building a better psychological science of gender.* Springer.

Rutherford, A. (Ed.). (2013). Teaching diversity: What can history offer? *History of Psychology, 16*(4), 1–5. https://doi.org/10.1037/a0034368

Rutherford, A., Vaughn-Blount, K., & Ball, L. C. (2010). Responsible opposition, disruptive voices: Science, social change, and the history of feminist psychology. *Psychology of Women Quarterly, 34*(4), 460–473. https://doi.org/10.1111/j.1471-6402.2010.01596.x

Settles, I. H., Warner, L. R., Buchanan, N. T., & Jones, M. K. (2020). Understanding psychology's resistance to intersectionality theory using a framework of epistemic exclusion and invisibility. *Journal of Social Issues, 76*(4), 796–813. https://doi.org/10.1111/josi.12403

Shields, S. A. (2007). Passionate men, emotional women: Psychology constructs gender difference in the late 19th century. *History of Psychology, 10,* 92–110. https://doi.org/10.1037/1093-4510.10.2.92

Shields, S. A. (2015). Transformational moments in feminist psychology. *Psychology of Women Quarterly, 39,* 1–8. https://doi.org/10.1177/0361684315574502

Shields, S. A. (2016). Functionalism, Darwinism, and intersectionality: How an intersectional perspective reveals issues of power, inequality, and legitimacy in psychological science. *Feminism & Psychology, 26,* 353–365. https://doi.org/10.1177/0959353516655371

Travis, C., & White, J. W. (Eds.). (2017). *American Psychological Association handbook on the psychology of women.* American Psychological Association.

Weisstein, N. (1993). Power resistance and science: A call for a revitalized feminist psychology. *Feminism & Psychology, 3,* 239–245. https://doi.org/10.1177/0959353593032011

CHAPTER 2

The Promise and Perils of Conducting Feminist Research

- **Jioni A. Lewis**
  University of Maryland, College Park

- **Marlene G. Williams**
  Texas Woman's University

In the current sociopolitical climate, feminist research is needed now more than ever to help us solve many social problems in the world, such as patriarchy, sexism, racism, white supremacy, heterosexism, capitalism, ableism, religious intolerance, and xenophobia (Collins, 2019). Historically, feminist research exposed sexism and patriarchy in knowledge production across a range of disciplines, which led to a challenge to the traditional research paradigm of positivism and assumptions about a universal truth that can be measured using the scientific method (Hesse-Biber, 2012). Given this, feminist research is inherently critical of patriarchal systems and thus requires moving beyond traditional research methodologies. Feminist research requires a process of critical self-reflexivity, which provides a deeper and more critical connection to the research and challenges one's own positionality in the research endeavor. Feminist research also has a commitment to the empowerment of women (Hesse-Biber, 2012). Feminist research inspires individuals to conduct meaningful scholarship that can seek to critically analyze and disrupt interlocking systems of power, privilege, and oppression. Feminist research also has an explicit focus on social justice and emphasizes the importance of using research to make an impact and implement social change at multiple levels in society, from the individual, community, and institutional/structural level (Collins, 2019; Riger, 2016).

In this chapter, we discuss the promises and perils of conducting feminist research. First, we share our personal and professional positionalities as a way to model critical reflexivity. Next, we discuss strategies on how to conduct feminist research, with a specific focus on intersectional feminist research. Then, we discuss some tips on how to navigate the challenges of conducting feminist research in academia.

Critical Reflexivity Statements

A researcher's background, sociocultural identities, and social locations cannot be separated from their approach to the research process (Cole, 2020; Hesse-Biber & Piatelli, 2012). Thus, first we think it is important to share our positionalities to contextualize our approach to conducting feminist research and to better situate the information we share in this chapter.

Jioni

My identities as a Black, cisgender, heterosexual woman, and first-generation college graduate, have shaped my gendered racial identity development and Black feminist consciousness both personally and professionally. My positionality is inextricably linked to my identity as a Black woman and my experiences with interlocking systems of racism, sexism, and classism. I am a tenured associate professor of counseling psychology at a large, public land-grant research-intensive university. I have over 10 years of experience in qualitative, quantitative, and mixed-methods research in the areas of racism, sexism, intersectionality, gendered racial identity, and Black women's health. My identity as a Black feminist psychologist serves as the foundation of my research and praxis, which centers on an understanding that Black women have a unique standpoint, as well as unique experiences, knowledge, and wisdom based on our race and gender that cannot be teased apart.

Marlene

My identities as a cisgender, heterosexual, middle-class Black woman are most salient to me and have played important roles in my academic journey. I am a tenure-track assistant professor at a feminist counseling psychology graduate program at a medium-sized public university in Texas. My research broadly applies Black feminist and intersectionality frameworks to exploring the gendered racial identity development and mental health of Black women. I have navigated both predominantly white spaces and predominantly Black spaces in different contexts. I am writing this section from a unique position having been the graduate student mentee of Jioni, the first author of this chapter, who has been an integral source of my identity development as a Black woman in academia. Support through mentorship in the academy and seeking feminist academic spaces have helped me navigate challenges with integrating my Black feminist research agenda within feminist academic spaces that are not explicitly Black feminist. Thus, my Black feminist and intersectional research experience inform much of the positionality and perspective I share in this chapter.

Strategies on How to Conduct Feminist Research

Drawing on our feminist values and positionalities, we chose to share some strategies we have found helpful when conducting feminist research, particularly intersectional feminist research. As Black feminist scholars, we employ Black feminist thought (Collins, 2000) as an epistemological framework in our research, which is centered on Black women's unique standpoint and challenges white, Eurocentric constructions of knowledge production. In addition, we conduct intersectional feminist research by applying an intersectional analysis throughout the research process as a paradigm to illuminate interlocking systems of oppression, power, and privilege (Cole, 2009; Crenshaw, 1989). Next, we offer five strategies on how you can engage in the process of conducting feminist research. Throughout this section, we use one of our own qualitative studies (Williams & Lewis, 2021), which explored gendered racial identity development and meaning making among Black women, as an example of how we employed each of these strategies in our own feminist research.

Develop Intersectional Feminist Research Questions

Feminist researchers often seek to ask questions that can explore new knowledge or experiences that have been marginalized (Hesse-Biber, 2012). Thus, the key to feminist research is to move beyond a focus on gender as a singular identity and shift toward a more complex understanding of gender and the role of sexism, patriarchy, and structural inequality in the lives of women from various racial, ethnic, cultural backgrounds and marginalized identities. For us, this involves grounding the research in an intersectional analysis throughout the research process, from the framing of the research questions to the types of research methods that are employed, to data collection and analysis and the interpretation of the findings (Bowleg, 2008; Cho et al., 2013; Lewis & Grzanka, 2016). For example, in our study (Williams & Lewis, 2021), we were intentional about the way we framed our research questions as well as the wording of our specific interview questions to ensure we were asking about participants' experiences as *Black women*, rather than asking them about their race and gender separately. For instance, one of the interview questions asked participants, "What does it mean for you to identify as a Black woman?" This way, we focused on participants' intersectional identities based on race and gender simultaneously. In addition, we also asked participants about their experiences of oppression at the intersection of race and gender to move beyond the notion that intersectionality is just about identities since it is important to connect our identities to interlocking systems of oppression and power.

Embrace Mixed Methods and Methodological Flexibility

Historically, feminist research has focused on challenging dominant narratives about who can be producers of knowledge and critiquing the idea of objectivity in research (Bowleg, 2008; Hesse-Biber, 2012; Shields, 2008). Although many of us as psychologists have been trained to primarily utilize quantitative research methods, we think it's important to have some methodological flexibility and be open to multiple research methods. Thus, we encourage feminist researchers to embrace utilizing both qualitative and quantitative research methods to better illuminate the role of sexism and interlocking systems of oppression on the lives of women, particularly women who exist at the margins (Else-Quest & Hyde, 2016; Lewis & Grzanka, 2016; Watson-Singleton et al., 2021). For example, after developing a conceptual framework of Black women's gendered racial identity development based on our qualitative findings (Williams & Lewis, 2021), we are now in the process of developing a quantitative scale to assess the developmental process and gendered racial ideologies that emerged from the data. This measure will allow us to expand the empirical quantitative research on gendered racial identity development. Thus, it can be beneficial to have methodological flexibility as a researcher to expand our understanding of a particular phenomenon under investigation (Watson-Singleton et al., 2021).

Situate the Research in a Structural and Multilevel Analysis

As feminist scholars, we also think it's important to situate your research in a sociocultural, structural, and multilevel analysis of oppression. We know that structural sexism and interlocking systems of oppression influence the lived experiences of our research participants, so it is important to interpret findings within this context. For example, in our study of Black women's gendered racial identity development (Williams & Lewis, 2021), one finding that emerged from the data was that Black women's experiences of gendered racism served as critical encounters that were integral to their increased awareness of their race and gender as Black women throughout their identity development. Thus, rather than try to tease apart or separate experiences of gendered racism from identity development, we highlighted the key role that experiences of gendered racism played in the process of gendered racial identity development for Black women, from the individual level through gendered racial microaggressions to the institutional level, such as experiences of gendered racial discrimination in schools, workplace environments, or society at large.

Engage in Critical Reflexivity and Cultivate Feminist Research Ethics

Feminist research praxis includes thoughtful consideration of research ethics, power, authority, and reflexivity in the context of feminist research (Hesse-Biber, 2012). One way we've learned to increase our awareness about issues of power and authority in the research process is through critical reflexivity. The process of critical reflexivity involves researchers identifying their positionality and acknowledging their multiple social identities and the interlocking systems of privilege and oppression that frame their research at every stage of the process, from the purpose of the research topic, development of the research questions, selection of the methods used, selection of data analyses, and interpretation of the findings (Cole, 2020; Hesse-Biber & Piatelli, 2012; Watson-Singleton et al., 2021). This practice challenges the myth of objectivity and neutrality in research and situates both the researcher and the participant in the research process (Cole, 2020; Collins, 2019). For example, during the process of conducting our qualitative study (Williams & Lewis, 2021), we utilized a grounded theory approach that assumes that researchers bring informed knowledge and awareness to the analytic process that interacts with the subjective realities of the participant data. We also utilized the technique of memo writing, which is a common technique to provide trustworthiness to our qualitative data (Charmaz, 2017; Levitt et al., 2017; Morrow, 2005). Our process of memo writing involved writing down notes on the previous knowledge and expertise we brought to the research, reflecting on our own gendered racial identity development and personal experiences of oppression, and noting any other reactions or perceptions we had about the research throughout the process. We encourage feminist researchers to continuously engage in critical reflexivity so that you can share the responsibility of ensuring that practices throughout the research process are aligned with the values of feminist research and social justice.

Commitment to Social Justice and Empowerment

As we've said, a primary goal of feminist research is a commitment to social justice and ensuring that research is being applied to solve social problems in the world (Cole, 2020; Collins, 2019; Rosenthal, 2016). It is important for feminist scholars to strive to conduct research that can seek social change and transformation to benefit the lives of women and dismantle sexism in society. As a feminist researcher, you can ask yourself how the findings or implications of your studies can inform public policy or lead to systemic change. In addition, you can try to develop interventions based on the findings of your research that can benefit the lives of women. For example, although our study of gendered racial identity development (Williams & Lewis, 2021) was not directly focused on systemic change, we have disseminated our research to the public, such as by incorporating our findings into public scholarship to educate the broader community about healthy Black women's identity development with the hope that our findings can support others engaging in public policy work. We have also applied our research to our clinical practice with Black women and girls to help them increase their gendered racial identity development and critical consciousness. At the heart of feminist research is also a commitment to the empowerment of women (Hesse-Biber, 2012). Another potential strategy is to empower women by inviting members from the community under investigation into the research process, such as through participatory action research or as stakeholders in hearing the dissemination of the results and providing iterative feedback throughout the research process (Watson-Singleton et al., 2021).

In summary, there are several ways to engage in feminist research, particularly intersectional feminist research. We encourage feminist scholars to ask intersectional research questions to uncover new knowledge about gender and sexism, particularly for individuals who experience multiple forms of marginalization. We also encourage early career feminist scholars to be open to mixed-methods research and to situate their research findings within a systems-level analysis. In addition, it is important for feminist researchers to engage in critical reflexivity to increase their awareness about power, privilege, and oppression throughout the research process. Lastly, feminist researchers have a strong commitment to social justice, so it is imperative that your feminist research seeks to critically analyze, disrupt, and dismantle sexism in society toward the goal of social transformation and social change. Next, we discuss strategies on how to navigate some of the challenges of conducting feminist research.

How to Navigate the Challenges of Conducting Feminist Research

Although we know the inherent value of our research as feminist scholars, we are likely to experience challenges in navigating academia on the path to promotion and tenure. Thus, we would like to share some tips on how to successfully navigate the challenges of conducting feminist research so that you can survive and thrive as a feminist scholar in academia.

Cultivate a Feminist Mentorship Network

Depending on the type of institution you are working in (e.g., research intensive, teaching institution, large public university, small liberal arts college), the size of your department will vary as well as the number of other faculty in your department who might be familiar with the type of research you do. In addition, it is common for any research focused on women to be marginalized in traditional psychology departments. Thus, many feminist scholars may be one of a few scholars in their department who share their feminist consciousness and critical lens on their research. Given this, it is important for early career feminist scholars to seek mentorship both within their department as well as outside of their department, college, or university to have support at multiple levels within and outside their institution.

Building your mentorship network is also important for when you go up for promotion and tenure. You want other faculty across campus to be familiar with the important and impactful research you're doing as a feminist scholar and support your work if they end up serving on your college- or university-level promotion and tenure committee. In addition, it is a good strategy to begin cultivating relationships with feminist scholars at other institutions who are familiar with and could speak favorably about your work and its contributions to the field if they are asked to write an external letter for you when you go up for tenure. Another helpful way to seek out feminist mentors in psychology is through getting involved in professional associations, such as the Society for the Psychology of Women (American Psychological Association, Division 35) or the Association for Women in Psychology. In addition, participating in professional research institutes, such as the Institute for Academic Feminist Psychologists, can help you cultivate a network of feminist mentors.

We view lifelong feminist mentorship as essential to survive and thrive in academia. Thus, it's important to continue to nurture the mentoring relationships you cultivated as a graduate student as you transition to a faculty position. For example, lifelong feminist mentorship was modeled to me (Jioni) by my mentor and advisor from graduate school, Dr. Helen A. Neville, who has continued to serve as a tremendous source of support as I navigated the challenges of obtaining tenure and promotion to associate professor at a research-intensive university. In addition, although my formal mentoring relationship with Marlene began when I was her graduate school advisor, we have continued our mentoring relationship as Marlene has transitioned to a tenure-track faculty position. We continue to collaborate on research together, work alongside each other as leaders in professional associations, and continue to meet regularly to provide support to each other as Black feminist scholars in academia. This type of lifelong feminist mentorship is essential to navigate the challenges of conducting feminist research on the tenure track.

Build Your Sister Circle of Support

It is also vital to build a broader sister circle of support and a community to survive and thrive as an academic feminist researcher. Building a broader community of support is in line with core feminist principles, which honor that we are relational beings. In graduate school, we both experienced the power of feminist community building, initially within our research teams of Black women. For example, as a graduate student I (Jioni) was fortunate enough to be trained in a research lab of mostly Black feminist scholars. Many of these women have become a part of my sister circle of support both within and outside of academia. Once I became an assistant professor and developed my own research lab, it was important for me to carry on a similar tradition of building a Black feminist research team, modeling how to cultivate a supportive and collaborative community of feminist scholars, and providing a nurturing space for feminist researchers to thrive. In graduate school I (Marlene) sought out supportive communities both within and outside of academia. Being involved in a research lab led by a Black woman and having a research lab of Black feminist scholars showed me the power of feminist community and support. I still have this tribe of support around me as I continue my journey of resistance as an assistant professor conducting feminist research.

In addition to building a supportive network within academia through a feminist research community, we also encourage you to actively seek out support outside of academia. It is important to develop a network of feminist women in your life to balance your resistance with rest. For example, I (Jioni) have been nurtured and supported through my circle of "sisterfriends" outside of academia to ensure that I don't forget my roots as a first-generation college graduate from a working-class background. Cultivating a community outside of academia can keep you grounded and can remind you about the larger importance of your feminist scholarship.

Resist Sexism and Push Back Against Dominant Research Paradigms

Along the path to promotion and tenure as an academic feminist psychologist, it is likely you will experience sexism and gender microaggressions, which may impact your feminist research. These experiences could occur within your department, college, or university as well as within the larger field of psychology. For example, we have experienced numerous incidents where our scholarship on gendered racial microaggressions has been dismissed or questioned in unprofessional ways at research conferences or by former colleagues or professors. For example, we've both experienced male psychologists challenging the legitimacy of our research on microaggressions by asking questions such as "How do you know microaggressions are real?" just because we have chosen to utilize qualitative methods that value the phenomenological experiences of Black women over utilizing an experimental design. We've often countered these attacks by citing the large body of research that supports the phenomena of microaggressions and the literature showing that dominant group members are often unaware of the ways they are perpetrators of microaggressions (Sue, 2010). Often, these exchanges support the theory and research on microaggressions, as our experiences have demonstrated that many of the individuals who critique our scholarship tend to be white and male and seem to question the objectivity of our work because we are Black and female.

At the core of these questions about the legitimacy of our research as feminist scholars is an assumption that we cannot be producers of knowledge (Collins, 2000). Given the history of epistemic exclusion and minimization of Black feminist scholarship in the field of psychology (Cole, 2020; Settles et al., 2020), we think an important strategy in how to navigate these challenges is to boldly push back against the dominant research paradigm. For example, when I (Marlene) was in graduate school, I was confronted by some professors in my classes who ascribed to dominant and patriarchal research methods, and I was publicly challenged in front of my classmates to defend the legitimacy of my feminist research on Black women. Through my mentoring relationship with Jioni, I have learned how to navigate academia as a feminist scholar through our regular mentoring meetings, which provided me space to process these experiences. She modeled how to effectively communicate the value of feminist research while pushing back against Eurocentric positivist research expectations. For example, she helped me hone my Black feminist research skills, which allowed me to boldly center Black women in my research and resist internalizing the narrative that I needed a white and/or male comparison group for my research to be more legitimate. I used these experiences as fuel to defend my work and resist Eurocentric and patriarchal research paradigms.

Our advice is to focus on conducting research that you are the most passionate about and stay true to yourself and your own sense of integrity in conducting your feminist research. For example, if you value qualitative research methods, then don't start trying to design experiments because you think your colleagues will respect you more if you do. The reality is they probably won't respect you more, because often these critiques about the legitimacy of feminist research are rooted in sexism and patriarchy. Also, make sure to publish in the journals that are the best fit for your research regardless of the prestige or impact factor of the journal. Of course, we know you must think about tenure and promotion, but it is important to push back against the narrative that a journal's impact factor is the most important metric to determine the value of your scholarship. For example, you could try to educate your department chair or tenure committee about the value of publishing your research in the journal that is the best for your work. We call on all academic feminist scholars to be bold in your vision about the contributions you want to make to your field and challenge the white supremacist, capitalist, patriarchal institutions that make you doubt the importance of your scholarship.

Protect Your Energy if Your Public Scholarship Is Targeted

Feminist scholars who are committed to social justice and want to disseminate your work broadly via social media, writing op-eds, and other forms of public scholarship, you unfortunately may run the risk of being targeted for your feminist scholarship. For example, when I (Jioni) was an assistant professor at a large public research university in the South, my research lab was targeted by a local conservative radio show host and "independent journalist" who initially invited me on his radio show to engage in a debate about microaggressions research. After I declined the interview, he continued to target and harass me by emailing me repeatedly to seek out information about my research lab, including the racial and ethnic identities of my research team, and how much public funding was being spent on my research. He then started contacting the university media and public relations office to get his questions answered using a Freedom of Information Act request. This harassment took place over the course of an academic year, and he ended up writing several negative blogs/op-eds about me and my work in the local newspaper.

I felt vulnerable as an untenured Black woman assistant professor. Although I received support from my department chair, the university administration was unaware of the larger systemic issues that contributed to these targeted attacks. I found myself being in the position of having to educate university leadership about the larger racist and sexist attacks that were happening nationwide to critical scholars, many of whom were early career women and faculty of color. One thing I chose to do during this time was push those in a position of power (e.g., university media and public relations office, legal/general counsel, the provost's office) to advocate for me and protect my scholarship. Thus, I chose to protect my energy and my peace during that time because I felt that it was more important for me to focus on my research and publishing rather than to waste my time and energy fighting white supremacist male patriarchy. Another strategy was to be transparent with my research team about what was happening to educate them about how to navigate the challenges they might face as Black feminist scholars in the future. Both of us have reflected on that experience and how it impacted us. For example, for me (Marlene), when our research was attacked by white supremacist patriarchy outside of academia, a sense of hypervigilance grew within me to further protect my research and resist against dominant narratives even harder. During that time, we both channeled Audre Lorde's powerful quote, "Caring for myself is not self-indulgence, it is self-preservation, and that is an act of political warfare." As feminist scholars, we know our work is inherently political, so when we engage in public scholarship, we are speaking truth to power, which will likely come with backlash. However, we encourage feminist scholars to continue to resist, disrupt, and dismantle white supremacist capitalist patriarchy through your research and scholar-activism.

In summary, although you might experience challenges as you navigate the process to tenure and promotion, it is important for you to remember the inherent power of your feminist research. So, please make sure to cultivate your feminist mentorship network, build your sister circle and "squad" of support, resist sexism and patriarchy, push back against the dominant research paradigm, and protect your energy against any haters, because your feminist scholarship is necessary to transform the academy.

Conclusion

In this chapter, we offered some practical advice on how to engage in the process of conducting feminist research so that you can be successful on the tenure track. We also shared some tips on how to navigate the challenges of conducting feminist research in academia. Our hope is that you realize how important your work is to the field of psychology and to transforming the academy. Feminist research can help to push historically white and male colleges and universities to truly embody their ideals of diversity, equity, and inclusion. It is important for you to remember that your feminist research is necessary to dismantle sexism, patriarchy, and interlocking systems of oppression in the academy. We need feminist scholars like you to carry on the legacy of our feminist foremothers as a way to continue the ongoing fight for freedom, justice, and liberation.

References

Bowleg, L. (2008). When Black+ lesbian+ woman≠ Black lesbian woman: The methodological challenges of qualitative and quantitative intersectionality research. *Sex Roles*, 59(5–6), 312–325. https://doi.org/10.1007/s11199-008-9400-z

Charmaz, K. (2017). The power of constructivist grounded theory for critical inquiry. *Qualitative Inquiry*, 23(1), 34–45. https://doi.org/10.1177/1077800416657105

Cho, S., Crenshaw, K. W., & McCall, L. (2013). Toward a field of intersectionality studies: Theory, applications, and praxis. *Signs: Journal of Women in Culture and Society*, 38(4), 785–810. https://doi.org/10.1086/669608

Cole, E. R. (2009). Intersectionality and research in psychology. *American Psychologist*, 64(3), 170–180. https://doi.org/10.1037/a0014564

Cole, E. R. (2020). Demarginalizing women of color in intersectionality scholarship in psychology: A Black feminist critique. *Journal of Social Issues*, 76(4), 1036–1044. https://doi.org/10.1111/josi.12413

Collins, P. H. (2000). *Black feminist thought: Knowledge, consciousness, and the politics of empowerment*. Routledge.

Collins, P. H. (2019). *Intersectionality as critical social theory*. Duke University Press.

Crenshaw, K. (1989). Demarginalizing the intersection of race and sex: A Black feminist critique of antidiscrimination doctrines, feminist theory, and antiracist politics. *University of Chicago Legal Forum*, 8, 139–167.

Else-Quest, N. M., & Hyde, J. S. (2016). Intersectionality in quantitative psychological research: II. Methods and techniques. *Psychology of Women Quarterly*, 40(3), 319–336. https://doi.org/10.1177/0361684316647953

Hesse-Biber, S. (2012). *Handbook of feminist research: Theory and praxis*. SAGE. https://doi.org/10.4135/9781483384740

Hesse-Biber, S., & Piatelli, D. (2012). The feminist practice of holistic reflexivity. In S. N. Hesse-Biber (Ed.), *Handbook of feminist research: Theory and praxis* (pp. 557–582). SAGE. https://doi.org/10.4135/9781483384740

Levitt, H. M., Motulsky, S. L., Wertz, F. J., Morrow, S. L., & Ponterotto, J. G. (2017). Recommendations for designing and reviewing qualitative research in psychology: Promoting methodological integrity. *Qualitative Psychology*, 4(1), 2–22. https://doi.org/10.1037/qup0000082

Lewis, J. A., & Grzanka, P. R. (2016). Applying intersectionality theory to research on perceived racism. In A. N. Alvarez, C. T. H. Liang, & H. A. Neville (Eds.), *The cost of racism for people of color: Contextualizing experiences of discrimination* (pp. 31–54). American Psychological Association.

Morrow, S. L. (2005). Quality and trustworthiness in qualitative research in counseling psychology. *Journal of Counseling Psychology*, 5(2), 250–260. https://doi.org/10.1037/0022-0167.52.2.250

Riger, S. (2016). On becoming a feminist psychologist. *Psychology of Women Quarterly*, 40(4), 479–487. https://doi.org/10.1177/0361684316676539

Rosenthal, L. (2016). Incorporating intersectionality into psychology: An opportunity to promote social justice and equity. *American Psychologist*, 71(6), 474–485. https://doi.org/10.1037/a0040323

Settles, I. H., Warner, L. R., Buchanan, N. T., & Jones, M. K. (2020). Understanding psychology's resistance to intersectionality theory using a framework of epistemic exclusion and invisibility. *Journal of Social Issues*, 76(4), 796–813. https://doi.org/10.1111/josi.12403

Shields, S. A. (2008). Gender: An intersectionality perspective. *Sex Roles*, 59(5–6), 301–311.

Sue, D. W. (2010). *Microaggressions in everyday life: Race, gender, and sexual orientation*. Wiley.

Watson-Singleton, N. N., Lewis, J. A., & Dworkin, E. R. (2021). Toward a socially just diversity science: Using intersectional mixed methods research to center multiply marginalized Black, Indigenous, and People of Color (BIPOC). *Cultural Diversity and Ethnic Minority Psychology*. Advance online publication. https://doi.org/10.1037/cdp0000477

Williams, M. G., & Lewis, J. A. (2021). Developing a conceptual framework of Black women's gendered racial identity development. *Psychology of Women Quarterly*, 45(2), 212–228. https://doi.org/10.1177/036168432098860

CHAPTER 3

The Tenure Clock

Understanding Your Tenure Process and Pacing

- **Leah R. Warner**
  Ramapo College of New Jersey

Tenure, a critical milestone in in the career of an academic, creates job security, pay increases, and other substantial benefits to faculty members. Notably, women, and particularly Women of Color, remain underrepresented in both tenure-track and tenured positions (Catalyst, 2015). At the current rate, it will take more than 100 years to achieve gender equity (Marschke et al., 2007). Widespread evidence indicates that bias contributes to this disparity. During the tenure process, white women and People of Color, as well as those from other marginalized social groups, report harsher scrutiny, as well as microaggressions, double standards, social exclusion, and other barriers to tenure (e.g., Arnold et al., 2016; Hart & Cress, 2008). Those who engage in work that addresses systemic oppression, such as feminist scholarship, teaching, and service, face additional barriers due to the politicized nature of their work (e.g., Adair, 2018).

This chapter focuses on tactics and strategies that help you, as a feminist scholar, navigate the tenure clock. While these strategies largely focus on the actions individual feminist scholars can take, I emphasize that these actions should not replace administration and senior faculty responsibilities for addressing systemic inequities present at their institutions. Thus, I end the chapter with recommendations for institutions to reduce structural barriers for junior faculty.

My positionality informs my perspective on the tenure process. I am a queer/lesbian cisgender woman from a highly educated family who helped me navigate my academic life. I entered academia with institutional knowledge, such as the need for mentorship. I am also currently a full professor at a mid-Atlantic teaching-oriented public liberal arts college, one that hired me for my feminist approach to scholarship and teaching. Because my department supported my feminist approach, I recognize that my personal experience does not represent experiences of feminists whose departments are resistant to their work. However, I still experienced challenges as a queer/lesbian woman who engages in feminist pedagogy and institutional activism, both in the classroom and in other domains at my institution.

Strategies and Tactics

As a feminist faculty member, you can maximize your potential to achieve tenure by understanding (a) your institution's tenure process; (b) how to package the research and scholarship, teaching, and service sections within your tenure dossier; and (c) pacing and work–life balance.

Understanding the Institution's Tenure Process

Tenure processes in institutions of higher education tend to be intensive, covering typically a 5- to 7-year pre-tenure period, with assessments along the way until candidates complete tenure dossiers. Many institutions also rely heavily on peer evaluations written by colleagues within the institution, along with external evaluations from discipline experts. Institutions often justify this extensive data collection by stating that tenure signifies a significant investment, and thus promotion and tenure committees, as well as administrators, need to ensure they are making the correct decision. Officially, institutions guide tenure-track faculty through this process through tenure policies and procedures as outlined in faculty handbooks and through trainings offered by employee relations and other designated offices.

During your tenure-track period, you will need to attend both to the stated tenure requirements as outlined in faculty handbooks and the "hidden" set of requirements that often accompany official policies. These hidden requirements often result from ambiguously stated policies and unwritten social norms within departments and institutions. Many faculty handbooks contain language left open to interpretation, such as a requirement that faculty maintain an "active" service record without providing guidance as to how much service meets an "active" standard. This ambiguity may subsequently influence tenure review committees' use of heuristics and other unconscious biases (Arnold et al., 2016; Hart & Cress, 2009), such as using unwritten social norms to measure "active" participation. See (2016), for example, described her experience of declining senior faculty's dinner party invitations to instead attend student-led social justice events. She was unaware that the faculty expected her presence and believed that these decisions, and other instances where she lacked institutional knowledge, contributed to her denial of tenure. Faculty who are marginalized from the institution, including feminists and those from historically underrepresented groups, often lack access to the knowledge of these hidden requirements, and their tenure prospects can suffer. Latino/a faculty have described this ambiguity as creating a culture of fear (Urrieta et al., 2014) and Black faculty report sociopsychological stress responses to experiences such as these that force assimilation into white, male-dominant culture in higher education (Arnold et al., 2016).

One central way you can address this ambiguity is to seek support for both the formal tenure process and the hidden requirements. Few et al. (2007) emphasize that new faculty should identify sources of support very early in their tenure-track positions, irrespective of whether the institution implements a formal mentorship program. These support individuals, preferably multiple folks who are knowledgeable about the institution's specific tenure process, can provide insight into early decisions, such as how many and what types of publications the faculty member needs to produce on an annual basis. Gaining information from multiple individuals is key to triangulating information about ambiguous language or unwritten departmental norms, given that any one individual will share their subjective interpretations of unclear parameters.

For example, at the beginning of my tenure-track appointment, I reached out to as many senior faculty who would be willing to answer my questions. I cast a wide net since I did not know who to trust nor who possessed the most informed perspective. From there, I was left with an array of varying and, at times, completely contradictory perspectives. I then went back to discuss these contradictions with the senior faculty members who seemed most receptive to supporting me. They then helped provide context for how faculty could arrive at such conflicting advice: (a) Some faculty were relying on out-of-date interpretations of faculty handbook information; (b) other faculty possessed a stubborn "vision" for the college that deviated from current practices; and (c) faculty varied in terms of their awareness of informal norms. Throughout my pre-tenure years I would repeat this practice, and over time I learned which combination of vantage points helped me arrive at the most accurate answers.

Feminist mentors, in particular, ideally offer what Martínez (2018) calls an "intimate, collaborative relationship" (p. 111), facilitating a critical lens to navigating inequalities within institutions of higher education. Feminist support not only provides individual-level advice, but also a shared critique of and call to action to address factors that contribute to inequalities in the tenure process. Outside of faculty mentorship, support can come from other domains, particularly for those who experience hostile or unsupportive environments. These domains, both within and outside one's institution, can include communities that share one's social location, such as an LGBTQ faculty group or local Latin American communities (Urrieta et al., 2014). Also see Chapter 4 (this volume) on building one's invisible college.

You can also address ambiguity by taking advantage of tenure checkpoints, although the nature of these checkpoints varies greatly between institutions. Some require annual reviews until faculty submit their tenure dossiers. These annual reviews may simply include information from a curriculum vitae, or they may require more intensive measures, such as peer teaching observations and documentation of service contributions. Other institutions require a midpoint check-in before the tenure process. Within these variations, you should take advantage of feedback on your progress. For example, if your scholarship is interdisciplinary or you possess a joint appointment, you should consult mentors to ensure a coherent narrative of your scholarly interests (Few et al., 2007). Further, you should take advantage of annual reviews to document evidence for all contributions. This documentation helps to avoid forgetting about your work and to decrease the record-collecting labor during the tenure process (Stewart & Valian, 2018). If you are not subject to annual reviews, you should engage in detailed record keeping on an annual basis. Record keeping should be contingent on the requirements for tenure and may include email confirmations of acceptance to conferences, fliers from a co-curricular event you organized, the number of hours spent on advising or mentoring research assistants, and other evidence. To simplify record keeping, create a habit of enacting low-effort, high-impact actions. For example, create email folders for quickly filing contributions. You can file service requests or invitations for invited lectures, and after you complete the action, ask the requester to send an email confirming that you completed the task. In addition, immediately write a reminder in your CV to add a new item and then designate space in your schedule at the end of the semester or quarter to record contributions during that time period.

In sum, when understanding your institution's tenure process, ask yourself the following questions: (a) What are my institution's stated versus hidden tenure requirements? (b) Who can I ask to help me navigate these requirements? and (c) What strategies will I adopt to gather data about my contributions toward tenure?

Research and Scholarship Requirements

Feminist scholars often find themselves experiencing tension between narrowly defined measurements of research quality and a drive to actualize feminist research ideals. Feminist research includes integrating scholarship and activism, where scholars work to dismantle oppressive societal structures as an execution of their research (Adair, 2018). Actions may include collaborating with local communities to address their experiences with inequality, organizing awareness campaigns around the findings of their research, or conducting research that challenges sexist practices within their home discipline. This approach directly, and often purposefully, challenges institutions' trends toward neoliberalism, which values research that is profitable and that meets private interests rather than valuing liberatory actions that center one's community (Richter et al., 2020). A real risk in challenging neoliberalism in the academy is that neoliberalism encourages a decrease in tenure-track faculty and an increase in contingent faculty as a "cost-cutting" measure. This trend can serve as a threat to faculty who fear retaliation (Richter et al., 2020). Further, institutions often label activism as service rather than as scholarship (Adair, 2018), which can be detrimental to faculty at research-focused institutions.

To address some of these issues, in your annual review and tenure applications you can contextualize your scholarship by specifying the standards for your field. For example, my work on intersectionality often necessitates the inclusion of multiple authors to ensure that diverse standpoints contribute to the scholarship. Because faculty from across my college served on the all-college tenure committee, including those whose disciplinary standards value single-author work, I foregrounded the scholarship section of my tenure package by explaining, with citations, how my work met the standards for my subfield. Stewart and Valian (2018) further advise faculty to contextualize disciplinary-specific language so that reviewers from outside one's field can understand one's research program. In addition, if you are allowed to choose or provide a list of your external letter writers, you can choose individuals who can appropriately contextualize your work. For more information on how to conceptualize, engage in, and communicate the value of feminist research during a pre-tenure time frame, see Lewis and Williams (Chapter 2, this volume).

Teaching Requirements

Like with research, feminist pedagogy disrupts systems of oppression, through both the process of teaching and course content. Packaging this work into a tenure dossier requires purposeful strategies, particularly when faculty experience pushback from students and colleagues. Faculty who teach about social justice and equity issues, such as feminism, report feeling disrespect from students that challenge their perspectives (Urrieta et al., 2014), especially in a broader cultural context that harasses instructors perceived as "pushing a leftist agenda." Adair (2018), for example, discussed the impact that the murder of Michael Brown and subsequent backlash from conservative whites at her institution in Missouri had on her ability to conduct Black feminist pedagogy. Students emboldened by the backlash issued formal complaints to administration of Adair's attempts to address the complex intersections of gender, race, and police brutality in her classroom. I also have faced substantial pushback from students. For example, a small group of students, emboldened by the 2016 election, made inflammatory remarks during every class session in Psychology of Gender. I took a three-pronged approach to this situation: (a) To head off any complaints I might receive, I notified my dean, a supportive administrator, that this dynamic manifested in my classroom; (b) I highly leaned on my invisible college of social justice faculty for support; and (c) I turned the students' behavior into a teaching lesson for the rest of my class, which sometimes meant deviating from my stated lesson objectives.

Often faculty who receive these types of complaints are reliant on administrators and senior faculty who are willing to protect them, something that cannot be guaranteed. When possible, you can reach out to peers and mentors to write letters contextualizing the importance of teaching "uncomfortable" content to students and the potential lower teaching evaluations that may result. You can also gather multiple measurements of teaching effectiveness, such as teaching observations, portfolios, and alumni surveys (Boyson, 2021). When resources are not available within your institution, you can look to local and national professional associations. As evidence of your teaching effectiveness, you can present your teaching at conferences, and you can apply (or ask a feminist mentor to nominate you) for teaching awards that support feminist pedagogy. As a member of several feminist-oriented teaching award selection committees, I observed that few feminist faculty apply for awards, with far fewer applicants than I see qualified candidates. White women and faculty from underrepresented racial/ethnic groups are more likely to receive criticism and less likely to receive recognition for their academic achievements than white men, which, if perceived as valid information, can lead them to underestimate their own performance (Stewart & Valian, 2018). This perspective could erroneously lead faculty to avoid applying for teaching awards and other measurements of high-quality feminist pedagogy.

Service Requirements

As with the other requirements, service expectations vary greatly by institution. Service generally entails participating in faculty governance at department, school, and university levels, contributions to the profession (e.g., participation in regional or national organizations), and service to community (e.g., offering lectures or through clinical work). Some institutions categorize advising and mentoring students as service and value other contributions, such as curricular and co-curricular programming.

One form of service that institutions increasingly require is diversity, equity, and inclusion work (Ahmed, 2012). As a feminist faculty member, you may find yourself desiring to and being asked to participate in this form of service. At times this work provides fulfillment of one's life passion, but at times faculty, particularly Faculty of Color, can feel overburdened by disproportionate diversity-related service expectations (Urrieta et al., 2015). Further, often institutions value performative diversity work, creating an outward appearance of valuing diversity but an inner unwillingness to change the structures that devalue them (Ahmed, 2012). Thus, feminists experience roadblocks when engaging in diversity work that is more than just performative (Richter et al., 2020).

Additionally, you may find yourself asked to serve as the face of feminist efforts on campus. You may find yourself providing support to students not just for choosing classes and letters of recommendation, but also counseling them on their activist efforts and serving as a source of support for experiences of marginalization. You may also experience pressure to engage publicly to politicized events. For example, Martínez (2018) described that students looked to women and gender studies and the Black studies department for support during a high-profile protest on her campus, service that her institution not only did not value, but potentially counted against her in pre-tenure evaluations. Further, some institutions require faculty to maintain a presence on social media to promote their research. Faculty whose work is explicitly political may face harassment and threats, which is particularly concerning since many institutions lack formal policies for protecting faculty against targeted attacks (Ferber, 2018). When considering both the desire to engage in diversity work and the pressure to serve as the face of it, faculty may also experience being devalued as "only caring about diversity" rather than other service responsibilities.

A strategic action you, individually, can take to avoid being pigeonholed is to ensure that you engage in non-diversity service as well. Stewart (2016) advised that faculty should engage in routine service opportunities, such as assessment, to develop rapport with other faculty and staff outside of a diversity context. By building a relationship in contexts that are less loaded, you can then rely on those relationships when you address diversity issues. I belong to an institution with high service requirements, which easily allowed me to apply this sage advice. For example, by belonging to general education curriculum committees, I developed connections with faculty from across the college, and then when I advocated with a group of faculty for an African American literature faculty line, I was more easily able to speak with these colleagues to convince them to join our efforts.

For faculty who cannot add more service, Few et al. (2007) recommend ridding oneself of nonessential demands and setting more realistic goals so that one completes fewer tasks well. You can make your priorities transparent, framed not as eschewing responsibility but as prioritizing focus, such as "I am prioritizing learning about assessment, and thus I cannot plan the department's holiday party at this time." New faculty, however, may face several challenges in implementing this advice, such as not knowing which demands are nonessential. Thus, you should include questions about essential demands in your conversations with senior faculty about the formal tenure process and hidden requirements. For example, at my institution, essential demands include service that increases visibility on campus, as it is an informal norm that faculty who are "known" on campus are perceived as more valuable than faculty who complete equivalent work in private. Another challenge facing white women and People of Color, in particular, is pressure to say yes to all requests, such as my experience when only the young women faculty were asked by an administrator to plan faculty parties. As I elaborate in a later section, institutions and senior faculty hold ultimate responsibility for ensuring equitable distribution of service. For more information, see Buchanan and Jones (Chapter 13, this volume).

Further, when you are overwhelmed by the number of service-related responsibilities, you can work to combine research, teaching, and service so that any individual effort serves multiple purposes at once; doing so serves to dismantle hierarchical valuing of faculty contributions and creates more efficient social justice actions (Richter et al., 2020). For example, I created a social science general education course that utilizes intersectional social justice pedagogical approaches. The creation of this course counted toward my teaching, particularly since I also applied for and received a teaching award. The creation of this course also counted as service and institutional action, both in ensuring that social justice was woven into the fabric of the course and, through my role as director, providing sources of support for faculty from marginalized groups and creating a fund for students in financial need. I then integrated these efforts into my scholarship, as I presented on this course at conferences and published scholarship based on the creation of this course. I thus combined all components to maximize this effort's impact on my promotion process.

When considering the three sections of your tenure dossier together, you can ask yourself three questions: (a) How will I contextualize my feminist research within my institution's measurements of research quality? (b) Which strategies will I employ to better highlight my feminist teaching, beyond student evaluations? and (c) How will I maximize my service input without being overburdened?

Putting It All Together: Pacing and Work–Life Balance

When considering research, teaching, and service responsibilities, coupled with the information-gathering process of the tenure process itself, many pre-tenure faculty experience an intense, high-stakes workload. Faculty report pressures that the tenure process not only feels like an evaluation of their professional achievements, but also an evaluation of their personhood (Stewart & Valian, 2018). Sifaki's (2016) interviews with feminist faculty reflect a struggle for balance, with folks stating that they lack time for sleep and that they are "just drowning" (p. 115).

Although not addressing the high-intensity workload in general, some institutions provide faculty an opportunity to stop the tenure clock when external barriers prevent productivity. The goal of stop-the-clock policies is to create an equal playing field for those who encounter life situations that decrease their ability to engage in faculty responsibilities. Many stop-the-clock policies initially were created for women to address the fact that pre-tenure periods often overlap with prime childbearing years (Manchester et al., 2013). Policies have since expanded to all genders to address other family reasons (e.g., caring for an ill family member), personal illness, unanticipated research delays, contractual issues, engaging in a temporary appointment elsewhere (e.g., working for the government), and during the COVID-19 pandemic (Arnold et al., 2016; Htun, 2020; Manchester et al., 2013).

While, in principle, an off-the-clock year may support work–life balance, pre-tenure faculty may be concerned about whether stopping the clock will violate unwritten departmental norms. Given the intense productivity norms for pre-tenure scholars, tenure dossier evaluators may use a faculty member's off-the-clock year as a heuristic to infer lack of effort or commitment to their position. While few studies have examined faculty perceptions of stopping the clock, the research that does exist suggests mixed findings. For example, Manchester et al. (2013) examined perceptions of stop-the-clock practices at a research-focused U.S. doctorate-granting institution. In this context, faculty members hired between 1998–2002 who stopped the clock for family reasons experienced a salary penalty compared to those who did not. Because productivity levels did not explain these differences, the authors suggested that biased perceptions of faculty members contributed to the difference. Fortunately, faculty who stopped the clock experienced higher promotion rates than those who did not.

In contrast, Antecol et al. (2016) analyzed policies at the top 50 U.S. economics departments from 1985–2004 and found that stopping the clock reduced women's and increased men's tenure rates. According to their findings, men were more likely to be productive while their tenure clock was stopped whereas women were much less able to do so, given the greater nonacademic responsibilities women faced. This broader study suggests that Manchester et al.'s findings were institution specific, and that you should investigate formal and informal practices at your institution before taking an off-the-clock year.

Beyond offering an off-the-clock year, feminist scholars advocate for resisting the pressure to produce at the expense of well-being and for challenging systems that support this culture (e.g., Adair, 2018; Few et al., 2007). For me, one of the more personally difficult aspects of the grueling pre-tenure experience was that it contributed to me staying in the closet. I was so focused on my job—getting tenure and succeeding professionally—that I ignored this central aspect of my life. When I was working 80 hours a week, learning how to teach, and trying to establish a research program at a teaching-heavy college, it was far too destabilizing for me to process my feelings about my sexuality and to engage in the significant life changes necessary for me to actualize that part of myself. I was bewildered when I experienced a crisis moment, no longer able to suppress this core essence of my being. That crisis moment occurred after I received associate professor and completed a significant leadership role at my institution. When I no longer faced relentless pressure to prove myself, I was left with fear and shame regarding how to finally live my life as a queer person. Perhaps my life would have been different if I had a model or a mentor who had experienced something similar or if I had been granted more mental or emotional space during my early career to address my own needs.

Given the strain that the pre-tenure process gives feminist faculty, I advise you to, as best you can, assert work–life balance to avoid burnout and associated mental and physical health consequences. In a chapter on avoiding burnout, Asia Eaton and I (2020) outlined steps that social justice scholars can take to engage in self-care. We emphasized Lorde's (1988) assertion that, in contrast to neoliberal notions of self-care that emphasize individual responsibility and consumerism (e.g., buying expensive fitness equipment), self-care can act as resistance against oppressive systems. As feminists, we can frame getting sleep, exercising, making doctor's appointments, and spending time with loved ones as challenging the self-sacrificing, workaholism, and individualistic success that is built into tenure processes. We can remind ourselves that restoring our energy will, eventually, better counteract systems designed to deplete feminists and prevent social change.

To address this struggle for balance, you can begin by asking yourself the following questions: "What are my institution's stated policies and informal norms for stopping the tenure clock?" and "How will I protect my well-being during the tenure process?" While individual feminist faculty can assert their own work–life balance, one cannot simply "advise" individual faculty to change their own behaviors. Instead, senior faculty and administrators need to assert responsibility for addressing institutional-level changes. Thus, the final question to ask is "How can institutions better support feminist faculty in their tenure process?"

Recommendations for Institutions

When faculty are denied tenure, the responsibility is typically placed on the faculty member's individual failures rather than institutional structures that create barriers (Baez, 2002). Here, I provide recommendations for changes to formal policies and procedures as well as informal practices that better support your path to tenure.

Institutions can most directly improve the tenure process for feminists by increasing the clarity and transparency of both the tenure criteria and the tenure process. Institutions must clarify fuzzy language in faculty handbooks, policies, and procedures (see Stewart & Valian, 2018, for detailed recommendations). Further, tenure processes are frequently shrouded in secrecy (Martínez, 2018), where candidates often lack agency over their information and evaluations, such as not allowing candidates to learn the names of their outside evaluators. Barring changes that give candidates themselves the ability to properly vet the qualifications of their outside evaluators, those in charge of the tenure process must take particular care in educating themselves about the types of evaluators who will most accurately represent candidates' work.

External reviewers with lived experiences that mirror those of candidates, as well as those who share feminist scholarly perspectives, will allow for the most rigorous reviews since those individuals can most deeply evaluate and communicate the candidates' contributions to the field (Urrietta et al., 2014). Pre-tenure faculty should be granted the opportunity to provide a mentor or a tenure and promotion committee member a list of potential external reviewers that can best speak to their strengths. In addition to greater clarity and transparency in stated policies and procedures, senior faculty need to increase transparency around unwritten norms to ensure feminist faculty know what actions departments and institutions value. Ideally, departments should pair junior faculty with a senior feminist faculty member that not only explains norms but advocates for changing norms that produce inequities.

In addition, institutions can build greater awareness of and motivation to address systemic inequalities in tenure and promotion processes. Empirically validated trainings and interventions can challenge unconscious biases that influence tenure committees' decisions and stimulate institutional changes. For example, the Workshop Activity for Gender Equity Simulation-Academic (Shields et al., 2011) is a simulation that demonstrates how gender biases accumulate over time to negatively impact women's advancement to tenure and promotion. WAGES-Academic leads participants to detect and report subtle gender bias in tenure and promotion materials (Cundiff et al., 2018) and leads faculty and administrators to change both their individual behaviors and policies at their institutions (Shields et al., 2018).

Trainings such as WAGES-Academic highlight the need for administrators to make policy changes. For example, administrators need to create greater oversight on the objectivity of salary setting, such as collecting and sharing data on the faculty demographics of pre-tenure and tenured faculty (Stewart & Valian, 2018). Further, institutions should ameliorate negative consequences of stop-the-clock policies through a variety of changes, such as allowing faculty to select a subset of pre-tenure years to consider for evaluation (Htun, 2020) and by creating flexible timelines depending on the nature of the external barriers to productivity. Also, institutions can increase positive perception of these policies by broadening faculty use of the policy, such as through implementing opt-out instead of opt-in enrollment (Manchester et al., 2013).

Other necessary policy changes include those that protect faculty against targeted harassment (Scott, 2018) and policies that protect academic freedom for feminist faculty on social media, particularly when social media serves as a job requirement. Further, upper administrators should decrease reliance on student-based teaching evaluations given that those metrics disproportionately produce lower ratings for white women and People of Color (Kreitzer & Sweet-Cushman, 2022). Finally, senior faculty should review the distribution of service responsibilities among the department to ensure that those with the least power are not disproportionately burdened with service work. Discussions of service contributions should be transparent and should utilize clear metrics, such as estimating the number of hours required for each contribution and limiting the time frame for serving.

Finally, to better support feminist research, teaching, and service, senior faculty and administrators should critically reflect on and re-create institutions' value systems around individual and community well-being and social equity (Richter et al., 2020). In particular, feminist activism should be counted as an academically rigorous contribution, similar to obtaining a grant or high-impact publication in research-intensive institutions (Few et al., 2007). With these systemic changes, feminist faculty will more likely receive the support they need to successfully navigate the tenure process.

Resources

Few, A. L., Piercy, F. P., & Stremmel, A. (2007). Balancing the passion for activism with the demands of tenure: One professional's story from three perspectives. *National Women's Studies Association Journal, 19*(3), 47–66.

In this article, April L. Few explains her story as Black assistant professor seeking tenure at a predominately white university. She discusses the balance between her commitment to diversity and social justice and the requirements for tenure. Adding to this discussion, her department head and department chair of the tenure and promotion committee reflect on this issue from their own social locations. All three then provide recommendations for faculty seeking tenure, particularly in terms of how to stay true to one's passions while navigating racism and sexism within institutions of higher education.

Stewart, A. J., & Valian, V. (2018). *An inclusive academy: Achieving diversity and excellence*. The Massachusetts Institute of Technology Press.

This volume provides guidance at each stage in the faculty job process, including tenure. In addition to providing guidance for administrators and senior faculty, Abigail Stewart and Virginia Valian describe strategies for pre-tenure faculty on how to advance to tenure, with a particular focus on individuals from historically underrepresented groups.

References

Adair, Z. R. (2018). Pretenure and Black: Teaching and research in the era of Trump. *Women, Gender, and Families of Color*, 6(1), 26–31. https://www.proquest.com/docview/2491992275

Ahmed, S. (2012). *On being included: Racism and diversity in institutional life*. Duke University Press.

Antecol, H., Bedard, K., & Stearns, J. (2016). Equal but inequitable: Who benefits from gender-neutral tenure clock stopping policies? *IZA Discussion Papers*, (9904). Institute for the Study of Labor (IZA). http://hdl.handle.net/10419/142343

Arnold, N. W., Crawford, E. R., & Khalifa, M. (2016). Psychological heuristics and faculty of color: Racial battle fatigue and tenure/promotion. *The Journal of Higher Education*, 87(6), 890–919. https://doi.org/10.1080/00221546.2016.11780891

Baez, B. (2002). *Affirmative action, hate speech, and tenure: Narratives about race, law, and the academy*. RoutledgeFalmer.

Boyson, G. (2021). Student evaluations of teaching: Can teaching social justice negatively affect one's career? In K. Case, W. Williams, & M. Kite (Eds.), *Navigating difficult moments in teaching diversity and social justice* (pp. 235–246). American Psychological Association.

Catalyst. (2015). *Quick take: Women in academia*. http://www.catalyst.org/knowledge/women-academia#us

Cundiff, J. L., Danube, C. L., Zawadzki, M. J., & Shields, S. A. (2018). Testing an intervention for recognizing and reporting subtle gender bias in promotion and tenure decisions. *The Journal of Higher Education*, 89(5), 611–636. https://doi.org/10.1080/00221546.2018.1437665

Eaton, A. A., & Warner, L. R. (2020). Social justice burnout: Engaging self-care while doing diversity work. In K. Case, W. Williams, & M. Kite (Eds.), *Navigating difficult moments in teaching diversity and social justice* (pp. 31–43). American Psychological Association.

Ferber, A. L. (2018). "Are you willing to die for this work?" Public targeted online harassment in higher education: SWS presidential address. *Gender & Society*, 32(3), 301–320. https://doi.org/10.1177/0891243218766831

Few, A. L., Piercy, F. P., & Stremmel, A. (2007). Balancing the passion for activism with the demands of tenure: One professional's story from three perspectives. *National Women's Studies Association Journal*, 19(3), 47–66.

Hart, J. L., & Cress, C. M. (2008). Are women faculty just "worrywarts?" Accounting for gender differences in self-reported stress. *Journal of Human Behavior in the Social Environment*, 17(1–2), 175–193. https://doi.org/10.1080/10911350802171120

Htun, M. (2020). Tenure and promotion after the pandemic. *Science*, 368(6495), 1075. https://doi.org/10.1126/science.abc7469

Kreitzer, R. J., & Sweet-Cushman, J. (2022). Evaluating student evaluations of teaching: A review of measurement and equity bias in SETs and recommendations for ethical reform. *Journal of Academic Ethics*, 20(1), 73–84. https://doi.org/10.1007/s10805-021-09400-w

Lorde, A. (1988). *A burst of light*. Firebrand Books.

Manchester, C. F., Leslie, L., M., & Kramer, A. (2013). Is the clock still ticking? An evaluation of the consequences of stopping the tenure clock. *ILR Review*, 66(1), 1–31. https://doi.org/10.1177/0019793913066001

Marschke, R., Laursen, S., Nielsen, J. M., & Rankin, P. (2007). Demographic inertia revisited: An immodest proposal to achieve equitable gender representation among faculty in higher education. *The Journal of Higher Education*, 78(1), 1–26. https://doi.org/10.1080/00221546.2007.11778961

Martínez, R. (2018). Fomenting fear and calling on our courage: Being Latinx on the tenure track in the time of Trumpism. *Women, Gender, and Families of Color, 6*(1), 110–117. https://www.jstor.org/stable/10.5406/womgenfamcol.6.1.0110

Richter, J., Faragó, F., Swadener, B. B., Roca-Servat, D., & Eversman, K. A. (2020). Tempered radicalism and intersectionality: Scholar-activism in the neoliberal university. *Journal of Social Issues, 76*(4), 1014–1035. https://doi.org/10.1111/josi.12401

Scott, J. W. (2018). Targeted harassment of faculty: What higher education administrators can do. *Liberal Education, 104*(2). https://eric.ed.gov/?id=EJ1183018

See, S. E. (2016). Talking tenure. In P. A. Matthew (Ed.), *Written/unwritten: Diversity and the hidden truths of tenure* (pp. 148–164). The University of North Carolina Press.

Shields, S. A., McCormick, K. T., Dicicco, E. C., & Zawadzki, M. J. (2018). Demonstrating the cumulative effects of unconscious bias with WAGES-Academic (Workshop Activity for Gender Equity Simulation): Short and long-term impact on faculty and administrators. *Journal of Women and Minorities in Science and Engineering, 24*(2), 147–163. https://doi.org/10.1615/JWomenMinorScienEng.2018014113

Shields, S. A., Zawadzki, M. J., & Johnson, R. N. (2011). The impact of the Workshop Activity for Gender Equity Simulation in the Academy (WAGES-Academic) in demonstrating cumulative effects of gender bias. *Journal of Diversity in Higher Education, 4*(2), 120–129. https://doi.org/10.1037/a0022953.

Sifaki, A. (2016). Which side are we on? Feminist studies in the time of neoliberalism or neoliberal feminist studies? *Women's Studies International Forum, 54*, 111–118. https://doi.org/10.1016/j.wsif.2015.06.011

Stewart, A. (2016, March 2). *Being a full-time feminist psychologist across the life cycle: Scholarship, teaching and service* [Keynote address]. Institute for Feminist Academic Psychologists. Pittsburgh, PA.

Stewart, A. J., & Valian, V. (2018). *An inclusive academy: Achieving diversity and excellence*. The Massachusetts Institute of Technology Press.

Urrieta, L., Méndez, L., & Rodrguez, E. (2014). "A moving target": A critical race analysis of Latina/o faculty experience, perspectives, and reflections on the tenure and promotion process. *International Journal of Qualitative Studies in Education, 28*(10), 1149–1168. http://dx.doi.org/10.1080/09518398.2014.974715

CHAPTER 4

Building Your Invisible College

■ **Ying Tang**
Youngstown State University

I grew up in Chengdu, China, in a family that believed in the transformative potential of education. Education showed its powerful effect in my grandparents and parents' generations, as they were among the first to pursue university and postgraduate degrees. Education allowed my father to leave his coal-mining hometown and gave my aunt a ticket to an international career. That was why I knew—as a teenager in a rather closed-off China in the 90s—that my admission to Wesleyan College in Macon, Georgia, offered me not only a ticket to the United States, but also a steppingstone to the world. My 4 years at college—one of the first in the world to grant university degrees to women—was empowering beyond measure. The small and engaged community propelled me to occupy central roles in research, leadership, and service opportunities, through which I found my love of psychology and a calling to help empower others. After college, I obtained a PhD in social psychology from Syracuse University, followed by a tenure-track faculty position at Youngstown State University, where I obtained tenure in the fall of 2020.

Building a career from the ground up as a young, foreign, and Asian woman in the United States with no family around may have been daunting, but I was never alone. I am keenly aware that my success took a village. Every step of the way, there have been individuals who graciously supported me, opened doors for me, and elevated me to higher grounds. Mentors turned into recommenders, friends evolved into collaborators, role models became colleagues, and coworkers grew as confidants. The teaching, research, service, and life that I have partaken in alongside these individuals have effectively fashioned the scope of my achievements and influence—they have become my *invisible college*.

The Origin and Conceptualization of an Invisible College

The "invisible college" can be traced back to mid-17th century in a series of letters that Robert Boyle wrote, in which he described the luncheon meetings of a group of well-educated lay members, who gathered for enthusiastic discussions about science (Coser, 1965). These informal meetings evolved over time and culminated in the formation of the Royal Society, the oldest scientific society in Great Britain. Since then, the term *invisible college* has been used to describe different groups in academia.

There are two broad approaches to understand the nature of invisible colleges. One approach is to focus on formal structures, such as the network of coauthorship (Newman, 2001) and bibliometrics, such as citations (Frost, 1979). A second approach argues that the invisible college may in fact be rooted in informal and personal communication throughout one's professional life (Crawford, 1971). Lievrouw (1989) critiques quantifying the invisible college through the measurement of structural indicators. Instead, she highlights the importance in considering the individual's subjective perception of an invisible college and the process that they may engage in to create their own reality.

In broadening the invisible college to include principles of feminism, it is imperative to contextualize modern academic life within a larger social (including professional and personal) network that demands much visible and invisible labor. In turn, we should be conscious of the process as much as the outcomes of professional and personal lives. This requires us to invest in ourselves and others for the long-term with strategies to effect transformation within ourselves, within institutions, and within society. A feminist approach to building an invisible college recognizes the imbalance of power and privilege from an intersectional lens, builds allyship in the office and at home, celebrates diversity and access, heeds sustainability and accountability in the pursuit of productivity, commits to personal and organizational growth, and increases equity for all.

The Need to Build an Invisible College

The invisible college, as conceptualized as a network of formal research collaborators and/or informal professional/personal relationships, is useful for thinking about building and using a feminist invisible college for yourself. For one, publication is the lifeline of early career academics; thus, it is essential for you to cultivate a targeted network that helps achieve such an end. Indeed, research collaboration helps individual academics increase research productivity (Sooho & Bozeman, 2005) and creativity (Dawson et al., 2011), which are strongly predictive of our impact and contribution to science (Simonton, 1997).

Its significance notwithstanding, research productivity is not the sole harbinger of professional success. Scholarship on career advancement in academia reveals that success not only relies on your individual knowledge or competence, but, rather frequently, whom you know (Austin & McDaniels, 2006). Such networks of influence facilitate our growth in social capital, which enables you access to institutional knowledge about the political processes of a given institution so that you can better capitalize on existing reward systems for professional gains (Wunsch & Johnsrud, 1992). Such networks provide you with instrumental support (e.g., knowledge about grant and job opportunities) as well as indirect benefits (e.g., friendship and mentorship) (Kezar, 2014), bolstering a variety of career-related outcomes, ranging from the invisible (e.g., power; Brass et al., 2004) to the visible (e.g., increased salary; Seibert et al., 2001).

Beyond research productivity and professional access, the invisible college must include a network of people who can support and strengthen your emotional and physical well-being both inside and outside the professional setting. This includes finding friendships with people in whom you can confide, deepening familial bonds that keep you grounded, and choosing romantic partners who will aptly share all your burdens and responsibilities (Sandberg, 2013).

Approaches and Strategies in Building an Invisible College

In addition to developing individual knowledge and skills, you should intentionally cultivate—as part of the overall professional capacity building—a network of collaborators and supporters that helps strengthen your work sustainability and career development. However, networks can take on many forms, and their effects are not identical. We all need to strategically engage in invisible college building that reaps the most fruitful results.

You could begin by identifying professional goals and priorities—better yet, long-term career paths: Which professional area(s) do you want to build or strengthen (scholarship, teaching, and/or service)? How can you benefit from a network of collaborators and supporters to succeed in your priority areas? What kind of an invisible college do you need to help you achieve your goals? Some of the answers may be readily available given your career stage. For example, if you are a faculty member on the tenure track, the urgency of receiving tenure may naturally necessitate your areas of focus (e.g., How can I build a research network to generate more publications given the tenure emphasis on scholarship?). How can you build your credentials as a nationally renowned educator in an institution that values teaching? For post-tenure or midcareer faculty, your path forward might be less delineated[1] and strategies for invisible college building less obvious.

Following prioritization and goal setting, the next step leads to the "how to" in building an invisible college. While there is not an all-encompassing formula for network building in the context of wide-ranging needs and goals, several general principles may be considered, accompanied by sample strategies. One useful principle is *propinquity*, which suggests that spatial proximity can lead to interpersonal closeness. Much research has shown that when people are geographically close to each other, they are more likely to become friends, due to mere exposure (Moreland & Beach, 1992), low social transaction costs (Kadushin, 2011), or an affordance for more frequent informal communication (Katz & Martin, 1997). The propinquity effect is evident in research collaborations. For example, Sooho and Bozeman (2005) found that among people who collaborate, more than half of existing collaborative relationships exist within one's own institution. Thus, turning physical proximity into social closeness and, in turn, to work productivity is important in building an invisible college. Sample strategies include the following:

- Make friends with colleagues in your department, college, and institution by meeting them through formal and informal events on campus. Follow up with in-person meetings or email correspondence to identify common interests and discuss potential collaboration opportunities.

- Build relationships with folks in local and community organizations through getting involved in community projects/services. Connect community needs with our academic work.

- Foster proximity with others by creating opportunities for encounters through:
  - attending conferences/workshops,
  - participating in social and professional programs,
  - joining and engaging with interest groups,
  - volunteering services at social and professional events,
  - connecting with local academic units (e.g., offer to give a talk or ask to visit labs) as you travel, and
  - organizing events where you invite individuals you want to connect with.

---

1. Please refer to Chapter 16 in this book for practical guidance. For individuals who are in search of a professional direction, the following resource may also be helpful in jumpstarting the process of exploration: https://www.insidehighered.com/advice/2017/10/11/how-select-best-path-after-gaining-tenure-essay.

Here's an example: Much of my invisible college is rooted locally through proximity. For instance, I have made many good friends in the foreign language department and have relied on these friends for friendship, as well as research opportunities and recommendation letters. They also connected me to service opportunities around campus. I have also actively volunteered my time for the local YWCA in the past few years, after having served on the board of directors. Through grant applications and community events, I have applied my expertise in psychology to meet the needs of the organization as well as to use the platform of the organization to disseminate academic work on psychology. Other times, I had to travel far to meet a local collaborator, such as meeting one colleague who lived an hour away from me in Japan through our participation in an APA-National Council–sponsored travel and mentorship program.

Homophily (Kadushin, 2011) is another mechanism for invisible college building based on the principle that similarity breeds connection. Individuals enjoy the comfort of interacting with others who are similar (Berscheid & Walster, 1969), and indeed often exchange ideas with others who are alike (McPherson et al., 2001). In the research context, there is evidence showing a positive relationship between similarity of beliefs and attitudes and the number of interactions (Borgatti & Foster, 2003). Research collaboration is more likely between researchers with the same rank than those with different ranks, and such research productivity proves to be more impactful as well (Stvilia et al., 2011). Thus, rather than trying to establish a new collaboration network, it may be effective to cultivate relationships with others who are similar, including leveraging the trust and homophily in existing networks. Sample strategies may include the following:

- Build relationships with those who share a part of your educational or professional history, such as graduate friends, previous colleagues, and fellow alumni from the same institution by intentionally seeking such individuals out to build collaborations.

- Work with individuals who come from a similar intellectual heritage, speak a similar academic language, and are like-minded in interests/passions.

- Form alliances with others based on similar personal characteristics, such as career stage, gender, race, nationality, ethnicity, and social status.

Here's an example: Many individuals became close members of my invisible college because we shared something in common. For example, after reconnecting with a colleague in China with whom I worked on my master's thesis, our shared history and similar academic ranks and professional goals energized us to successfully build an international program for our current respective students. Furthermore, many of my graduate school friends have become collaborators even though we are now scattered around the world and are typically separated by disciplinary divides. We are able to continue our personal and professional relationships because of familiarity and overlapping interests. In more formal manners, one could easily find allyship and support in professional organizations that capitalize on shared identities or cultural heritage, such as the SPSP group for Chinese scholars that many of my friends are actively a part of.

Counterintuitive to the last principle, the principle of *heterophily* (i.e., seeking out or being attracted to others who are different from oneself) may also be essential for success, as it increases diversity in network connections (Niehaus & O'Meara, 2015), breeds creativity (Leung et al., 2008), and promotes innovations (Rogers et al., 2005). In social network analysis, having diversity means to have many weak ties in one's networks (Granovetter, 1973), which are relationships that lie outside the core, existing relationships within a coherent social network. Weak ties connect otherwise separate circles (e.g., two unconnected groups of colleagues) and increases your access to wider ranges of networks. Evidence shows that weak ties can effectively facilitate the availability of instrumental resources (Ibarra, 1993), career change and opportunities (Higgins, 2001), and upward mobility (Polodny & Baron, 1997). Sample strategies may include the following:

- Engage with others who come from a different training background and/or expertise domain to generate synergistic work.

- Participate in ongoing conversations with colleagues who may hold different views about the issues that you work on.

- Expand the diversity in your collaboration network by participating in multi-site/multi-national projects.

- Dialogue with people whose experiences are different from your own through social activities, such as book clubs.

- Develop your skill sets in new domains of interest (e.g., data analytics, creative writing, yoga, gardening) and incorporate the expanded network/expertise into your existing work.

- Form alliances with colleagues who are on the margin, whose unique perspectives are sidelined in the mainstream but have the potential to challenge and transform.

Here's an example: Some of our most energizing work can come from collaboration with friends and colleagues who are dissimilar to us in terms of personality, experience, and training. For example, I have worked with computer scientists to apply psychological principles to smartphone applications after having met them in data science classes in graduate school. A fellow social psychologist has collaborated with tech entrepreneurs to package psychological insight for the masses. A colleague cordially engages thinkers on the opposite end of the political spectrum to demonstrate fruitful intellectual debates. Another friend helps diversify the field of mathematics by contributing to a network that expands access and opportunities for underrepresented students and colleagues.

Lastly, there is the pertinent issue of *centrality*, which approximates the importance of your position in a network. This principle is reserved for last as it, with its elitist connotations, may seemingly threaten the spirit to democratize the invisible college. Such a preface aside, it is undeniable that in much scholarship on the invisible college, centrality has been identified as a defining feature, in that invisible colleges are often characterized as networks of/around "elite," "high-producing," and "outstanding" figures of "status" (Weedman, 1993, p. 756). Based on this principle, there is value in occupying a large degree of centrality because such an individual has contact with many others in the network, commands much relational and instrumental power, and is the producer of knowledge whom others referentially discuss (Knoke & Burt, 1983). Possessing centrality has indeed been found to predict many positive professional outcomes, such as job performance (Sparrowe et al., 2001), leadership, popularity, positive reputation, power, influence (Zhang & Luo, 2017), and scholarly outcomes (Vardaman et al., 2012). Nevertheless, a feminist approach to centrality requires us to first heed the quality of our own positionality in the network and/or that of those we connect with. Engage in consciousness-raising activities (e.g., conversations, books, films, workshops, self-examination) to examine how the unique locales of our gender, age, ethnicity, sexual orientation, class, nationality intersect in implicating our power and privilege. Cultivate strategies toward personal success while protecting and strengthening the empowerment of others. Treat central positions of power and influence not just as an end but a means to maximize access for success and prosperity for a maximum number of people. Sample strategies may include the following:

- Position yourself and your work in high-impact venues to attract networking interest from others.

- Build collaborative or mentoring relationships with colleagues possessing high centrality through strategies such as direct requests, introductions by mutual friends or colleagues, presenting tangible collaboration plans, or building relationships through professional events.

- Collaborate with friends and colleagues who may have access to high-impact figures.

- Approach prominent researchers directly to discuss research questions or to pitch collaboration ideas.

- Meet and work with central figures in a network through service opportunities.

- Join leadership academies or develop one's own leadership skills to access power.

- Solicit feedback or mentorship from elite members of a group.

- Organize or participate in high-impact events that feature prominent colleagues.

Maintaining an Invisible College

An invisible college begins with relationship formation but requires careful maintenance over time. The following strategies may be of value as you attempt to bridge the gaps across power differentials, disciplinary norms, and individual styles in order to create an equitable network and to generate productive outcomes:

- Collaborate with members of the invisible college (MIC) on sustainable projects to which all parties can uniquely contribute.

- Beware of power dynamics yet not be overwhelmed or constrained by them. When approaching someone higher in power, have confidence in your unique ability to contribute without appearing arrogant; meanwhile, express eagerness without compromising sincerity. When interacting with someone lower in power, show respect and curiosity without condescension; furthermore, demonstrate generosity and kindness without relinquishing your own boundaries.

- Negotiate with the MIC a process of interaction that is fair, equitable, and effective. Allocate divisions of labor justly and reasonably.

- Address communication issues by acknowledging different disciplinary norms and work styles, especially with others who come from dissimilar backgrounds. Assume humility, flexibility, and open-mindedness when seeking compromises.

- Keep in touch with the MIC by sharing news/updates and scheduling regular check-ins.

- Ask the MIC for feedback, advice, and opinions about your own work.

- Share with the MIC resources, opportunities, or information that may be of interest to them.

- Use the MIC as a sounding board to pitch new ideas and discuss creative solutions.

- Help the MIC by providing them with feedback, recommendations, and support.

- Maintain an active, informative, and appropriate social media presence by sharing about yourself and engaging with the MIC's content.

- Recruit the MIC as accountability and/or writing partners.

Issues and Challenges in Building an Invisible College

A primary challenge with the invisible college is that by nature, it is "invisible." Such invisibility renders its impact immeasurable and its pursuit elusive. While many believe that universities are meritocratic institutions based on academic excellence (O'Connor et al., 2017) and individual productivity (Ryazanova & Jaskiene, 2022), more researchers are highlighting the importance of nonmeritocratic (and often hidden) elements—such as useful contacts and the depth of their interconnectedness within networks—in professional advancement in academia (van den Brink at al., 2014). Moreover, an invisible network of support in our personal lives proves to be an essential backbone of our professional life, serving to alleviate the burdens of invisible emotional and physical labor, particular relevant to working parents' "second shift" (Hochschild & Machung, 1990).

However, everyone does not have equal access to the invisible college. Women have traditionally not been strong constituents of this network, and as a result experience limited professional advancement (Ibarra, 1993). The lack of accessibility to effective networks is exacerbated for those who also belong to an ethnic minority (Hall & Sandler, 1983). Evidence shows that individuals with two or more marginalized identities face isolation and underrepresentation, responsibility overload, struggles to achieve work–life balance, as well as challenges and mistrust from students on campus (Turner, 2002). Among underrepresented groups, the invisible college proves to be a particularly vital source of support to help faculty persist in the academy by way of providing networking and mentoring opportunities (e.g., Jones & Osborne-Lampkin, 2013).

Furthermore, the invisible college may be challenging to maintain. Due to its informal nature, an invisible college may be more organic and less stable than an existing hierarchical structure (Bradeley et al., 1993). Scripts, roles, and norms of interaction must be negotiated from the bottom up among network members, requiring continuous exertions of intentional efforts. Paradoxically, such managerial responsibilities may often fall on the person in direct need of such networks, who may coincidentally be on a lower academic rank and already stretched thin. Thus, the spontaneous nature of building an invisible college and the energy it constantly commands may prove the network-building process strenuous.

Moreover, many aspects of the invisible college require balancing. One, quantity does not necessarily predict quality. In the case of research collaboration, scholarship shows that the size of your research collaboration network does not have a linear relationship with research productivity. While there is evidence suggesting that research quality increases with the group size (Kenna & Berche, 2011), productivity may in fact plummet once the group size exceeds a particular threshold (von Tunzelmann et al., 2003), even though such collaborations strengthen information diversity and knowledge creation (O'Leary et al., 2011).[2] Second, while diversity holds a multitude of benefits (Katz & Martin, 1997), too much heterophily in the network may ironically impede effective knowledge cross-fertilization due to communication challenges between individuals who are drastically dissimilar. However, the good news is, as the frequency of communication increases even heterophilous interactions may become homogenized over time, drawing interaction partners closer in similarity (Kadushin, 2011).

Finally, one should be aware of the limitations of the invisible college. One caveat is that, over time, there is a tendency for groups to reach homophily or homogenization by developing similar preferences and standards of conduct. While this effect may, in the long-term, unite members with a shared sense of identity and intensify collaboration effectiveness, it could constrain the innovation of ideas and curb the evolution of purposes for the individual and the group (Woolcock & Narayan, 2000). Perpetual vigilance is required to ensure the invisible college remains a steady source of accountability and inspiration, and not of constraint and obligation.

Conclusion

Since its inception, the invisible college has positively contributed to the advancement of science and the development of individuals. In a competitive

---

2. Heinze et al. (2009) imply that there may an optimal group size for research productivity, such as a group size of five to six members for researchers in natural science, which could be a point of reference for psychologists.

age of knowledge economy and harsh academic climates, its value is more indispensable than ever. Through the interconnectedness in the invisible college, the individual academic is transported from a position of isolation and self-reliance to a more inclusive and effective realm of collaboration, productivity, opportunities, and resources. While each person's invisible college may differ in terms of proximity, homophily, heterophily, and centrality among its members, it undoubtedly has the equal potential to spawn many personal and professional benefits.

Beyond the ripe personal benefits, there is arguably an epistemological necessity to promote invisible colleges in the field of psychology. In the age of a "replicability crisis" (Nelson et al., 2018) and among the ensuing calls to bolster the validity of psychological research, there is increasingly less value placed on individual work (Vazire, 2018) and more demand for collaborative research (Byers-Heinlein et al., 2020). Furthermore, to challenge the hegemony of particular cultural values and suppositions about the human condition in psychology (Duarte et al., 2015; Henrich et al., 2010), outreach to and inclusion of diverse perspective are sorely welcome. As debates continue and diversity of thoughts flourishes, the invisible college may fundamentally strengthen and expand the insights that our field offers to the world.

The initial invisible college originates from a grass roots movement some hundreds of years ago that sought to subvert the dominant intellectual powers of the day (Lomas, 2003). The moral and political implications of this historic fact resonate loudly today. United through the invisible college, those who used to stay on the sidelines—including colleagues with marginalized identities (Turner, 2002) and graduate students (Byers-Heinlein et al., 2020)—can now access platforms of resources, alliances, and opportunities. Manifesting empowerment, collaboration, and resourcefulness for the individual, the invisible college may very well be the ground that nourishes a more inclusive, equitable, and creative world for all.

References

Austin, A. E., & McDaniels, M. (2006). Preparing the professoriate of the future: Graduate student socialization for faculty roles. In J. C. Smart (Ed.), *Higher education: Handbook of theory and research, XXI* (pp. 397–456). Springer.

Berscheid, E., & Walster, E. H. (1969). *Interpersonal attraction*. Addison-Wesley.

Borgatti, S. P., & Foster, P. C. (2003). The network paradigm in organizational research: A review and typology. *Journal of Management*, 29(6), 991–1013. https://doi.org/10.1016/S0149 2063_03_00087-4

Bradeley, S., Hausmann, J. A., & Nolan, R. (1993). *Globalization, technology and competition*. Harvard Business School Press.

Brass, D. J., Galaskiewicz, J., Greve, H. R., & Tsai, W. (2004). Taking stock of networks and organizations: A multilevel perspective. *Academy of Management Journal*, 47, 795–817.

Byers-Heinlein, K., Bergmann, C., Davies, C., Frank, M.C., Hamlin, J.K., Kline, M., Kaminsky, J. F., Kosie, J. E., Lew-Williams, C., Liu, L., Mastroberardino, M., Singh, L., Waddle, C. P. G., Zetttersten, M., & Soderstrom, M. (2020). Building a collaborative psychological science: Lessons learned from ManyBabies 1. *Canadian Psychology/Psychologie canadienne, 61*, 349–363. https://doi.org/10.1037/cap0000216

Coser, L. A. (1965). *Men of ideas: A sociologist's view.* The Free Press.

Crawford, S. (1971). Informal communication among scientists in sleep research. *Journal of the American Society for Information Science, 22,* 301–310.

Dawson, S., Tan, J. P. L., & McWilliam, E. (2011). Measuring creative potential: Using social network analysis to monitor a learners' creativity capacity. *Australasian Journal of Educational Technology, 27*(6), 924–942. https://doi.org/10.14742/ajet.921

Duarte, J., Crawford, J., Stern, C., Haidt, J., Jussim, L., & Tetlock, P. (2015). Political diversity will improve social psychological science. *Behavioral and Brain Sciences, 38,* 1–58. https://doi.org/10.1017/S0140525X14000430

Frost, C.O. (1979). The use of citations in literary research: A preliminary classification of citation functions. *Library Quarterly, 49,* 399–414.

Granovetter, M. S. (1973). The strength of weak ties. *American Journal of Sociology, 78*(6), 1360–1380.

Hall, R. M., & Sandler, B. R. (1983). *Academic mentoring for women students and faculty: A new look at an odd way to get ahead.* Association of American Colleges.

Heinze, T., Shapira, P., Rogers, J. D., & Senker, J. M. (2009). Organizational and institutional influences on creativity in scientific research. *Research Policy, 38*(4), 610–623.

Henrich, J., Heine, S. J., & Norenzayan, A. (2010). The weirdest people in the world? *Behavioral and Brain Sciences, 33*(2–3), 61–83. https://doi.org/10.1017/S0140525X0999152X.

Higgins, M.C. (2001). Changing careers: the effect of social context. *Journal of Organizational Behavior, 22,* 595–618. doi:10.1002/job.104

Hochschild, A., & Machung, A. (1990). *The second shift.* Avon Books.

Ibarra, H. (1993). Personal networks of women and minorities in management: A conceptual framework. *Academy of Management Review, 18,* 56–87.

Jones, T. B., & Osborne-Lampkin, L. (2013). Black female faculty success and early career professional development. *Negro Educational Review, 64*(1/4), 59–75.

Kadushin, C. (2011). *Understanding social networks: Theories, concepts, and findings.* Oxford University Press.

Katz, J. S., & Martin, B. R. (1997). What is research collaboration? *Research Policy, 26*(1), 1–18. https://doi.org/10.1016/S0048-7333(96)00917-1

Kenna, R., & Berche, B. (2011). Critical masses for academic research groups and consequences for higher education policy and management. *Higher Education Management and Policy, 23*(3), 9–29.

Kezar, A. (2014). Higher education change and social networks: A review of research. *The Journal of Higher Education, 85,* 91–125. https://doi.org/10.1353/jhe.2014.0003

Knoke, D., & Burt, R. S. (1983). Prominence. In R. S. Burt & M. Miner (Eds.), *Applied network analysis: A methodological introduction* (pp. 195–222). SAGE.

Leung, A. K.-Y., Maddux, W. W., Galinsky, A. D., & Chiu, C.-Y. (2008). Multicultural experience enhances creativity: The when and how. *American Psychologist, 63*(3), 169–181. https://doi.org/10.1037/0003-066X.63.3.169

Lievrouw, L. A. (1989). The invisible college reconsidered: Bibliometrics and the development of scientific communication theory. *Communication Research, 16*(5), 615–628.

Lomas, R. (2003). *The Royal Society, freemasonry and the birth of modern science.* Headline.

McPherson, M., Smith-Lovin, L., & Cook, J. M. (2001). Birds of a feather: Homophily in social networks. *Annual Review of Sociology, 27,* 415–444. https://doi.org/10.1146/annurev.soc.27.1.415

Moreland, R. L., & Beach, S. R. (1992). Exposure effects in the classroom: The development of affinity among students. *Journal of Experimental Social Psychology*, *28*(3), 255–276. https://doi.org/10.1016/0022-1031(92)90055-O

Nelson, L. D., Simmons, J., & Simonsohn, U. (2018). Psychology's renaissance. *Annual Review of Psychology*, *69*, 511–534. https://doi.org/10.1146/annurev-psych-122216-011836

Newman, M. E. (2001). The structure of scientific collaboration networks. *Proceedings of the National Academy of Sciences*, *98*, 404–409. https://doi.org/10.1073/pnas.021544898

Niehaus, E., & O'Meara, K. (2015). Invisible but essential: The role of professional networks in promoting faculty agency in career advancement. *Innovative Higher Education*, *40*, 159–171. https://doi.org/10.1007/s10755-014-9302-7

O'Connor, P., Lopez, E.M., O'Hagan, C., Wolffram, A., Aye, M., Chizzola, V., Mich, O., Apostolov, G., Topuzova, I., Sağlamer, G., Mine, G. T., & Çağlayan, H. (2017). Micro-political practices in higher education: A challenge to excellence as a rationalising myth? *Critical Studies in Education*, *61*(2), 195–211. https://doi.org/10.1080/17508487.2017.1381629

O'Leary, M. B., Mortensen, M., & Woolley, A. W. (2011). Multiple team membership: A theoretical model of its effects on productivity and learning for individuals and teams. *Academy of Management Review*, *36*(3), 461–478. https://doi.org/10.5465/AMR.2011.61031807

Polodny, J. M., & Baron, J. N. (1997). Relationships and resources: Social networks and mobility in the workplace. *American Sociological Review*, *62*, 673–693.

Rogers, E. M., Medina, U. E., Rivera, M. A., & Wiley, C. J. (2005). Complex adaptive systems and the diffusion of innovations. *Innovation Journal: The Public Sector Innovation Journal*, *10*(3), 1–26.

Ryazanova, O., & Jaskiene, J. (2022). Managing individual research productivity in academic organizations: A review of the evidence and a path forward. *Research Policy*, *51*(2). https://doi.org/10.1016/j.respol.2021.104448

Sandberg, S. (2013). *Lean in: Women, work, and the will to lead*. Knopf.

Seibert, S. E., Kraimer, M. L., & Liden, R. C. (2001). A social capital theory of career success. *Academy of Management Journal*, *44*, 219–237.

Simonton, D. K. (1997). Creative productivity: A predictive and explanatory model of career trajectories and landmarks. *Psychological Review*, *104*, 66–89. https://doi.org/10.1037/0033-295X.104.1.66

Sooho, L., & Bozeman, B. (2005). The impact of research collaboration on scientific productivity. *Social Studies of Science*, *35*(5), 673–702. https://doi.org/10.1177/0306312705052359

Sparrowe, R. T., Liden, R. C., Wayne, S. J., & Kraimer, M. L. (2001). Social networks and the performance of individuals and groups. *Academy of Management Journal*, *44*, 316–325. https://doi.org/10.2307/3069458

Stvilia, B., Hinnant, C.C., Schindler, K., Worrall, A., Burnett, G., Burnett, K., Kazmar, M. M., & Marty, P. F. (2011). Composition of scientific teams and publication productivity at a national science lab. *Journal of the American Society for Information Science and Technology*, *62*(2), 270–283. https://doi.org/10.1002/asi.21464

Turner, C. S. V. (2002). Women of color in academe: Living with multiple marginality. *The Journal of Higher Education*, *73*(1), 74–93.

van den Brink, M., & Benschop, Y. (2014). Gender in academic networking: The role of gatekeepers in professorial recruitment. *Journal of Management Studies*, *51*(3), 460–492. https://doi.org/10.1111/joms.12060

Vardaman, J. M., Amis, J. M., Dyson, B. P., Wright, P. M., Van de, R., & Randolph, G. (2012). Interpreting change as controllable: The role of network centrality and self-efficacy. *Human Relations*, *65*(7), 835–859. https://doi.org/10.1177/0018726712441642

Vazire S. (2018). Implications of the credibility revolution for productivity, creativity, and progress. *Perspectives on Psychological Science, 13*(4), 411–417. https://doi.org/10.1177/1745691617751884

von Tunzelmann, N., Ranga, M., Ben, M., & Geuna, A. (2003). The effect of size on research performance—A SPRU review. Retrieved from http//www.sussex.ac.uk/Users/prff0/Publications/Size%20HE%20research.pdf

Weedman, J. (1993). On the "isolation" of humanists: A report of an invisible college. *Communication Research, 20*(6), 749–776. https://doi.org/10.1177/009365093020006001

Woolcock, M., & Narayan, D. (2000). Social capital: Implications for development theory, research, and policy. *The World Bank Research Observer, 15*(2), 225–249.

Wunsch, M. A., & Johnsrud, L. K. (1992). Breaking barriers: Mentoring junior faculty women for professional development and retention. *To Improve the Academy,* 269. https://digitalcommons.unl.edu/podimproveacad/269

Zhang, J., & Luo, Y. (2017). Degree centrality, betweenness centrality, and closeness centrality in social network. *Proceedings of the 2017 2nd International Conference on Modelling, Simulation and Applied Mathematics, 132,* 300–303.

CHAPTER 5

Publishing 101
Manuscript Preparation and Navigating the Editorial Process

- **Jan Yoder**
  The Pennsylvania State University

Although I spent most of my 40-plus-year career navigating the editorial process as an author, I was surprised by how much new I learned as an editor. My goal here is to share some of these insights, starting with my own journey toward being an editor (See Yoder, 2021, for reflections on what I learned from editing *Sex Roles* about doing feminist research on gender and gendered contexts). When I applied to be editor of *Psychology of Women Quarterly* (*PWQ*), I had completed 156 reviews as an ad hoc reviewer for 29 different journals as well as served *PWQ* as a consulting editor for 12 years and an associate editor (AE) for 2 years. Being an editor was not a sought-after career goal for me; without the pedigree of a top-tier university, I thought I would never qualify. Rather, my trajectory toward becoming an editor evolved over my years of participation in the process, and my expectations that being an editor would offer me opportunities not only to contribute meaningfully to feminist scholarship but also to serve as a mentor to authors, reviewers, and aspiring editors.

I found being an editor highly challenging as well as rewarding; still, there are many other good reasons for being involved in the editorial process. Serving as an ad hoc reviewer made me a better researcher and writer because I not only saw what other researchers/authors were doing but also was privy to the expert feedback authors received from other reviewers as well as editors' decision letters. I further gleaned an insider's view of the editorial process itself because I was, at times, part of the revision process, observing authors' successful and failed responses to revision requests. Reviewing also opened up networking opportunities by making me known to the editors/AEs who solicited my reviews, wrote promotion letters for me, and included me on their editorial boards. Although there were times I felt overwhelmed by requests to review, being part of the process was enriching, exciting, and gratifying.

I spent 14 months with *PWQ* as its incoming editor, then 6 years as its editor (2010–2015), and finally 5 years as editor of *Sex Roles* (2016–2020). At *Sex Roles* alone, I handled 3,206 manuscripts, making almost 5,000 decisions (Yoder, 2021). I soon discovered that as an editor I was more frequently asked to contribute letters for colleagues' tenure and promotion cases, directly expanding my opportunities to support junior feminist scholars. My academic jobs have spanned universities that weighed both research and teaching in their promotion decisions (University of Wisconson-Milwaukee, University of Akron, and Kent State University) as well as a more teaching-focused institution (Webster University). As a senior scholar with fewer worries about my own research productivity, I was able to manage being editor of *PWQ* without university support; however, to take on the more intense demands of *Sex Roles* as a monthly journal, I was very grateful to negotiate a position at nearby Kent State where I had limited teaching responsibilities.

What I fundamentally came to appreciate across all these experiences is that by publishing feminists' scholarship, we ensure that feminist scholars will be present, valued, and influential in the academy where publication records matter. My goal with this chapter is to offer advice to researchers, reviewers, would-be editors, consumers of published works, and even teachers and activists by sharing some of the insights I gained as an editor. Of course, I cannot speak for all editors, but my hope is that you will find something valuable here, whatever your experiences and aspirations regarding published scholarship may be. First, I focus on manuscript preparation by offering some tips for successful writing and for targeting a specific journal, then move on to suggestions for navigating the editorial process by shedding some light on the review process, sharing ideas about how to successfully revise a paper, and highlighting the importance of being part of the editorial process as a reviewer and possible future editor. I conclude with some thoughts about expanding being published beyond traditional research to include work relevant to teaching and feminist activism, making the argument that, as academics and as feminists, we all have a stake in publishing.

Manuscript Preparation

In the next section, I focus on how to prepare your manuscript and how to target particular journals.

Tips for Successful Writing

Every empirical paper can only be as strong as the research it reports; however, even sound research can struggle toward publication if it is not conveyed effectively. Toward this end, I cannot overemphasize the importance of telling a *well-organized*, *coherent* "story." From my vantage as an editor, this story's focal point is the research question(s) and/or hypotheses. It is these that "walk" a reader through your story, leading them to the handful of major takeaway points you target. It is imperative that you be clear in your own mind about what these points are and that you state them precisely. One strategy for pinpointing your takeaways is to explain your paper in lay terms to a naïve audience; as an editor, I often tried to sum up a paper in a few nonjargony sentences. When a research question or hypothesis is muddled, your story loses coherence and can readily become what others read into it, should they persist at all, rather than what you want to convey.

A precise research question or hypothesis provides the focus for your introduction. This section typically opens with a general argument about the importance of your work by drawing on theory, past research, and/or real-world practices. Basing this argument on the grounds that "no one has done this before" is weak because, unless you are doing replication work, this point is assumed and because there may be compelling reasons no one has found this work worthy of their efforts. Ultimately, the introduction funnels to clear statements of your precise questions/hypotheses. It does not summarize everything you read on the topic, but rather it is confined to the logical steps you need to make the case for what you propose. These questions/hypotheses then guide the reader through your data collection in the "Method" section, making clear all the decisions you made regarding your sample and sampling, choices of variables, and so on. As an editor, I made liberal use of online supplements (i.e., ancillary materials that accompany a published paper electronically and that authors append to their submitted paper) to make sure authors disclosed their complete methods while confining what was reported in the published paper to details relevant to the paper's main "storyline."

Similarly, I expected the "Results" sections to be question/hypotheses centered, not statistics centered. Statistics are the means to address an end (e.g., Is hypothesis 1 supported?), not be ends themselves. Operationally, this approach means clearly structuring a "Results" section around what you asked or hypothesized, such as "To test hypothesis 1, which predicted ..., we did this test, finding that ... and concluding that hypothesis 1 was supported." Although the Results section should be guided by what you proposed, there are instances when analyses raise points beyond the paper's major storyline. As an editor, I was committed to erring on the side of fully reporting research by offering authors two possibilities regarding unanticipated supplemental findings: (a) adding a "Supplemental Findings" section to the Results section of the published paper or (b) reporting the finding(s) in the online supplement. A key to choosing between these options is a judgment about how wide an audience of scholars might be intrigued by these ancillary findings.

I also urge you to ask whether and how effectively to use tables and figures to complement your story by making sure that they are not gratuitous. Figures should add visual clarity to the text, and their main point should stand out for readers. For example, I asked authors to make significant lines and pathways black, and nonsignificant ones gray, so that key findings "popped." Useful tables serve to unclutter the text by confining statistical details to them, and tables in either the Method or Results sections can serve as easy-to-consult summaries for demographic and quantitative details as well as for categorizations in qualitative work or content analyses. Given that readers come to any paper with varying levels of research sophistication, I suggest that you summarize your findings in the opening few paragraphs of your Discussion section. Ambiguities only open your paper up to misinterpretations.

I further urge you to tell a *complete* story. Good reviewers understand that research is not an endpoint, but rather it is an ongoing process so that it is more honest and ultimately in authors' best interests not to hide, but instead to discuss, shortcomings. It is critical to report data collections and analyses in full. An online supplement is a useful resource to balance comprehensive, along with streamlined, reporting, and by cataloguing extraneous variables there, it can serve as a safeguard against p-hacking (running multiple unplanned tests to eventually find one that crossed the $p < .05$ threshold). Additionally, clear references to authors' related papers within the manuscript itself and at submission in a letter to the editor (American Psychological Association [APA], 2020) are critical to avoiding allegations of piecemeal publication. Handy checklists of what information should be reported in a complete manuscript are available in the APA publication manual (2020, pp. 77–81; 95–99; also see Levitt et al., 2018, for qualitative research), and complete reporting has long been a cornerstone of feminist publishing that is now being taken up by the open science movement more broadly in psychology (Matsick et al., 2021).

Lastly, take some time to think about the title, abstract, and keywords (i.e., search terms) for your paper. These final touches often come when you are feeling burned out, but to editors they are highly important because they "sell" your papers to potential readers. Your abstract should summarize all sections of your paper and entice a broad audience of readers, extending (when possible) beyond scholars to counselors and therapists, activists, educators and students, policymakers and administrators, and lay readers, including media outlets. Keep in mind that where your goals and those of an editor overlap is in having your paper widely read and cited. (The single most frequently used indicator of an academic journal's quality is its 2-year impact factor, that is, the average number of times papers published in the prior 2 years are cited in the indexed year.) Do, however, avoid overselling your paper; be cognizant of its limitations and the basic fact that research is a building process in which your work arguably takes some steps forward.

Reflection question: What is the core story I want to tell with my paper? Do all parts of my paper focus on telling this complete story?

Targeting a Specific Journal

Selecting a journal to target is a major key toward successful publishing. It may make you dig deep into your own, sometimes competing, values and goals (e.g., a high-risk, top-tier journal that will lend academic prestige; where you are on your career path; a journal that will target a specific audience whom you want to inform). One useful resource is your own reference list—the journals that you are citing will provide cues about where your work will fit. And, "fit" is a key here. Editors typically screen new submissions and make upfront judgments about fit, including both topical and methodological (and possibly even ideological) appropriateness. A key indicator of fit for me was a paper's reference list; it most clearly suggested a good fit if papers from the journal were cited or, at the very least, the broader gender literature was represented. It is important to frame or tailor your paper to the specific journal to which you are submitting. Given the high rejection rates of solid journals in psychology, it is important to appropriately reframe a paper that was previously rejected at another journal. A rejected paper need not signal its end; instead, the feedback gleaned from the process may help to strengthen your paper for another outlet. Like many of my colleagues, I have had solid, previously rejected papers successfully published.

There are various resources to help you enhance the suitability of your paper for a specific journal. Exploring the journal's website, especially the journal's "Aims and Scope" statement, will lay out the editor's vision for their journal. For example, *Sex Roles*' Aims and Scope statement fundamentally described the purview of the journal (despite its outdated name) as focused on understanding gender and gendered contexts (Yoder, 2016). Oftentimes, an editor's vision for the journal is further detailed in published editorials (e.g., Yoder, 2010, 2016, 2021). A journal may also publish papers that outline its specific standards (e.g., in *Sex Roles*, Neuendorf, 2011, on content analysis; Chatfield, 2018, on qualitative methods). Most informative is the presence of papers similar to yours, both topically and methodologically. When still in doubt, you might send a brief email to the editor.

Reflection questions: Who do I want to reach with this paper? Why should they want to read it?

Navigating the Editorial Process

As you prepare your manuscript, it is also important to understand the peer review process and how to successfully respond to reviews. In this section, I focus on how best to navigate the editorial process.

Understanding the Review Process

Although journals have different editorial structures, the APA (2020) publication manual is unwavering in assigning "final editorial authority on decisions regarding manuscripts" (p. 377) to the journal's lead editor(s). Some journals, such as *PWQ*, rely on AEs to serve as the action editor on some subset of submissions by handling all stages of consideration up until the final acceptance. Other journals may employ AEs to handle specific content areas and relegate varying levels of decision-making responsibility to them. Journals' editorial boards commonly include consulting and/or advisory editors who expand the topical and methodological expertise of the core editorial staff who might be called on to mediate conflicting reviews.

All journals relying on peer review draw heavily on ad hoc reviewers who are recruited to provide input regarding an individual manuscript. Although reviewers' comments are generally masked to the author, journals frequently acknowledge the service of ad hoc reviewers by publishing a list of names in an issue of the journal (typically the December issue), and journals' online tracking systems for manuscripts often keep an internal log of reviewers for each submission, including editors' evaluations of reviewers' input. A journal's website should provide information about the specific editorial structure of the journal as well as identify all members of the editorial board.

Although there are various editorial structures, editorial functions are generally similar across journals. These functions begin with an administrative review to ensure that a submission is complete and masked (if required); approved submissions are then passed to the editor for desk review. The editor may opt to "desk reject" the paper at this point, most commonly citing "fit" (topical or methodological) or judged quality. With papers I judged to be high risk, I tried to strike a balance between rejecting so that an author might move forward with their work elsewhere and proceeding with peer review when I thought there might be some chance for success and/or that the author might benefit from expert feedback beyond my own. At both journals, I tried to complete my desk review within 2 weeks of having a paper forwarded to me by the system administrator (*Sex Roles*) or assistant (sometimes "managing") editor (*PWQ*).

The editor's second option at desk review is to either recruit reviewers themselves or assign the paper to an AE, who may either recommend desk rejection or recruit reviewers. Some submission processes require or allow authors to recommend peer reviewers, and I appreciated savvy authors who offered reasonable suggestions, especially those who drew from relevant experts identified on my editorial board. Alternatively, I was put out by authors who recommended clearly inappropriate reviewers such as coauthors, students, and colleagues. A source that I frequently used to identify relevant reviewers was a paper's reference list, and I used the keywords authors provided to search our electronic database of topically expert reviewers.

I was surprised by the number of times I recruited a reviewer who had reviewed the submitted paper for another journal. In those cases when reviewers asked me if I considered this history a conflict, I would leave it to the comfort of the reviewer to decide if they could make an unbiased judgment (with most accepting the review). Given the high rejection rates of many psychology journals, a previously rejected paper is not necessarily an unpublishable paper, especially if the author strengthened the paper in light of previous reviewers' comments. What reviewers generally found most disturbing was encountering a "flipped" paper, that is, a paper that was resubmitted having ignored previous feedback. Given that editors may elect to tap the same experts for reviews, authors are taking a risk when they fail to benefit from generously provided prior feedback from their colleagues.

My general philosophy regarding the solicitation of reviews is that I continue until I feel I can make a clear, defensible judgment that I can reasonably convey to the author. Different editors determine how long they give a reviewer to complete their review; I generally asked for 3 weeks, at times granting extensions and offering longer periods at demanding times of the academic year and taking into account holidays. The APA (2020) sets initial review at 2–3 months, recommending that an author track a paper's progress online and avoid contacting the editor or AE until at least 3 months have passed. Probably most confusing to authors is when they saw their paper come back to me but then go back out for review, a process that I always explained by noting (honestly) that I needed further input, oftentimes wanting to resolve a difference between two reviewers by seeking out additional advice from a member of my staff (which included methodological consultants, both quantitative and qualitative) and/or board.

If this initial decision does not result in rejection, then the editor or AE will monitor revisions, including whether additional review is needed and by whom (i.e., original and/or new reviewers). There may be multiple rounds of revision, so the timeline for the processing of a paper will depend on how timely authors are with their revisions as well as the responsiveness of reviewers. A paper may go through major then minor revisions and then be provisionally accepted when only small, usually formatting and writing, changes remain. A paper is formally accepted when a letter from the editor (or possibly the handling AE) makes acceptance clear and forwards the paper to the publisher for final copyediting and production with page proofs later approved by the author (commonly taking about 30 days). At this stage, a paper is "in press;" it is considered "published" when it is assigned a DOI (digital object identifier) by the production editor of the publisher. Overall, the timeline from submission to formal acceptance can take months (during my term at *Sex Roles*, averaging over 7 months), obviously shortened or extended by the number of required revisions and turnaround by authors, reviewers, and editors/AEs. Oftentimes, journals publish statistics about average turnaround times on their websites, but given that few papers are accepted outright (I had one in my lifetime as an author and can think of none during my editorships), submitting a successful paper to any journal is not a quick nor final process.

Submitting a paper to a journal involves complementary rights and responsibilities of authors and editors, ultimately resting on the mutual respect shared by both parties (see Figure 5.1). Many misunderstandings between authors and editors can be avoided by being transparent about the review process. I find it helpful to think about this process by picturing a continuum of editorial processing from rejection at one end to acceptance on the other (see Figure 5.2). Between these two endpoints are categories of major revision, minor revisions, and provisional acceptance. Each step incurs some probability of rejection, from 100% with either a desk rejection or editor's rejection after peer review, to 0% at formal acceptance. Major revision can have a wide range of rejection probabilities, from a very high to a more moderate level of risk. This range narrows for minor revisions and trends

Author's Rights	Editors' Responsibilities
Timely processing	Make informed decisions by soliciting advice as needed
Get feedback	Share constructive feedback, recognizing that reviews are advisory to the Editor
Get helpful directions on how to revise	Provide direction by reviewing reviewers' requests and answering authors' questions
Understand the Editor's plans for the re-submission	Outline the Editor's *expected* processing of the re-submission
Understand editorial decisions	Provide a rationale for each decision
Withdraw a paper	Make all final decisions (accept/reject)
Contest decisions with a rationale	Give full consideration
Authors' Responsibilities	**Editors' Rights**
Ensure that their submission is not under review elsewhere, follows ethical guidelines, and is not a duplicate or piecemeal publication; Pledge to make a good-faith effort to revise if requested	Know that the Editor's time and the journal's resources are not being wasted
Submit detailed revision notes	Expect timely and complete revisions
Submit complete and unambiguous papers	Have the information necessary to make an informed decision
Not re-submit rejected papers to the same journal (unless reconsideration is approved by the Editor)	Know that rejected papers will not be re-submitted

FIGURE 5.1 The complementary rights and responsibilities of authors and editors.

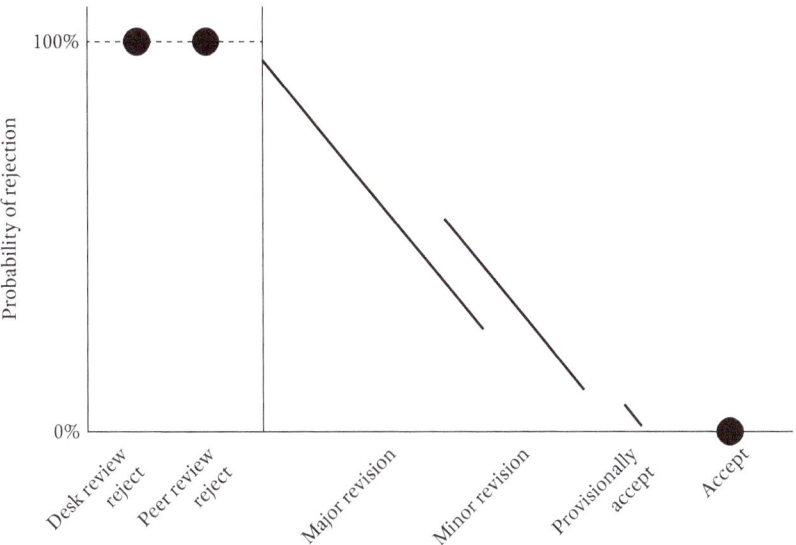

FIGURE 5.2 A continuum of editorial processing and the probability of a submission's rejection.

toward lower rejection probabilities, and at provisional acceptance this range shrinks even more and moves toward an even lower probability of rejection. The points I am trying to help you visualize here are that papers can be rejected anywhere along the continuum, from major revision to provisional acceptance, and that your goals as an author are to understand how likely your paper's probability of rejection is and what you can do to narrow it.

There are common cues in decision letters from the editor/AE to help authors decipher where they fall on this rejection-to-acceptance continuum and their probability of rejection. The certain key to knowing that your paper has been rejected is the absence of directions for resubmission. I do not know if other editors take this approach, but there were select occasions when I issued a rejection because I could not determine whether a revision would be successful (most commonly, when extensive re-analyses were required). Although these infrequent letters did not include directions for resubmission (signaling rejection), they did offer a chance to submit a *new* paper should a reconstructed paper meet the standards I outlined. They also made clear that by rejecting the original paper, I was freeing the author to submit it elsewhere. Ultimately, I did have a handful of papers that came back as new submissions, which then were successfully published. More commonly though, rejected papers cannot be revised and resubmitted to the rejecting journal, and authors can always take them elsewhere. At the other end of the continuum, accepted papers have information about the paper being sent to the publisher for final processing and often have a statement about being "in press."

There is a wide gray area from major revision to provisional acceptance that can be better understood by figuring out how to decode an editor's/AE's decision letter. Typically, a decision of major revision conveys this judgment with wording such as "rejected in its present form but …" This phrasing makes clear that the editor is not interested in an unrevised version, and the "but," along with subsequent information about how to resubmit, communicates that the editor is open to a revise-and-resubmit. Further cues regarding the riskiness of the revision can be gleaned from what the editor says about their expected handling of the revised paper, most notably whether the editor expects to recruit new reviewers (highest risk), return only to the original reviewer(s), or just involve an AE or the editor (lowest risk). Obviously, what an editor actually does with a revision is their prerogative given their guiding responsibility to make informed decisions. The distinguishing difference between a minor revision and provisional acceptance likely will come in lead wording of "may" and "will," respectively, and "accept pending changes." Overall, any expectations for involving parties beyond the editor/AE convey a higher risk of rejection.

Reflection question: Do I realistically understand where my paper stands in the review process?

Successfully Revising a Paper

Although decisions, ultimately, rest with editors, authors play a major role in moving their papers toward publication through their responses to revision requests. The most common reasons I have seen for failed revisions involve core re-analyses or new analyses that failed and clarified methodological details that revealed critical weaknesses. It also is imperative that an author respond to *all* requests, most efficiently and comprehensively by copying and pasting first the editor's letter and then the reviewers' comments into a file and then responding to each and every point (even if simply noting "done"). Each party tends to concentrate on their own input so that an author may be better served by redundancies than by assuming that one party's points were resolved in their responses to another party.

Successful revisions often entail a lot of work, thought, diplomacy, openness, and having a thick skin. As an author, I developed my own process for dealing with reviewers' and editors' comments, starting with some downtime to let the decision sink in (sometimes accompanied by cathartic venting around the dinner table) followed by an initial reading of the comments, more time to absorb those comments, and finally a more cool-headed, longer period to work thoughtfully and thoroughly through each comment, genuinely discovering that doing so strengthened my paper. Although your end goal as an author is to be published, it is important to recognize that an editor's main concern is to protect the journal. I consistently and deeply felt that because my name was at the top of the journal's masthead, I ultimately was responsible for its quality and contents. At some level then, an editor's safest decision is to reject a paper, and for journals with high rejection rates, passing on what may be a fine paper is less risky than accepting a paper that may prove problematic (e.g., nontraditional analyses). Thus, reassuring an editor or an editor's advisors (AEs and reviewers) is much more productive than being defensive or aggressive. And, remember that you as an author and the editor have a core goal in common: publishing papers that will be widely read and, most importantly for the prestige of the journal, cited.

Always use the editor's letter as your central guide, keeping in mind that editors diplomatically write these letters knowing that they are shared with both the author and the reviewers. These recipients create difficulties for an editor when reviewers offer conflicting advice, although I have most frequently found that useful middle ground can be found that satisfies both reviewers. As an editor, I took it upon myself to help the author find that path in my decision letter. If this advice from the editor remains unclear or is not offered, I think it is reasonable for an author to email the editor for advice prior to resubmitting. I certainly am not suggesting that you dismiss a reviewer's comment in your revision notes; indeed, the editor may return to this reviewer for input regarding other points. However, I am suggesting that you can respectfully decline to follow some reviewers' suggestions by providing a well-reasoned rationale for doing so.

As an author, you can respectfully argue against any undesired request regardless of the source. Indeed, there are times when, as a conscientious scholar, you may not be able to abide with a request. One often successful possibility is to open an interchange about the point in question by laying out your case in your revision notes (or in an email exchange with the editor prior to resubmission) about why you disagree with a request. Most unnerving for me as an editor were instances when an author followed one of my requests yet when I saw the changes I was taken aback about how mistaken I was. Even more distressing were a few times when the authors made ill-conceived changes despite their own unspoken reservations so that I discovered their concerns only when I came to realize that the changes I requested were not worthwhile.

Another tactic for revising authors is to offer the requested change along with the original, putting your preferred version in the paper itself and the less preferred in your revision notes. This approach implies that either version is acceptable to you as an author so that you are giving the editor/reviewer a preview of what both versions might look like. If both approaches are deemed to have merit, one possibility is to put the one that better fits your paper's storyline in the text itself; the other in an online supplement. My point is that you might consider being open to compromise and creativity and that there are multiple options for signaling this openness. Of course, there are times (thankfully very infrequently) when an author's integrity as a scholar and an editor's judgment of quality and content cannot be reconciled so that withdrawing a paper and seeking its publication elsewhere is in the author's best interests. My guess is that few, if any, editors will give in to an ultimatum; in the rare instances when I faced such a threat, I immediately rejected the paper.

As an author, I was sometimes frustrated by comments that suggested to me that the editor/reviewer did not closely read my paper. On further reflection, however, I generally came to realize that the need for stronger clarity rested with me, even if this meant being briefly redundant about a core point. As an editor, this call for clarity became even more vivid because, over the handling of many, many papers, I saw firsthand how different readers brought different vantages to a paper. Thus, I saw it as imperative that authors take responsibility for conveying precisely the points they want to make rather than leave openings for readers, who come to papers with a wide range of backgrounds and skills, to misinterpret their work. My mantra to authors became "better to make your points clearly than leave these to someone else." Oftentimes, authors are too close to their papers to see their gaps and ambiguities, so having less involved readers provide feedback, both prior to first submission and through editors and reviewers, can improve a paper's clarity, completeness, and conciseness. And finally, given the importance of submitting a strong revision, there is little harm in requesting an extension for resubmission if needed. Within reason, I always valued solid revisions over rushed ones.

Reflection question: If I put myself in the editor's or a reviewer's place, how might I react to my revisions and arguments?

The Importance of Reviewing

As an editor responsible for making informed decisions about manuscripts, I relied constantly and heavily on the expertise of others. Although all staff and reviewer inputs are advisory to an editor, there is no doubt in my mind that being an editor depends on the generosity of expert colleagues so that I am an unwavering supporter of peer review. Although reviewers' input certainly varied in how valuable it proved to me and authors, it was rare that it was of little use or was demeaning to the author and even rarer when it was not offered in good faith. In these highly infrequent cases, editors are empowered to not pass a review on to an author and to delete inappropriate portions of a review forwarded to the author.

Journals may provide some guidelines for doing reviews, often with a link within the invitation to review from the action editor. Two general points to keep in mind are (a) that you are being asked to provide expertise that the editor does not have and (b) that you are likely to be part of a group of reviewers. Given the former point, there is no need to contribute detailed editing of a paper; the editor and the publisher's copyeditor can handle these details. Given the latter point, it is common for an editor to seek out a team of two or more reviewers from whom they are seeking different expertise. If as a reviewer you have some relevant expertise as well as some limitations, simply note those limits in your review. For example, I may solicit input from a reviewer with broad topical expertise but not with relevant methodological expertise so that this reviewer's comments might highlight the former and note the absence of the latter. From the editor's perspective, our goal for any paper is for it to have a wide audience that is not limited to readers whose skills fit it exactly so that input across a group of knowledgeable reviewers can be most informative.

The inputs that are most valuable to an editor are your expert judgments about the soundness of the research/arguments and the value of the paper to the scholarly literature, as well as your constructive feedback to strengthen these contributions. Constructive reviews offered with kindness and respect provide invaluable opportunities to mentor and be mentored by knowledgeable colleagues. Although the review request often will include the decision you recommend regarding the paper (e.g., reject, major revisions), this confidential information is advisory to the editor but should not be shared with the author because decision-making is the exclusive purview of the editor.

Many review requests provide opportunities to share confidential information with the editor as well as (often masked) feedback to the author, which is also shared with other reviewers. Given this dissemination of feedback to the author, it is an opportunity for a senior reviewer to mentor junior colleagues. One of my biggest frustrations as an editor was when reviewers were inconsistent in their confidential feedback to me and in their more open comments to authors, particularly when they made a compelling case to me for rejection but then failed to repeat that case to the author. I believe that if a study has an identified fatal flaw that no amount of revision can remedy, then consistently say so, provide feedback for moving forward with follow-up work rather than revising, and decline the opportunity to review a revision.

There are various avenues to take toward becoming a reviewer. Most journals draw on published authors as potential reviewers, so publishing your own work may itself bring reviewer opportunities. One often-overlooked way to be published is to contribute a review of a book; for example, both *PWQ* and *Feminism & Psychology* publish book reviews and their book review editors are often looking for scholars willing to contribute a review of the books they target. The APA outlines the qualifications for reviewing for APA journals, offers a sign-up link, and identifies reviewer mentoring programs offered by APA journals (n.d.). *PWQ* maintains its own student advisory board (https://doi.org/10.1111/j.1471-6402.1991.tb00802.x). Many faculty welcome opportunities for graduate students to c-review a paper for which they received a review request, and by identifying their coreviewer to the action editor when the review is submitted, a journal may extend an opportunity to the coreviewer to be included in its online file of potential reviewers. How many reviews you take on as a junior scholar likely depends on your time and interests as well as whether your home institution values reviewing. Targeting journals central to your own scholarship for the bulk of your reviewing service work can further your own professional networking, whereas taking on reviews for a broader array of journals can be a good way to promulgate a feminist perspective throughout psychology.

Reflection question: How might my expertise as a reviewer most constructively advance scholarship and help the authors? the editor? the other reviewers who read it?

Publishing Is for All of Us

I targeted much of this chapter toward researchers, but I believe that whether being a published scholar is at the core of one's academic appointment or is more peripheral, we all as academics have a stake in sound, useful published scholarship. I contend that it can be productive to combine our work as researchers, teachers, and feminist activists, for example, by publishing about our own teaching (e.g., *PWQ*'s Teaching Briefs; Matlin, 2011), by conducting research regarding our own teaching effectiveness, and by using our own classes to do research that contributes to meaningful feminist scholarship (Yoder, 2018). We also can bring published research directly into the classroom (e.g., with the teaching supplements in *PWQ* that I spearheaded) and consider the meaningfulness of our scholarship for feminist activists and other practitioners (as I requested from most authors first in *PWQ* and then in *Sex Roles*).

Having served as part of the editorial process, from being an ad hoc reviewer through being an editor, I know that I have grown not only as a researcher but also as a teacher and feminist. Further, I believe that I helped others develop their own work and made a lasting contribution to our base of knowledge in psychology. My hope is that by sharing here some of what I learned as an editor I helped demystify the process as well as inspired you to take part in it at some level. My motto is not "publish or perish" but rather publish and prosper.

Reflection question: What role might my own participation in the editorial process play in my professional development and work?

References

American Psychological Association. (n.d.). *Call for reviewers*. https://www.apa.org/pubs/journals/resources/call-for-reviewers

American Psychological Association. (2020). *Publication manual of the American Psychological Association* (7th ed.). Author.

Chatfield, S. L. (2018). Considerations in qualitative research reporting: A guide for authors preparing articles for *Sex Roles*. *Sex Roles*, 79, 125–135. https://doi.org/10.1007/s11199-018-0930-8

Levitt, H. M., Bamberg, M., Creswell, J. W., Frost, D. M., Josselson, R., & Suárez-Orozco, C. (2018). Journal article reporting standards for qualitative primary, qualitative meta-analytic, and mixed methods research in psychology: The APA Publications and Communications Board Task Force report. *American Psychologist*, 73, 26–46. http://dx.doi.org/10.1037/amp0000151

Matlin, M. W. (2011). Editorial: Creating a home for teaching the psychology of women and gender. *Psychology of Women Quarterly*, 35, 628–631. https://doi.org/10.1177%2F0361684311423365

Matsick, J. L., Kruk, M., Oswald, F., & Palmer, L. (2021). Bridging feminist psychology and open science: Feminist tools and shared values inform best practices for science reform. *Psychology of Women Quarterly*, 45, 412–429. https://doi.org/10.1177%2F03616843211026564

Neuendorf, K. A. (2011). Content analysis—A methodological primer for gender research. *Sex Roles*, 64, 276–289. https://doi.org/10.1007/s11199-010-9893-0

Yoder, J. D. (2010). Editorial: A feminist journal at the cutting edge of a psychology for women. *Psychology of Women Quarterly*, 34, 1–4. https://doi.org/10.1111%2Fj.1471-6402.2009.01535.x

Yoder, J. D. (2016). *Sex Roles*: An up-to-date gender journal with an outdated name. *Sex Roles*, 74, 1–5. https://doi.org/10.1007/s11199-015-0560-3

Yoder, J. D. (2018). Challenging the gendered academic hierarchy: The artificial separation of research, teaching, and feminist activism. *Psychology of Women Quarterly*, 42, 127–135. https://doi.org/10.1177/0361684318762695

Yoder, J. D. (2021). Reflections about what I learned as an editor making judgments about gender and gendered contexts with a feminist perspective. *Sex Roles*, 85, 233–247. https://doi.org/10.1007/s11199-021-01235-4

CHAPTER 6

Publishing 102
Navigating the Peer Review Process

- **Sarah J. Gervais**
  University of Nebraska-Lincoln

- **Kathryn J. Holland**
  University of Nebraska-Lincoln

Congratulations! You submitted your manuscript for publication. Submitting a paper represents a summit. Many people start climbing the publication mountain with a research idea, but veer off the path during study design, data collection or analysis, or drafting the paper. Publishing represents a central avenue to share knowledge, advance feminist psychology, and foster positive social change. Not to mention that academics must publish to get and keep their jobs, promote their students, and establish credibility with funding agencies, community partners, and the public. Celebrating the submission of a paper, however, marks the beginning of another, often harder, journey—the peer review process. In this way, initial paper submission represents a false summit. You're close, but you must persist to reach the actual summit. And this last leg is particularly important and challenging.

The peer review process is difficult. With 90% rejection rates at our top journals, manuscript acceptance represents the exception rather than the norm, and it may take several tries to find a home for your paper. Likewise, negative reviews are disheartening: Strengths are briefly mentioned followed by a long list of weaknesses. As gatekeepers to the scientific literature, peer reviewers frequently focus more on your paper's flaws than its merits. In many cases, the peer review process is constructive; our papers improve because of thoughtful reviewer feedback. At the same time, the peer review process can sidetrack us when we interpret negative reviews as indicators of our professional inadequacies; fail to follow through on revise-and-resubmit invitations; or abandon rejected papers altogether.

In an already difficult landscape, the peer review journey can be precarious for feminist scholars. Feminist research is routinely minimized and belittled by some so-called "mainstream" researchers. Advice to submit research papers on women and gender to "specialty" journals because of the "niche" focus often accompanies rejections from top journals in the field of psychology. How could a focus on women, half of the world's population, represent anything but a human issue? Bias also pervades the peer review process. One of us has been told that studies of queer women require a "control group" of heterosexual women, suggesting that empirical knowledge related to queer women's experience is only important in comparison to "regular" (i.e., heterosexual) women's experience, and that a study focused on women's experiences was flawed because it neglected men. Ad hominem attacks by peer reviewers are also common. One of us was accused of "hijacking" cognitive psychology for feminist aims by one particularly ornery reviewer. Such attacks often come from reviewers who are protecting their own theoretical, methodological, or professional turf and under the guise of identifying our work as too "political" and not "scientific" enough.

These facts should not discourage you from submitting your feminist psychological work. Indeed, whether you submit and resubmit your papers will help determine your success as an academic. This statement is bold, but true given the established norms and reward systems in academia, where publications are one of our main currencies. In this chapter, we work to demystify the peer review process and offer advice to help keep your research program moving. Specifically, we provide a roadmap for the peer review process, including (a) submitting a high-quality paper to the right outlet, (b) tracking your article after submission, (c) interpreting decision letters, (d) dealing with negative emotions during peer review, (e) revising and resubmitting your paper, and (f) keeping manuscripts moving along the pathway to publication. We draw from our considerable experience publishing papers to offer tips and tools to help you expedite the journey and avoid common detours in the publishing process. We also have peer reviewed and edited many manuscripts, so we understand the process from both sides. To ground our stories and advice, we offer our positionalities: Sarah identifies as a white heterosexual, cisgender woman who was a first-generation college student, while Katy identifies as a white lesbian (with attraction to more than one gender) cis woman with a disability. These experiences and identities inform our perspectives on how to best navigate the peer review process.

Step 1: Submitting a High-Quality Paper to the Right Outlet

Our first tip is to submit a high-quality, polished paper from the start. Although this may seem obvious, we have reviewed and edited many manuscripts that were simply not ready to be submitted. Peer reviewers work for free, and as you know, academics' time is often stretched thin. A poorly written and disorganized manuscript not only makes it harder for the reviewer to evaluate the strengths and weakness of the paper, but it also gives reviewers and editors low-hanging fruit to deliver a rejection. In our experience, submitting a highly polished paper speeds the peer review process considerably. Yoder (Chapter 5) emphasizes this as a key part of publishing. In addition to the tips Jan offered, here are some additional points we would like to emphasize that can help to hone the most common type of paper feminist researchers submit: original research.

First, ensure that the organization of your paper is clear and consistent following the APA-recommended sections, including an introduction, method, results, and discussion. Your opening paragraph should clearly convey the importance of the work, concisely outline what you will cover in your introduction, and end with a statement of the research purpose. The main body of the introduction should then summarize the relevant literature related to your specific research questions and/or hypotheses. The introduction should end with a short summary of the research aims and an explicit statement of your specific research questions and/or hypotheses.

Next, your method section should allow the reviewer to walk away knowing exactly how you collected your data; who was in your study; how you operationalized and measured your variables (for quantitative research); what questions, prompts, and probes you asked (for qualitative research); and how you plan to analyze your data. There should be no surprises in the method section; for instance, if you describe examining gender as a main variable, gender must be introduced and justified in the introduction. If you don't, the editors and reviewers will be left wondering what happened and why gender matters. The results section should then follow exactly the analysis plan you just described. Finally, the discussion section should not simply reiterate the findings. Instead, think about your research aims and results and why the reader should care about these findings.

Second, if there are multiple authors who have contributed to the manuscript, edit their respective sections so that they are written in the same "voice" and blend seamlessly. There should be one or two people on the team who read the entire manuscript after a draft is complete and edit it in this way (e.g., the first and second author). Third, identify and fix any grammatical and spelling mistakes in the paper. Occasional typos or errors are inevitable, but many are distracting. Reviewers may conclude that the paper was not given the care it should have had before submission and may signal deeper problems (e.g., sloppiness with data collection or analyses). Some ways to catch these errors can include submitting the paper to a program like Grammarly or the Belcher Editing Diagnostic Test (a convenient macro can be downloaded into Word; Belcher, 2019). Reading the paper out loud can also help. Fourth, you can ask a colleague outside the research team to read the paper and give any initial thoughts and feedback. This functions as a mini prereview, where you learn how people outside the writing team respond to the content and flow of the manuscript. You can then fix any issues before submission.

Selecting the right outlet for the work is another key step to take before submission. There are multiple considerations to keep in mind when selecting an outlet. There are different places that academics can publish, including peer-reviewed journals, chapters, and books. However, not all publications are created equal. While there can be good reasons for working on chapters and books (e.g., you often have more latitude in chapters than peer-reviewed articles; books allow for more in-depth considerations on scholarly topics), peer-reviewed outlets are counted most favorably on the job market and toward tenure and promotion. For that reason, we will discuss some steps to help you choose the right peer-reviewed journal for your paper.

Some journals may readily come to mind, including those that are highly regarded in your field as well as those with articles that inform your research questions, study design, or analytic approach. Another useful tool is a searchable database. For example, Sarah has used Journal/Author Name Estimator (JANE) when trying to identify an outlet for a new line of research. It allows you to insert a paper title, abstract, or keywords and provides journals with similar articles. One benefit of JANE is that it provides transparency around potentially predatory publishers (i.e., counterfeit scholarly publishers who invite researchers to pay to publish their work, promising high visibility with open access and swift turnaround times) and denotes high-quality open access journals (based on the Directory of Open Access Journals [DOAJ]). It is important that tenure-track faculty consult with mentors, particularly those in your department who make promotion and tenure decisions, about which journals "count" most toward tenure. While there are an increasing number of reputable, peer-reviewed open-access journals in psychology (e.g., *Frontiers in Psychology*, *PLoS ONE*), some researchers remain skeptical of these outlets, given the large numbers of manuscripts they publish each year. Some open-access and non-open access journals are perceived as lower quality and therefore detract from your tenure dossier, so getting feedback from people "in the know" is critical (e.g., the chair of your promotion and tenure committee).

Once you have identified some possible journals, ask yourself some key questions to determine whether to submit your manuscript there: Are the journal's aims and interests aligned with the research? Will the audience of that journal be interested in the work and its findings? If you have already submitted to the journal successfully in the past, this will be easy to know. If it is the first time you are submitting to a journal, there are a few ways to determine this. One is to read the journal description. Another is to look at the editors and editorial board. Do you recognize any of the associate editors or board members? Have they published similar research? Which associate editor might be assigned as the action editor for your manuscript (i.e., selecting reviewers, providing feedback, and facilitating the review process)? The last is to look at the types of papers that have been published in recent issues. Do you see research similar to your own? For example, if it is a qualitative or mixed-method study, has the editor published research using these methods within the past few years? If you are having trouble determining fit from these steps, you could also email the editor (see Chapter 5, this volume).

Another tip for choosing the right outlet is considering the journal's turnaround time: how long it takes the editor to collect peer reviews and send an initial decision on the original manuscript; how long it takes between resubmission and the final editorial decision (acceptance or rejection); how long it takes between acceptance and publication online; and how long it takes for publication to reach print (i.e., finally having a volume, issue, and page number). Long lag times at any of these stages can be detrimental for graduate students and pre-tenure faculty who need to build a strong body of work in a short amount of time. Unfortunately, it can be difficult to know up front how long each of these stages will take if you have not published in a journal before. Some journals publish stats related to turnaround times on their websites, which offer important information. There are also emerging databases such as Academic Accelerator that provide average durations for peer review, such as days to initial and final decisions. As these resources continue to be honed, they will provide more reliable data (at present, they are based on an algorithm that contains journal home pages, Wikipedia pages, and a limited number of user responses). In our experience, it also helps to ask colleagues about their recent experiences with a particular journal before you select it. For early career scholars, if time from first submission to first decision letter is more than 3–6 months, go elsewhere.

As feminist scholars, you will also run into unique issues and biases that are helpful to consider at this stage. For instance, a feminist psychological journal, such as *Psychology of Women Quarterly* or *Sex Roles*, is a good and clear choice for submitting feminist psychological work. However, if you are submitting to a journal that is not explicitly publishing feminist work (which is often the case for other top journals in your area of specialization), it may require a different "pitch." In many social psychology journals, for example, editors will consider papers with an explicit gender and/or feminist focus, but only if the work relies on a social psychology theory. To illustrate, Sarah recently published a paper on the effects of critical and complimentary objectification experiences on women in *Personality and Social Psychology Bulletin*, which integrates objectification theory, a decidedly feminist framework, with balance theory, a classic social psychological approach that incorporates considerations of positive or negative sentiment from others. If you go this route, you'll need to have the journal in mind when you're planning the research. Despite the challenges, we encourage feminist scholars to submit papers to a range of journals as many of our subdisciplines would benefit from more feminist research. But it is an important consideration when selecting an outlet for the work.

It is helpful to identify your top/first journal choice as you are drafting your paper so that you can edit the tone, structure, and length to best fit the journal. It isn't fun to finish a draft of a manuscript and then learn that you'll need to cut the word count in half due to page limits or restructure the sections in your introduction or discussion. Likewise, you should identify a second and third priority journal with similar aims and formats, which will allow you to quickly resubmit your manuscript should it be rejected from your first-choice journal.

Step 2: Tracking Your Article After Submission

Even under ideal circumstances, the back and forth of the peer review process can take many months, if not years. And early career scholars don't have the luxury of time. Tracking your article and nudging the action editor (when appropriate) can speed up the process. After submitting your paper, you want to record the journal's response time. Sometimes people set alarms in their calendars to check on a paper after a certain amount of time has passed.

After submitting your paper, you should receive a receipt with a manuscript ID. If you don't, follow up within a week to assure that the journal received your manuscript. Nothing is more frustrating than thinking you've submitted a paper, only to find it sitting, unsubmitted, in the submission portal. A month after submission, confirm the paper has been sent to reviewers. The submission portal usually tracks this information, but sometimes you will need to email the managing editor. Editors are often as motivated as authors to find peer reviewers after manuscript submission. Occasionally, though, a manuscript will slip through the cracks. Finding reviewers can be difficult. Editors might also desk reject a paper, and we've had instances where the rejection email goes to spam.

If you haven't received a decision within the typical timeline, then check on the status of your article with the action editor. If decisions are usually rendered within 3 months, send an email 3 months and 1 day after submission. If you don't hear back after a week, email again. The tone of these emails should be direct: "I'm emailing regarding the status of my paper, entitled [title of paper (manuscript ID)] that I submitted on [date of submission]." Good editors will respond promptly. Nine times out of 10, they are waiting on reviewer feedback. That's good news. Your manuscript is one step closer to publication and you should wait patiently. Remember that editors are also frustrated by slow reviewers. However, your emails can gently nudge your manuscripts along through the peer review process.

Sometimes your article will be under review much longer than expected and no decision appears imminent. This is a difficult situation, especially for early career scholars, because the clock is ticking very loudly (e.g., until your tenure year). It can also be useful to remind editors of the urgency of feedback when the academic job market or tenure dates are quickly approaching (e.g., late in your 4th year and beyond). For instance, Katy disclosed to an editor that she was on the tenure clock and that her coauthor was a year away from going on the academic job market, which was well received by the editor, who moved the paper forward with the two reviews that she had received rather than continuing to wait for the tardy third reviewer. Additionally, you may weigh the pros and cons of leaving the manuscript under review or withdrawing and submitting it elsewhere. If the editor has been responsive to your queries, we encourage you to wait. After all, starting the clock over at another journal will take months to complete. However, if the editor has been unresponsive with no forthcoming decision, no one will fault you for withdrawing and submitting the manuscript to another journal.

Step 3: Interpreting Decision Letters

After months of waiting, you've now received a decision on your paper. Acceptance on first submissions is clear-cut, though exceedingly rare. Language in the decision letter might include, "I would like to conditionally accept your paper" and "it will require minor editorial revisions." In these cases, the editor may also state that they will not be sending the paper back to the reviewers. Rejection at this stage is also pretty straightforward. While the editor may mention some strengths, they will focus on fatal flaws and discourage resubmission. This editor doesn't want to see the paper again. Here, you should identify a new outlet for the work (e.g., the second- or third-choice journals you identified while writing the paper). Before submission, consider the issues raised by the reviewers. If an issue is easy to fix or represents a major weakness, you should revise the paper before submitting it to a new journal. That new journal may send it to one (or more) of the same reviewers, and nothing is more frustrating as a reviewer than to see the same manuscript and find none of your comments addressed. It can be useful to give yourself a time limit (a week is often sufficient) to revise and submit the manuscript for a new outlet. Procrastination after a stinging rejection is normal, but with a full draft and one round of critical feedback, rejected papers are still a step closer to accepted papers (see also the section on dealing with negative emotions during peer review).

Occasionally, an editor may reject your paper, but the reviewers identified no fatal flaws (e.g., in terms of fit, significance, approach). Finding a new journal is best following most rejections. In rare circumstances, however, you might request that the editor reconsider the decision. Usually, the editor will affirm the original decision. Valuable time can be wasted arguing with editors, so this option should be chosen sparingly. However, in our experience, men are more likely than women to dispute decisions and eventually get their papers published, so if you are on solid ground in requesting to submit a revision, occasionally asking doesn't hurt.

Requested revisions usually fall into two camps: minor or major revisions. Minor revision decisions may include language such as "before your paper can be published" or "I believe the paper can make a significant contribution to the literature," and the editor may indicate that they will not send the paper out for further peer review. Major revision decisions may include language such as "I am offering no guarantees that the paper will be published" or "I must reject the paper *in its current form*." As the name suggests, major revisions will likely require *major* changes and your paper may not be accepted (see also Chapter 5, this volume). For minor revisions, you should revise and resubmit the paper as soon as possible. For major revisions, you need to decide whether you're willing to make major changes to your paper. In these instances, you should almost always revise and resubmit your paper. In our experience, major revise-and-resubmits eventually translate to publications. If you think peer reviewers are being unreasonable, vent to a coauthor or colleague, and then make the revisions anyway.

Regardless, don't procrastinate. Most journals will give you a couple of months to revise your paper, and if you miss the deadline your manuscript may be treated as a new submission rather than a revise-and-resubmit (though editors are often willing to extend the deadline, if you request an extension). If the revisions are straightforward, why not move your paper from a revise-and-resubmit to an acceptance more quickly? It might still be months before the paper appears in print at the journal and counts toward your job market CV or tenure dossier. And if you can return the manuscript to editors within a few days or weeks, your manuscript will be fresh in their mind, and they may proceed quickly. After all, at that point they want to get the paper off their plates as much as you do.

Step 4: Dealing With Negative Emotions During Peer Review

The peer review process is inherently negative. Disappointment and frustration are inevitable. In short, after spending months (or years) conducting research, the peer review process can feel like a kick in the gut. Furthermore, patriarchy (not to mention white supremacy, hetero- and cis-normativity, capitalism) are inherent to the peer review process, making it challenging for feminist researchers. While strides have been made to reduce sexism in the peer review process (e.g., more women as editors; incorporating double-blind reviews), bias remains. Thinly veiled attacks on feminist topics and approaches (e.g., qualitative methods, participatory action research) sometimes make the peer review processes brutal for feminist researchers. And the peer review process does not occur in a cultural vacuum. It proceeds in a larger context that excludes women, especially women with racial, ethnic, gender, and sexual minority identities, from the scientific community. The negative emotions inherent to the peer review process may result in belonging uncertainty for feminist researchers. Such experiences can cause counterproductive behaviors, such as procrastinating on revise-and-resubmits or failing to submit rejected papers to new journals. These instances do not indicate a "broken" system, but rather that the system is operating as designed—to keep women in their place. Reducing women's publications reinforces patriarchy and other systems of oppression in science.

We share this context because negative feedback during peer review feels so personal. How can it not? Most of us study issues that are deeply important to us. We believe that our research can help facilitate social change. Submitting the work for peer review is an act of courage that can elicit feelings of vulnerability. Rejection makes us feel that the work—and sometimes by extension ourselves—is not good enough. It can be easy to catastrophize and wonder if you'll ever get a job or tenure, following a rejection. If you feel this way, you are in good company. We have both received many more rejections than acceptances over our careers. During her 1st year on the tenure clock, for example, Katy had a particularly devastating rejection. She submitted a manuscript to a violence journal and received a revise-and-resubmit decision (R&R); two reviewers offered both praise and constructive suggestions and one (who was, fittingly, reviewer 2) listed a litany of the paper's "failings," recommending the paper be rejected. She revised the paper and received another R&R, with feedback from the same reviewers—two were satisfied with the revision, but reviewer 2 listed a whole new set of "reservations" about the manuscript. After resubmitting, she received yet another R&R, this time with rude and off-topic comments from reviewer 2 (e.g., an entirely different research question would have been more interesting). Again, she responded to each criticism and resubmitted the paper. After an entire year and three rounds of revisions, the editor rejected the article without weighing in once. Feelings of confusion, frustration, and hurt crashed down. She worried that her research was terrible, would never be published, and that she would be evaluated negatively during her 2nd-year re-appointment decision. These feelings are normal. These feelings are not personal pathologies;

they represent predictable responses to difficult and (often) rigged systems. While structural problems require structural solutions, we can also exercise individual agency within the system. Her story has a happy end—after following the advice outlined, the paper was accepted for submission at a different journal 6 months after the first submission. We hope this advice helps you move through negative feelings that come with rejections.

First, when a decision letter email pops up in your inbox, take a deep breath. Remind yourself that this decision does not represent the final say on the quality of the project or your competency as a scholar. Peer reviews are mostly negative, the process is subjective, good manuscripts are often rejected (just as bad papers can be accepted), and a rejection does not represent the end of the road. Rather than focusing on every detail, we often skim the decision letter for the gist of the decision. Is the paper rejected? Is there an option to revise and resubmit? We then set aside the letter for a day or two (but no longer) so that we can interpret the specific comments with a better mind-set. Editors and reviewers bring multiple and new perspectives and can help identify and correct our blind spots. They help us to clarify our arguments, methodological approach, analysis and interpretation of our data, and the implications and limitations of our findings for a broader audience. We might initially feel defensive about the issues raised (which is normal). If we sit long enough with it, however, we usually decide that the reviewer makes a good point and opt to make a change in response.

Second, while our initial urge may be to bury the email deep in our inbox, airing reviews with others—coauthors, colleagues, or mentors—can be empowering. Such conversations allow us to gain some distance from the process. For example, others might help us focus on the positive comments, rather than solely on the negative ones. We can also lament on the slights or errors. Other people can also help us brainstorm fixes for issues raised. Finally, once you've had a chance to process the decision, we urge you to quickly mobilize to revise. A revise-and-resubmit decision (even an onerous one) is one step closer to publication, so it should move to the top your writing priority list (see also the next section). Challenge yourself to see just how quickly you can get the revisions turned around! Doing so will help to speed the publishing process and keep your research program moving. This means that you may need to examine what is on your plate and push something off. You may need to pause work on a paper that has not yet been submitted until you complete your revisions (at the same time, how might you keep that paper moving forward—could you pass it to a coauthor for the time being?). You may need to spend less time making your lecture slides (you can always edit them the next time you teach the class). You may need to say "no" to some service requests (recognizing that the power differentials for early career faculty make it difficult to do this), such as strategically saying no to requests to being a peer reviewer (early career faculty might want to cap the ad hoc reviews they do in a year, e.g., three to six, or decline review requests from journals or on papers that do not strictly fall in your area of expertise) or asking for an extension for reviews.

Finally, we must all consider how our own conduct contributes to negative review norms within our field. When we feel passionate about a particular issue that comes up when reviewing a paper, it can be easy to pour our heart out in ways that reflect our own emotional state (e.g., incredulity, irritability) without stopping to consider how such words will feel for the authors. Words have power. As feminist researchers let's see if we can challenge ourselves to change the toxic norms. While criticism is a necessary component of the peer review process, we should also be constructive. When you review, how often do you point out aspects of a paper that are really good, giving praise where praise is due? Tone of voice also matters. Replace combative questions with constructive comments. Other things to avoid are writing in ALL CAPS (we don't need to yell at each other) or stating that the research is uninteresting (just because you do not find it interesting does not mean no one will). Sarah finds it helpful to imagine signing her review; with her name attached to comments, she finds herself moving from criticizer to helper. As feminist researchers, we also need to think about the implications of insisting on the inclusion of dominant, privileged groups in research on minoritized and stigmatized groups (e.g., they must be compared to majority groups). Research on the lived experiences of marginalized and stigmatized groups offers valuable knowledge to our field and a better understanding of human experience. This does not mean that you should always give positive reviews, especially when the paper you are reviewing is a complete disaster. In that case, we recommend that you complete the review in a limited period of time (e.g., 60 minutes), articulate the three main issues of the work, edit for tone where needed, and note your wish to advance the work.

Step 5: Revising and Resubmitting Manuscripts

Next we offer practical tips for how we tackle the revision process (see also Chapter 5, this volume). First, take the decision letter and translate it into a series of numbered reviewer concerns. We recommend copying and pasting all the issues from the decision letter into a Word document, separating the comments by person (i.e., a section with the editor's comments, a section for reviewer 1's comments, a section for reviewer 2's comments, etc.), and then number each issue raised. This will give you a point-by-point list of action items based on direct quotes (or summaries) from the decision letter. Below each numbered point, describe your response in a different font (e.g., in bold or italics) so that the editor and reviewers can easily see how responsive you've been to their feedback. Your responses should be detailed enough that the editor and reviewers can understand how you addressed the concern by reading the reply letter but should not overexplain or describe every change verbatim from the manuscript (reviewers can read it in context). If applicable, your response should also contain a page number so reviewers can see the edits you made in more detail and in the context of the paper. For example, "Reviewer comment #3: I was wondering about the sample ..." A good reply: "Thank you for raising this question. We have clarified that our sample was XX on page 28." A not-so-good reply: "We included more information about our sample." We also recommend that you try to revise the paper in response to *every* comment. Yes, every single one. Don't worry if your response is long—we've had letters that are longer than the manuscript itself.

What should you do with conflicting comments? This happens frequently for feminist researchers. For example, we are often told by one reviewer that the interpretation of our findings should be made even more explicitly feminist (reviewer 1 says, "Institutional responses to sexual violence deliberately hinder gender equality in higher education—say this!") while another reviewer says that the interpretation is *too* feminist (reviewer 2 says, "You have taken these findings much too far! Institutions' hands are tied in how they can respond to sexual violence—there are no deliberate actions that reduce gender equity!"). We first laugh at this impossible situation. Then, we see if the editor indicated how much we should count feedback from each reviewer or weighed in on the conflicting advice, and if so, we follow the editor's lead. You can also (a) email the editor to ask for some clarity on how to proceed; (b) choose a particular reviewer to go with, make changes accordingly, and justify that decision in your response letter; or (c) go with the reviewer's recommendation that you make the research even more explicitly feminist (i.e., reviewer 1)—it should come as no surprise that the authors of this chapter believe we need more feminism in science. Finally, when choosing not to make a suggested change, we also recommend explicitly stating that you are willing to consider alternative changes if the editor requires them for publication.

Step 6: Keeping Your Manuscripts Moving Along the Pathway

As you continue to make progress toward the summit, we also offer some advice on how to keep multiple manuscripts moving along the publication pathway. As you revise and resubmit your papers, developing a writing routine is useful. You might have skated by with all-nighters to finish term papers during your undergraduate years, but most academic work won't move forward with solely a "binge-writing" approach. How many people start spring break, the holidays, or the summer months with ambitious plans to write feverishly, only to fritter away the time with little to no progress? Writing in fits and starts yields few high-quality papers and is physically and emotionally taxing. Empty pages and half-done manuscripts cause anxiety, guilt, and shame. Plus, we like to spend time with our families, relax and rejuvenate, and engage in nonacademic pursuits (e.g., reading books for leisure, traveling) during breaks, and we don't want to return from a break more burned out than when we started it.

A writing routine is simple to plan, but not necessarily easy to implement. We must sit down regularly—such as an hour each workday or one workday each week—to write. The specifics of your writing plan will depend on your unique situation. While faculty at R1 universities with fewer teaching responsibilities may be able to write daily, those at liberal arts colleges may find that writing once per week on a light teaching day is practical. You should also factor in your personal life and preferences. While Sarah routinely wrote on Saturdays earlier in her career, she has two small kids that require care on the weekends, so she schedules her writing time during the week. She also attends a 2-day annual writing retreat during the work week and acts as if she were away at a conference (e.g., finds a substitute for her classes; cancels all meetings). Having long hours to write and make more progress when you have the luxury of time can be gratifying. While the details will vary, the bottom line is that you need to schedule writing time *and stick to it*. We do this with our other responsibilities; we don't miss our classes, but we often miss writing time. Women are further thwarted from writing compared to men. Due to bias in the classroom, we overprepare for our classes, and we squander time completing a disproportionate amount of service (see also Chapter 13, this volume). We must have clear boundaries around our writing time and expect that others will test the limits.

What will you write during your writing time? A comprehensive list of projects is a useful place to start, followed by rank ordering the projects from highest to lowest priority. Few people multitask effectively, and we find that we can only advance one to two projects in a given week or month. After creating this list, we divide the top two projects into action items. For instance, "write the introduction" might convert to write (a) the introductory paragraph; (b) the first, second, and third section of the literature review; and (c) hypotheses. It is nice if action items for one project involve heavy lifting (e.g., writing the introduction), while action items on the other are low-hanging fruit (e.g., proofreading, revising references, or finalizing a note).

Note when you accomplish your goals and when you don't. This exercise will allow you to translate your writing aspirations to your writing realities. We usually hope to write much more than we can actually write in a set period of time (e.g., an hour a day for a 15-week semester; see Chapter 7, this volume). When we dissect a goal into action items, we might see that it is impossible to complete all our projects, and we can prioritize different projects, depending on which of them help us best advance our current goals. For a PhD student, a dissertation proposal might eclipse a paper, whereas for a tenure-track faculty member, a peer-reviewed paper might trump a chapter. As noted, revise-and-resubmit decisions should go to the top of the list (and if you have a writing routine when you receive the R&R, you won't have to "find time" to write, because that time will already be scheduled). A list of action items also guarantees that projects won't slip through the cracks. The format can be simple. An Excel file or whiteboard can be sufficient, though many apps and other electronic tools are also available. You will want to regularly update this list, such as during a weekly planning meeting.

Once you've established a writing routine and plan, the next step is to create an accountability structure. Tracking your progress is one approach and can be accomplished in many ways. Some folks set content goals for each writing session. They plan to write an abstract, and the abstract is written when the time ends. They enjoy crossing items off their list. Others write a set number of words (e.g., 300). Still others focus on having their butt in the seat rather than specific products or word counts. Knowing that quality and quantity ebb and flow, they write for a set time, regardless of output. Any one of these approaches is better than nothing. Like the list, pragmaticism is the key. If you're just developing a writing habit, writing an introduction or 1,000 words in one session is unrealistic. While lofty goals can initially inspire, they eventually disappoint, causing people to abandon the process.

Working with someone else is another accountability approach. The students in our classes would notice if we didn't show up to teach, but no one notices if we don't show up to write. In addition to accountability, writing with others is more fun than writing alone. Celebrating successes (e.g., I wrote every day this week!) or commiserating over challenges (e.g., Am I wrong or did this reviewer miss this entire paragraph in the discussion?) is better with others. Anyone can be an accountability ally, but someone at a similar career stage is often best. Friends can be good accountability allies, but will they hassle you after a missed deadline, or will they let you off the hook? Knowing this pitfall, you might create additional carrots or sticks to keep you on track. One of us pledged a donation to a detested organization if we didn't meet our goal. While our friend was ready to enforce it, the threat proved sufficient to follow through.

Finally, collaborating with others can be a terrific way to keep manuscripts progressing along the pathway. Writing with people who share your interests can result in more publications that are better and published faster. Plus, it is more fun to write with good collaborators rather than going it solo (as we can attest after having collaboratively written this chapter!). Nevertheless, people vary in their working styles, goals, and priorities, and it is important to have frank conversations about how the collaboration will "work" prior to beginning it. For example, a tenure-track faculty member might note that she needs to submit a paper by a certain date, so it will count toward her tenure dossier. Likewise, a faculty member with extensive teaching responsibilities might comment on drafts during the school year but only write first drafts during the summer months. Routinely keeping a "minutes" document (e.g., via Google Docs) with these and related conversations (e.g., authorship decisions, use of measures or data from respective labs) can help jog people's memories down the road. Another question to pose is "What will you do when inevitable conflicts arise?" You and your collaborator may have different priorities and capacities at a given moment (e.g., an R&R due during finals week)? If there is a hard deadline, is everyone willing to hold a quick planning meeting and divvy up the responsibilities? Are there issues you'll be able to anticipate from the outset (e.g., I reserve my weekends for family responsibilities; my time will be limited during finals week)? What compromises are you willing to make (e.g., asking editor for extensions; adding a coauthor to pick up the load)?

We also recommend consulting with mentors prior to starting collaborations as well as beginning small (e.g., conducting secondary data analysis from one person's data set and doing a poster rather than submitting a grant application or starting new data collection). It is acceptable to decline working with others, even senior folks, if it is not a good fit. You might say that you appreciate their interest in collaborating, but you can't add another project to your plate right now. If you feel more comfortable, you can always keep the door open for later.

Conclusion

We hope this chapter has provided you with useful perspectives on to how avoid and overcome common hurdles as you navigate the peer review process on your way to the summit of the publication mountain. Even with our experience, we still lose our footing from time to time and will likely reread this chapter after a particularly difficult decision letter. We hope you also can put some of these tools in your backpack as you hike toward your own summit.

Reference

Belcher, L. W. (2019). *Writing your journal article in twelve weeks.* University of Chicago Press.

CHAPTER 7

Developing a Research Program at a Teaching (Nonresearch) Institution

- **Alexandra I. Zelin**
  University of Tennessee at Chattanooga

- **Sahana Mukherjee**
  Gettysburg College

At small liberal arts colleges, as with most U.S. universities, there are three criteria by which candidates for tenure and promotion are evaluated: teaching, research/scholarship, and service/governance. However, when in graduate school, most students are taught "publish, publish, publish" as the only part that matters for an academic position, especially one on the tenure track. We offer a different perspective on this narrative—one that suggests that exceptional teaching can be balanced with productive feminist scholarship. Throughout this chapter, we discuss our experience working at institutions that prioritize teaching and provide tips on what worked (and what didn't) for us. We explore an essential question, "What is *sufficient research*?" and how this research can align with feminist values of working toward equity. We then provide some insight onto developing collaborations, building egalitarian research labs, and successfully working with students. We end with something we both are still working on: protecting our research time and having balance.

Who We Are

I, Alex, am a recently tenured associate professor at a midsized predominantly White university in the southeast. While I do not have PhD students, I teach masters' and undergraduate students and conduct research with— all while maintaining a 4 × 4 teaching load. I am a White, cisgender heterosexual woman who was born in the United States and recognize the immense amount of privilege from my background. I also grew up mostly in the so-called Bible Belt (and still live in the Bible Belt) as a Jewish person and experience a few masked health issues. My experiences in this chapter and how I conduct research with my other required duties are heavily based on my undergraduate experience conducting research at a small, public liberal arts university with my inspirational mentor, Mindy Erchull.

I, Sahana, am a recently tenured professor at a small, liberal arts college that is predominantly White and located in a predominantly White rural town. I was born and raised in India and moved to the United States to pursue graduate school in social and cultural psychology, after which I got a tenure-track job at my current institution. As with everyone else, I have many majority group identities as well as nonmajority group identities. Aside from my female sex and gender, most of my identities were aligned with majority group experiences in India (e.g., being cisgendered, heterosexual, upper-caste Hindu, and middle class). However, when I moved to the United States, my racial and national identity came to the forefront and became a strong foundation for personal and professional experiences. Having a majority group member experience in India and minority group member experience in the United States influenced my research and teaching philosophies. My undergraduate training in psychology and sociology exposed me to perspectives such as critical race theory, postcolonial theory, and critical psychology and allowed me to consider teaching and research as tools for liberation and social change (see also Martín-Baró, 1994; Freire, 2015). My graduate training in cultural psychology further expanded my interest in social justice and motivated me to always strive for equity and inclusion in my research, teaching, and service. However, over the years, I have also learned that I have to carefully prioritize and balance my professional goals—in research, teaching, and service—if I want to not just survive but thrive in academia.

General Tenure Requirements at Teaching-Focused Schools

Though all faculty are expected to contribute toward service, few (if any) faculty members have ever been denied tenure on the basis of insufficient service. And, while all faculty are required to demonstrate their commitment toward teaching and success in being effective teachers (e.g., through student interviews and evaluations, reflection of challenges and accomplishments, revision of existing courses and development of new courses), outstanding teaching by itself will not guarantee someone tenure or promotion even at most teaching-focused institutions. Teaching, however, is a major factor for the successful completion of 3rd-year or pre-tenure review.

Research is often the decisive factor for tenure and promotion, and if a candidate's research is considered insufficient or not scholarly enough, no amount of teaching or service will compensate for this. This emphasis on research for tenure and promotion is not unique to our institutions and is prevalent across all disciplines at both 4-year teaching institutions and larger research-focused institutions. But what *exactly* constitutes sufficient research? Well, that is where our experiences differ, and we strongly recommend following advice from Warner (Chapter 3) on how to parse the differing opinions within your department in addition to reviewing your department's tenure and promotion guidelines. What we do want to emphasize, though, is that figuring out what "sufficient research" looks like is critical so that you can begin to plan and prioritize which scholarly activities to focus on.

What Is Sufficient Research?

We first want to talk about sufficient research in terms of feminist work because it is not just about how many manuscripts you can get published as check marks for tenure. Rather, feminist research must work toward the goal of equity (and some may argue justice and liberation). Thus, as feminist academics, we must consider the research projects we undertake and how they contribute to the feminist movement. One area I (Alex) prioritize in my research is intersectionality, so I often ask myself "Whose stories am I missing?" This helps guide my present and future research projects. For instance, the bystander model for sexual assault and harassment prevention is well documented in the literature as effective for college students (Cadaret et al., 2019). However, when applied to the workplace and the inherent power differentials (plus, keeping one's job is tied to it), the bystander model will not be as effective as overall community change (Zelin & Magley, 2021). Furthermore, bystander intervention may look different depending on the type of job environment (e.g., office-based, retail), which has guided my research attention to understanding what people are experiencing in different workplaces to better address (and prevent) workplace sexual harassment.

Essentially, there may be a disconnect between what your university deems "sufficient" research productivity and what might be needed in order to add to the feminist literature. For instance, it is easier and faster to obtain college student samples for research than it is to find an organization with which to partner and collect data to inform work focused on organizational change (e.g., culture change away from sexual harassment). However, a longer data collection process inherently increases time between project development and manuscript submission; this can create a challenge to achieving the required number of publications for tenure. What I (Alex) have found helpful in this case is to think of smaller pieces of the research that can be more quickly done and set the stage for your eventual larger-scale data collection. For instance, although my long-term goal is studying bystander intervention for gender-based violence within an organization, I can lay the groundwork by obtaining college sample data on bystander interventions for harassment of other marginalized populations, such as LGBTQIA+ populations and/or people with disabilities. These important projects are still related to my overall feminist goal of ending sexual harassment and assault. If you specialize in longitudinal research, you might build-in analyses and papers that focus on the cross-sectional data you collect in the process. Or you might consider smaller projects that will pave the way for multiyear studies once tenure is obtained.

What we were told: I (Sahana) was encouraged to pursue publications in high-impact peer-reviewed journals, and this outranked publishing book chapters or textbooks. Additionally, colleagues dissuaded me from publishing in open-access journals even if those journals were peer reviewed and aligned with the scope of my research. The content of the publication and my research area was also ranked: Publishing purely theoretical or "basic" research that utilizes quantitative methodologies outranked applied or activist-oriented research. These were some of the written and *unwritten* rules of publication that reflect what was considered important.

Likewise, I (Alex) learned that peer-reviewed publications in journals held the highest prestige in the tenure process, regardless of if they were theoretical, applied, or quantitative/qualitative based. While there is no departmental policy against publishing in journals that collect a fee, it is heavily frowned upon (and also, as smaller teaching institutions, the money really isn't available for that)! However, unlike Sahana, as long as the impact factor was above "1" or the journal was considered tier 2 or 3, that was sufficient to "count."

I (Alex) was also encouraged to publish with students, and having a student as a first author was perceived as doing the same amount, if not more work, than if I were the first author. This is not the case at all schools; some require your name to be first, but others, especially teaching schools, are likely to look positively at students appearing as authors before their supervising faculty. Edited book chapters also counted as peer-reviewed publications, though too many book chapters over peer-reviewed journal articles would be cause for an eyebrow raise.

Conducting research with undergraduate or master's students can create challenges to developing publishable manuscripts. For example, although it can be a great learning experience for undergraduates to conduct replication studies, many journals, at least in psychology, do not typically accept replication studies or studies that do not further the research area (make a "significant contribution"). Further, since students may not be able to continue working on a project once they graduate, you will have to consider what can be completed in the time you have together. You may need to pick the projects that have the most potential for publication and/or have the most student help. You may not be able to publish in a journal that requires three or more studies in the paper. Some alternative strategies include submitting research briefs to journals. We recommend investigating to see if journals you usually publish in, or those within your field, offer a chance to submit these smaller, more condensed manuscripts that present findings from a one-time data-collection study. Another strategy is to publish with your students in journals that focus on student research. The Council of Undergraduate Research maintains a detailed list of undergraduate research journals on their website.

Don't forget presentations! Depending on your institution, publishing may not be considered a key part of the tenure decision (e.g., at one of our colleagues' institutions, a minimum of one peer-reviewed manuscript is needed for tenure and promotion). However, it is likely that peer-reviewed conference presentations will often supplement and/or replace the need to publish (e.g., at both of our institutions it is expected that a tenure candidate will have more peer-reviewed conference presentations than publications). Typically, presentations at national/international professional conferences outrank presentations at regional conferences and on-campus presentations. Keep in mind that there are usually feminist conferences within every discipline, which may be a great option for you and your students. If posters contribute to a successful tenure portfolio, it is often easier to walk students through a project that is perfect for a poster but may not reach publication level.

In sum, to figure out what is sufficient research you need to understand what your institution requires. Do they encourage student participation? Is there a specific number of publications and/or posters that are required as a minimum for tenure? What outlets are acceptable for publishing? We found it helpful to answer these questions through consulting official departmental and college-level bylaws, directly asking others (e.g., a mentor, recently tenured colleagues), and through indirect approaches, including looking at CVs of recently tenured colleagues and publication records for those who win internal research awards. Considering these questions can help you determine how to best build your research program.

I Know My Requirements. Now What?

We are all familiar with the popular advice while flying: *In case of a cabin pressure emergency, put on your own mask first before assisting others.* In other words, you can't help others if you aren't taking care of yourself first.

The same is true for how to begin to think of your research productivity. Most faculty who work at a teaching institution generally like teaching and mentoring students. You might be that person! As enriching as it is to work closely with students, you also need to keep the tenure clock in mind. Because the publication process can take a while (see Chapters 5 and 6, this volume) and acceptance is not always guaranteed, you will likely need to have more than one paper in process at the same time. For faculty at teaching institutions, a good strategy is to work with collaborators on projects. Collaborators often help a project get written quickly for submission to a journal, since you can each work simultaneously on different pieces of the paper.

It can take time to find and develop working relationships with colleagues, especially from other institutions. We recommend starting with the network you already have, such as graduate student cohort mates or former mentors. You can also find collaborators by attending conferences and applying to networking opportunities, like the Institute for Academic Feminist Psychology. In finding collaborators, you are also finding and building your feminist community (see Chapters 4 and 14, this volume), something that is incredibly important as you might be the only feminist scholar within your department. Finding like-minded people will help remind you that you are doing the right thing, something hard to remember when others may not see your work as important.

But this begs the question: *How* do I find collaborators? What do I look for? The first thing we suggest is to look for others researching in the same areas. If you are lucky enough to attend conferences where a researcher in your area is presenting, cold-emailing them in advance to see if they have time for a coffee at the conference is an option. You can also typically approach them after the presentation, but as timing is short, be sure to keep it brief and then follow up with an email later. We have both found excellent collaborators on projects this way. If you don't feel comfortable reaching out to someone you don't know, see if any of your colleagues can introduce you. If meeting someone at a conference is not plausible for any number of reasons, reaching out through email and offering what you are interested in and how you think a collaboration might work can also be successful. Even if none of these ideas work out for an immediate project collaboration, know that you are still building that invisible college and can keep in touch with people you have reached out to for advice.

Since you are already teaching a lot, it also may be beneficial, at least until tenure is achieved, to focus on publishing about your teaching. For example, are you developing a new hands-on learning experience? Are you planning to redevelop one of your courses? Can you do some pre/post surveys related to course content knowledge around these new ideas? Many professional organizations have subsections focused on best practices for teaching, and they are always open to new ideas for pedagogy. If you are using feminist and inclusive novel strategies in your classes, these are of particular interest in the field right now, so go ahead and write it up! For instance, I (Alex) just revamped my Psychology of Women class and integrated the use of a makerspace so that students can complete hands-on projects related to the material. I published an article about this new course design in a teaching of psychology book. By sharing innovative class designs, you can increase access and inclusion for students at other universities. You don't only have to focus on success. You might write something along the lines of "I tried this, and it stunk. But then I tweaked something, and it worked out well." (e.g., randomly assigning groups of four to do outside-the-classroom work is a bad idea; too many conflicting schedules!). These types of publications about teaching offer a type of mentoring to other scholars in your field and may be highly valued at a teaching institution. Publishing on what you are already doing in the classroom is an easy way to turn it into something that benefits both your teaching *and* research portfolios. And while you are at it, don't forget to apply for some teaching awards in the process.

The same can also be true for some of the service in which you are engaging. For instance, if you are actively working in the community, is there something you can publish related to the work that you are doing? Are there changes you can document that others may want to consider trying? How can you tie in your service with a social justice framework? Sharing what has worked in your community (and, alternatively, what has *not* worked) can help other communities develop similar programs to serve their members. Similar to using your classes as potential for publication, the same can be said for your service.

Working With Students

Because faculty at teaching institutions are heavily encouraged to have students working with them on research, and having students be first author on presentations and publications is often considered a positive, you have the opportunity to build a large research lab. As someone who is very much known as the "Oh new research idea! PIVOT!" person when it comes to research, I (Alex) love having the space for new and different ideas that are not focused in just one niche area. My approach is to let students know I am interested in women's experiences, diversity, the workplace, and so forth, in general, and we can work from there on developing a specific topic for a research project. I have found success in having students tell *me* what they are interested in, and we work together to build out a research study. I (Sahana) have also found that when students work on a project of their choosing, they feel more empowered in the research project and are often more invested.

While our goal is always to develop research projects that become peer-reviewed publications, our minimum expectation is that all projects are of high-enough quality that they can be presented as a conference presentation. Thus, by having so many students in my research lab, I am also co-author on numerous poster presentations each year. This is mutually beneficial: It is a huge benefit to students to present at national/international conferences (i.e., they can have an important professional experience; it helps them have a strong undergraduate record), and it simultaneously helps build my CV in ways that are valued for tenure.

While having multiple different research projects with a variety of student collaborators can be overwhelming, having a designated lab meeting time where everyone provides updates, advice, suggestions, and support has been instrumental. An advantage of a large lab with fixed lab meetings is the collective brain power: Many minds can help ensure we are not missing anything in project planning. For example, as my (Alex's) lab worked through a sexual harassment vignette, I heavily depended on the students to create a plausible character (e.g., that the person in the vignette was dressed in something that seemed appropriate).

It has also helped us to build labs where each semester we welcomed new faces and experienced lab members act as mentors. Our egalitarian methods of having peer mentors rather than a starker hierarchy contributed to our building of an ever-growing feminist community. Students who may not have found classmates with similar feminist ideals now feel like they have a "home." By utilizing egalitarian values, all students believe that their projects are worthy (they are!) and that they each have an important contribution to make. Even after graduation, many students want to stay involved as mentors for current students, including discussing graduate school, job hunting, and general life advice. I (Alex) even presented at a conference in 2022 with a lab member from my 1st year (2016–2017) running a lab; in our presentation, we talked about what it is like to build a research lab at a teaching-focused institution: myself from the faculty advising side and my student from the mentoring side and the applied job skills they obtained.

Building Your Research Lab/Team

There are a few important questions to ask when you decide to mentor students through the research process. For example, do you want students working on just one project, or are you open to having more than one project that students are working on? How many students do you think you can feasibly manage while also balancing other responsibilities, including how many new-to-research students can you help supervise? Will your students be earning credit or volunteering, and does this count toward your teaching load?

We have found a few successful methods and some key pieces of advice based on our own experiences. If you have one project in mind that you need help with, you should pitch that particular project to students with a clear timeline and set of expectations. Something we have both experienced is that if a student is not genuinely interested in the research topic, having them complete tasks and assignments for that project takes a lot more patience and a little more frustration. Being open and honest with students about the project(s) they will work on from the beginning is important. You want a good match based on interest and capability.

If you are open to having multiple projects and/or having students develop their own projects, you can also pitch it that way. Asking students what they are interested in and being clear about on what topics you can and cannot provide guidance on can help you set up a fruitful research lab. For instance, one student came into my (Alex's) lab wanting to study recruitment techniques of private drug rehabilitation centers. Other than qualitative coding, I knew the project was far outside of my wheelhouse, so I asked a colleague who studies drug use and abuse to join us. I also had my student look through the Communications faculty to see if any of them worked with media. We then had a three-person comentoring faculty team for the one student to get her the experience she needed (and increased our feminist community)! However, other students have asked me to mentor them in a research project in which I am not familiar with any portion of the proposed study. In these cases, I let them know that I am not an expert and, when possible, introduce them to another faculty member who might be able to help.

As mentioned before, we have found this method of having students select their research project area to be empowering for everyone involved if the timing and level of involvement is good. However, in a large lab with multiple projects, it may be hard to cover everything in one research lab meeting a week. You will often need to schedule additional one-on-one meetings, such as for data cleaning and analysis. Around conference time, this can lead to a schedule full of finalizing posters—and not much else. While having other students provide templates and review posters is helpful in easing the load, you may still be doing significant oversight of many students new to making posters, especially if more experienced students have since graduated.

Another question to ask yourself is "How many students do you think you can handle?" Our recommendation is to start smaller and grow your research team from there. Starting with a smaller group allows you to get your feet wet and learn what does/does not work for you and your research leadership style. For instance, we learned that early morning meetings were not working for us *or* our students! There is also the possibility of having too many students. On one large project, for example, there may not be enough work to go around, or students may not feel like they are making as large of a contribution.

More students, especially those with individual projects, requires a lot of upkeep on your part and can get incredibly overwhelming. Starting small can help you determine your management style, your capacity for mentoring, and how many people it will take to work on particular projects. As you master the skills involved in running a lab, you can also grow your lab.

We also believe recruiting students as early in their career as is reasonable (but after they have taken a statistics and/or research methods class) is a good decision. You will likely only have students in your lab for a maximum of 3 years, and more often 1–2 years. Because you are at a teaching-focused school, you will not have the luxury of a dedicated PhD student for multiple years to help you run your research labs and long-term projects. Therefore, if you have students start research with you as 2nd-years, you can provide more in-depth mentoring and can work with them longer on developing research for publication and/or presentation. Recruiting strong students from research methods and statistics courses, in addition to content-related courses that you teach, allows you to get to know the student and form a positive relationship prior to starting a project. Simply emailing them or asking them after class if they are interested in research is perfect! Many may not have thought they "could do research" or just didn't know how to start. Reaching out first opens a lot of doors, especially for students who may be too nervous to ask (e.g., first-generation students may not know that they can ask for this opportunity). We both had the experience of asking students to join our labs whose responses have been, "Really? You mean I could do that? I am good enough to do that?"

Starting recruitment early also provides the added benefit of word of mouth: Students can recruit other students who are interested in similar topics and who are typically similarly high performing. Over time, you will find that you do not need to actively recruit as many students will come to you wanting to join your lab. That said, it can pose a problem if too many students are actively trying to work with you. You may need to eventually become more selective, especially if you know a particular semester coming up will be heavy with other responsibilities and duties, both work and nonwork related.

When you consider the standards for acceptance and the point at which you say no, keep in mind feminist philosophy. Grade point average might not be the best indicator of success in research and might actually be a barrier for many talented students. Additionally, consider accepting students who are not planning to attend graduate school. Research experience teaches many new skills that can easily translate to the workplace (e.g., adhering to timelines, presentation skills, information synthesis). Both of us have had a number of research lab students who have not gone onto graduate school; they are as likely to reach out to thank us for the experience and connect it to their job success.

Protecting Your Research Time

As a faculty member at a teaching-focused institution, there are often fewer faculty to go around when it comes to service (and even the number of new courses you have to prepare). New meetings are constantly popping up and, by mentoring a lot of students, we often have multiple research-focused meetings per week, even if we have one major lab meeting. We have both found that purposefully blocking off time to conduct research is the only way that we are able to make sure we stay focused. First, consider how you write best. There are some who say that a little bit at a time works, even if it is just an hour. However, you may be someone who can only really get things done if you have a chunk of time available. Or maybe you are a mix: You need longer blocks of time to write the paper, but can use shorter blocks of time for literature review, reference checking, or drafting an outline. Determine what works best by initially recording your actual productivity. Once you know your style, you can then schedule your writing time accordingly. If it means creating an "appointment" for yourself in your calendar with the name of the research project so people cannot schedule over it, do it! If it means physically blocking off time in a written agenda, do it! This will help you stay true to your promise and commitment to working on research. And make sure you do it more than a week in advance; our weeks fill up quickly. All too often, I (Alex) loosely schedule time for research each week only to have it magically disappear with meetings/additional grading/course preparation. By committing to research time and not letting anything else interfere, we have been a lot more successful in our writing and publication process.

Another way we have successfully found to schedule in designated research time is to develop writing and accountability groups with supportive colleagues. We have both joined accountability groups of colleagues at other universities, often sponsored by overarching organizations. For instance, the Society for Personality and Social Psychology offers writing accountability "Zoom" group time to help people block off time in their schedules. A colleague of mine (Alex) also brought the idea of writing and accountability groups to our department; they sent out an email at the start of the semester to see who was interested, and we scheduled weekly meetings where we provided updates on what we accomplished. However, we found that scheduling weekly meetings was getting tough with all of our other responsibilities, so we transferred to an online format with a shared Google sheet of goals and accomplishments for writing each week. Other semesters we have found success scheduling 2–3-hour writing blocks every 2 weeks where we report our goals and then at the end our accomplishments. The best part is that, for all of these groups, we could *turn off our email* and actually focus.

Importantly, blocking off time for writing and committing to it models positive behavior to our students: It is important to spend time researching (including time reading research articles). It also allows students to recognize that we do more than just teach, which in turn results in boundary setting around when we are available. Something we have also found helpful is to have students email us their work, and we spend our research time independently reviewing. This strategy has allowed us to provide more in-depth feedback that can help advance projects. So while we support having research team meetings, setting aside time to really focus on a specific project has yielded better results for us.

Additionally, as the only BIPOC and non–U.S. citizen faculty member in my department, I (Sahana) have often served in informal capacities of an advisor and mentor to Black, Indigenous, and people of color (BIPOC) and international students. These identities also impact my service/governance responsibilities to my institution. Additionally, my department is located within the Natural Sciences division, and because of how underrepresented BIPOC women faculty are in this division, I am often invited to serve on multiple committees. This is not to say that I do not enjoy serving my institution, and I am grateful to have opportunities to do so in meaningful and purposeful ways. But, over the years, I have (somewhat) learned to balance my desire for collective change with my individual success (i.e., tenure and promotion). This means learning to balance being available to my students and to serve on committees where I believe my voice is impactful and important versus protecting my time to write academic papers and maintain a programmatic line of research. It also means learning to balance how many research assistants to train and mentor versus doing the research myself to get it out sooner. Learning to voice my challenges and network with supportive colleagues, within and outside of my institution, was an important process for me. Essentially, it has taken me a while to learn that I cannot say yes to every committee request even if I believe that my voice is needed and can make an impact. But most of all, I have learned that I must protect my research and writing, which means saying no to students who want to meet, or at the very least not offering meeting times during my dedicated research slots.

Our Parting Advice

Much of success comes from finding a balance to make sure there is enough time to devote to research. We still admit that we are not perfect! And the best piece of advice we both got for our 1st years: Worry about teaching and know that you probably won't have a ton of time for research as you get settled in and prepare multiple new classes. Give yourself grace at the start, and plan for the 2nd year to be the time you really dig into research, once your classes are mostly prepared. And know that it is a constant balancing act, with some semesters looking wildly different from others; remember, any bit of time you can set aside each week, even if it is just 2 hours, adds up in the long run.

References

Cadaret, M. C., Johnson, N. L., Devencenzi, M. L., & Morgan, E. M. (2019). A quasi-experimental study of the bystander plus program for changing rape culture beliefs. *Journal of Interpersonal Violence*, 36, 19–20. https://doi.org/10.1177/0886260519872981

Freire, P. (2015). *Pedagogy of indignation*. Routledge.

Martín-Baró, I. (1994). *Writings for a liberation psychology*. Harvard University Press.

Zelin, A. I., & Magley, V. J. (2021). Sexual harassment training: Why it (currently) doesn't work and what can be done. In R. Geffner, J. W. White, L. K. Hamberger, A. Rosenbaum, V. Vaughan-Eden, & V. I. Vieth (Eds.), *Handbook of interpersonal violence and abuse across the lifespan: A project of the National Partnership to End Interpersonal Violence Across the Lifespan (NPEIV)* (pp. 1–21). Springer.

CHAPTER 8

Building a Lab at a Research-Intensive Institution
A Feminist and Sustainable Approach to Productivity

- **Jes L. Matsick**
  The Pennsylvania State University

- **Natalie J. Sabik**
  University of Rhode Island

> *To build feminist dwellings, we need to dismantle what has already been assembled; we need to ask what it is we are against, what it is we are for, knowing full well that this we is not a foundation but what we are working toward.*
>
> —Ahmed (2017, p. 2)

In *Living a Feminist Life*, feminist scholar Sara Ahmed reminds readers of the tools required for creating a life of feminist work, including the resources, spaces, personnel, and care that are needed to make feminist projects enjoyable and sustainable. We adopt a similar outlook for building a research laboratory. We suggest that constructing a *feminist* lab requires faculty to assess their values, including the academic norms they wish to unlearn ("what it is we are against") and the feminist principles they aspire to promote ("what it is we are for"). A lab offers feminist faculty the opportunity to counteract oppressive forces within academia and bring their feminist vision for academia to fruition. Indeed, feminist faculty likely find themselves at odds with the academy's masculinized culture. Born from a longstanding tradition of sexism, racism, capitalism, and colonialism, mainstream academic norms often foster competition, reward independence, prioritize productivity, exclude marginalized scholarship and scholars, and devalue teaching and mentoring (e.g., Bagilhole & Goode, 2001). We propose that a carefully developed lab can offer much-needed feminist space within the institution and provide resources that pre-tenure faculty can use to flourish in doing their feminist work.

This chapter focuses on strategies for developing sustainable research practices and thriving collaborations for feminist research within a lab. We draw upon our experiences as feminist psychologists at research-intensive institutions and discuss best practices for building a feminist lab culture. We address the following: establishing a vision, starting the lab, mentoring students while meeting pre-tenure goals, creating space for collegiality and collaboration, and sustaining oneself as a feminist academic. Throughout, we provide practical strategies toward productivity and sustainability for the feminist psychologist on their way to tenure.

Jes: I direct a large lab in Psychology and Women's, Gender, and Sexuality Studies. On average, I mentor three PhD students in a primary capacity, six in a secondary capacity (e.g., working on one project with each student), and five to seven undergraduate research assistants. Most of my pre-tenure publications involved PhD students. Finding synergy between graduate training and my research agenda has been a challenging but positive part of my pre-tenure experience.

Natalie: I run a lab in an interdisciplinary public health program and collaborate with undergraduate students as well as faculty and graduate students from other departments. Mentoring graduate students from other departments (typically 4–6 per year) while working with undergraduate students in my lab has challenged me to think creatively about how to structure mentorship across these different levels to align with my research program and goals.

Attending the Institute for Academic Feminist Psychologists in 2016 and 2018 sparked what has now become a thriving collaborative relationship and supportive friendship between us. We recognize shared values and goals in one another; namely, we both aspire to create a healthier and more just version of academia. Our philosophy of feminist work includes the promotion of equity and inclusion, anti-exploitation, respecting rest and sustainability, practicing self-awareness, and "working smarter not harder" (e.g., embracing organization strategies for work). We appreciate that feminist psychologists play a significant role in institutional change through our efforts to disrupt the status quo of the university (Stewart, 2016). Although our values are somewhat at odds with mainstream academic culture, we believe that these values are the foundation for lasting careers in academia and high-quality lab conditions that facilitate thoughtful and impactful research.

Developing a Vision for Your Research Program

Advice is often given to early career researchers to develop a 5-year plan, and developing and adapting a vision is central to building a lab. To do so, you need to consider your core values and sketch out your projects, research arcs, and goals. It is well worth the time, even though the task may feel nonessential in the short-term. Writing down an outline of your plans and values—allowing room for this to change and grow—can guide decisions about what projects to pursue within the lab, how to allocate time, which projects to prioritize, and with whom to collaborate. We recommend allocating time (even 20 minutes per week can have a big impact) to write and brainstorm your responses to some of the following questions as applicable: What do you think is most important and exciting in your work? What area, theory, or method do you want to shape? What impact do you hope to have? What collaborators do you thrive with, and how does your work intersect with theirs? What skills or resources will you need to acquire for the work you're imagining? How do you want your work to make you feel? What would make you proud of the lab you have created? Be specific and record your responses somewhere that you can easily retrieve to consult and update.

Allowing Your Vision to Take Shape Within the Constraints of Your Institution

We recommend updating this planning document at regular intervals. Opportune moments to do so are when identifying projects to move forward (e.g., at the beginning of an academic term), when preparing for an annual review, and when reflecting at the end of the year. Are your values, goals, and career expectations aligned with how you are spending your time? In addition to learning about criteria for tenure at an institution, while starting a lab, faculty must consider how their institution evaluates different activities (e.g., graduate training, student-led publications, undergraduate research). New faculty should aim to gather this information sooner rather than later so that their vision can be calibrated accordingly. It is important for you to note where your vision and that of your institution align; however, it is acceptable (and often necessary!) to pursue aspects of your vision that do not mimic institutional values. The key is to know how and why your work leads you in directions that may depart from the norm. Be ready to defend your vision. For example, articulating why you publish in the journals that you do, why you attend specific conferences, or why you pursue certain topics or methods should be integrated into your annual reviews and tenure dossier. Connecting with the "why" behind your plans and aligning your values with your vision is a cornerstone of building a sustainable and evolving research program.

Getting Started

Labs can take on many different formats, and the labs we build as feminist psychologists may differ from those of other colleagues. Though setting up a lab is not a one-size-fits-all endeavor, thinking through the following processes has helped us to get started.

First, we address *cultivating a lab identity*. Establishing a lab name, often using keywords to describe the lab's interests, is a common way to signal your research program. As one example, Jes named her lab the "Underrepresented Perspectives (UP) Lab," which is general enough to accommodate her research as it evolves in different ways but specific enough to highlight her core values of centering historically excluded people, theories, and perspectives in psychology. She then used her lab name to form the basis of a website to publicize her work.

Second, we emphasize the importance of *building a lab team*. Recruiting graduate and undergraduate students in the early years on the tenure clock lays a solid foundation for the lab. You should ask questions of other faculty and administrators to learn how graduate admissions work at your institution. To recruit graduate students who share research interests with you, it is important to advertise your intention to admit students. This information should be announced on your lab's website, via social media, and to colleagues at other institutions who may have students applying to graduate school. In addition, Jes created a frequently asked questions (FAQ) handout to circulate to prospective students, which includes unique information about the graduate program, lab interests and future directions, and the lab's values. To select students, we use a rubric that facilitates a fair and effective evaluation process (Posselt, 2016). For example, Jes evaluates applicants on research experience and academic preparation, alignment with the lab's interests and future goals, readiness for a PhD, and commitment to improving DEI in academia; the components of assessment are noted in the FAQ handout. Jes then uses interviews with prospective students to gain more insight into students' compatibility with her values of collegiality, sustainability, and prioritizing underrepresented perspectives. The decision to admit students and which students to admit must be considered in light of your vision so that the benefits gained from an advisee–advisor relationship are mutually beneficial.

To recruit undergraduate students, seek out department- or university-based websites or listservs that can advertise research opportunities or contact students who have performed well in class with you. Approaching students from your classes allows you to recruit students who may be less familiar with why research opportunities are advantageous and thus not searching for these positions on their own. We often recruit students who have taken our classes and have undergraduate students contribute to ongoing lab projects to build their skills before we agree to a larger project (e.g., honors thesis) with them. Students collaborate with each other in Natalie's lab, so determining who works well together and building expectations around supportive collaboration among students is a focus for her. Finally, streamline your process for engaging undergraduate students in the lab. For example, create an online application for interested students to complete, maintain a list of tasks that could require assistance, and design a lab syllabus that conveys policies, procedures, and expectations.

Third, we recommend strategies for *maintaining the lab*. Lab maintenance requires good record keeping and planning. We suggest keeping a spreadsheet of personnel as students come and go (e.g., semester, course credit, projects, contact information). A list is convenient when needing to provide student information for the tenure review process, writing letters of recommendation, and avoiding gaps in personnel (e.g., graduating students). Another strategy for maintaining the lab is to prepare tutorials for common tasks (e.g., conducting literature reviews). Writing down or recording how to complete a task can yield an impressive set of resources, and skilled students can help to create these resources. Natalie also encourages detailed memo making in the lab and writing meeting minutes so that work can be easily picked up from where it was left or checked by other lab members. Having an organized lab facilitates your progress on current projects while making future work within the lab more straightforward.

Mentoring Students Within Your Lab

Working with students can be highly rewarding. Students contribute to the lab's growth, reputation, and culture, and may provide a space for shared feminist values that help to sustain you. However, incorporating students into your research is also time-consuming. You thus need to learn how to balance the need to meet tenure criteria at your institution with your desire to support students in research. That is, consider how mentorship can advance your vision.

Establishing Boundaries

You should be empowered to select which student(s) with whom to work and in which capacity, and accept that there will be times when you have to say "no." One strategy for the "no" decision-making process is to consider when you want discomfort to occur: in the short-term of saying no to something you do not have the capacity to do, or in the long-term when you may not have the resources (e.g., time, energy) to meet the demand. We notice that we are more likely to decline requests that coincide with upcoming commitments (e.g., preparing a new course, serving on a time-consuming committee). Recognizing the obligations we already have—and having that list readily available—validates our need to say no. Also, keep in mind that women and/or people of color are often asked to do the most in terms of service and special requests. Practicing saying no is especially important for them to prevent an overload of demands on their time and energy.

When deciding when to decline a request, think about whose needs you should prioritize. The needs of your department head or chair might be high on the list. Requests from people with more power than you may be understandably difficult to refuse. However, ideally those people already have your best interests in mind and would understand and respect your decision if you had to say no. In contrast, the needs of some students (i.e., students on campus but not in your classes, students who you do not already advise) will likely be ranked lower on your list and therefore might be the recipients of your no. While pre-tenure, Jes was surprised by the number of requests she received to work with students, and she quickly realized that it would not be sustainable to say yes every time. She found it helpful to consider (a) the alignment of a student or new project with her goals and interests and (b) the stages of graduate and undergraduate students in her lab (i.e., those to whom she has already committed). It feels more feasible to say yes when knowing that a current student will be busy dissertating, graduating, or otherwise requiring less guidance. In contrast, it feels stressful to say yes when already feeling overwhelmed with trying to meet the lab's needs. It can ease the letdown if you continue to encourage the student, provide an alternative suggestion, or remind them that you are a limited resource and have already overcommitted at this time.

Mentoring Processes

Both students and faculty benefit when faculty provide students with clear goals and constructive feedback. Investing in students' development, such as by editing their writing or teaching them how to perform a task correctly, ensures that students are growing and have the capacity to contribute to your research. You can inspire students to thrive within the lab by instilling confidence in students, nurturing their autonomy, and strengthening their social connectedness (Alon, 2010). You should thus aim for students to feel sufficiently capable and valued, which will strengthen their contributions to the lab. Another benefit of investing in mentorship is that it may work toward building the feminist version of academia that you envision. Faculty serve a powerful role in repopulating the academic workforce, and your investment in feminist-minded students, particularly those from underrepresented backgrounds, helps to disrupt hegemonic perspectives and foster institutional change. Feminist labs can be safe havens for many students and faculty, especially those who experience their identities and scholarly interests as marginalized (e.g., see notions of epistemic exclusion; Settles et al., 2020).

Feminist mentoring tends to be less hierarchical, which can be a strength for working through interpersonal and work-related challenges in the lab. Open communication is key. When you decide to work with a student on research, it is important to clarify roles and emphasize that discussing responsibilities and defining authorship roles will be ongoing as the project unfolds. We state the resources (e.g., time, attention, skills, data, funding) we can offer and what our limitations are (e.g., timing for feedback, other priorities, bandwidth for collaboration). We also consider what projects we want to prioritize, what progress we envision for various projects, and what self-imposed deadlines we want to put into place. This conversation helps to determine whether a student–faculty collaboration will be a good fit.

Open communication also includes listening to and respecting students' circumstances, ideas, and plans; practicing nonjudgment (e.g., not making immediate top-down decisions about collaborative work); and working to be approachable and trustworthy so that students know they can have honest conversations within the lab when needed. As a feminist academic, you may feel a greater responsibility in your mentoring and be compelled to invest more than others do. Indeed, feminist mentoring sometimes includes providing psychosocial support that goes beyond mentoring academic performance. This requires emotional labor that is often unrecognized but essential for helping students navigate challenges. The benefits students may experience from your mentorship are often well worth the investment. However, we aim to be conscious of the time and energy that we put into this aspect of mentoring, and we often identify this mentoring in annual review forms. Even if you are not provided with space to document this mentoring work, thorough mentorship is consistent with feminist values and thus consistent with your scholarly identity. Try to create a space for it that your evaluators will have to recognize.

Mentorship for Yourself

Mentoring others is important, but you should build mentoring networks that support you too (see Chapters 3 and 4, this volume). You can begin by creating a mentor map: a visual to display people in your network who you can rely on for advice and support. The National Center for Faculty Development and Diversity (NCFDD) has a useful example of a mentor map structure (search engine term: "NCFDD Mentor Map"). Mentoring can be valuable for research and for navigating institutional norms, conflict, student issues, promotion processes, and career decisions. Including "sponsors" in your mentor map can also be used to identify colleagues who would be willing to help make your work visible and put you forward for opportunities. A map will illuminate gaps in your network that you can seek to close by cultivating new relationships. Thinking about what you can offer as well as what you need can make new relationships mutually beneficial. We also suggest protecting time for peer support. We recommend forming a small group with people who seem trustworthy, noncompetitive, and at a similar career stage. Attending the Institute for Academic Feminist Psychologists could facilitate these connections. Two options to consider are forming a writing group or a peer mentoring group. In our experience, smaller structured groups (approximately three to five people) work best. More information and suggestions about creating and maintaining peer mentoring and writing accountability groups is available at www.sustainableacademic.com.

We have engaged in an online writing accountability group and peer mentoring group and have found them to be helpful for counteracting isolation, providing dedicated time to exchanging advice, navigating challenges (e.g., in running a lab), and tracking research goals. Our peer mentoring group that developed from the Institute for Academic Feminist Psychologists has provided support for thinking through lab-related issues. For example, we discussed how to communicate our limited time to students so that they have a reasonable and realistic perception of how we are working (e.g., when to expect feedback). Crafting language with our peers helped us to feel empowered to communicate our boundaries to students. Writing groups and peer groups can be incorporated into the lab too, and we have encouraged our students to create them. For example, students can meet in person or virtually to write or take turns hosting grading "parties" to work on small tasks in the company of others (something that we have enjoyed doing together from afar too!). In sum, it is important to us that we teach our students about the strategies that help us to sustain our work as feminist psychologists.

Promoting a Feminist Lab Environment

Great labs that produce great research do not occur by chance. Such lab environments require us to imagine the culture that we wish to create and work within. Prevailing notions of academic culture—and its emphasis on competition, ego, and hierarchy—are often at odds with feminist principles such as valuing community, collaboration, and valuing outcomes that center marginalized groups. Rather than ascribing to a mainstream approach to academic productivity, we propose another path forward. At the helm of a new lab, you are responsible for the environment and will benefit from asking yourself, "How can I create a space that fosters research toward tenure while I uphold and model feminist values?" The duty of infusing feminist values into the academy requires us to unlearn (mentally) and undo (behaviorally) mainstream academic culture and approaches to research (Bagilhole & Goode, 2001; Matsick et al., 2021). To build a feminist lab we encourage you to promote collegiality and collaboration, as we believe in their transformative potential to advance a feminist academic culture more broadly.

We stress the need for trust in building a feminist environment. Trust must exist within the lab if you intend to resist pervasive, nonfeminist academic norms. Without trust, it will be difficult to nurture feminist approaches because feminist processes for research often counter what students learn elsewhere. One approach to building trust is to speak honestly with students about feminist struggles against mainstream academia. Discussing both the rewards and challenges of being a feminist psychologist shows students that, as feminist psychologists, we often push conventional boundaries (e.g., the journals in which we publish, the institutions we seek to change) but we deem those "risks" to be worth it and we prepare to overcome them.

For example, in conversations with students, we have shared our experiences of feeling like we do not "fit" within psychology, which likely characterizes the feelings of many scholars who have interdisciplinary roots or personal backgrounds that are undervalued or underrepresented in their discipline. Our lack of fit is salient when attending mainstream conferences in which feminist work is underrepresented. We have thus learned to offset those feelings by also attending more feminist-leaning conferences, such as those by the Society for the Psychological Study of Social Issues or the Association for Women in Psychology. This is a strategy that we share with our students. Another example of the challenges encountered when belonging to a feminist lab involves our refusal to thoughtlessly buy into dominant standards. As one example, our labs tend to reject currently valued metrics of research impact (e.g., impact factor) and instead use other criteria to measure the value of our work (e.g., contributing to communities, advancing knowledge for equity and justice, promoting feminist theory and methodology). We prioritize placing research in journals that have a record of appreciating and promoting feminist work, even when we have heard that others perceive these journals as "specialty" outlets because they often center research and researchers that have been historically excluded from mainstream publishing. As feminist psychologists, we willingly choose not to play by the same rules as other psychologists in defining success, but we recognize that our students may feel conflicted as they encounter more traditional messaging. We therefore aim to prepare students to be thoughtful and confident when challenging the status quo, and we have found it useful to remind our students (and ourselves!) that survival of feminist scholarship requires us to become champions of our work and that of other feminist psychologists.

Collegiality

We recognize that we will thrive the most when we build supportive and collegial environments for ourselves. To us, collegiality facilitates peer-to-peer support and noncompetitiveness, collective pride and teamwork, respect for individual differences, inclusion and belonging, and psychological safety (i.e., comfort in vulnerability). The potential for labs to also be sources of joy also should not be underestimated; indeed, work within a lab can provide relief to the otherwise solitary aspects of our work. In our experience, the best lab environments provide fun, companionship, and a lot of laughter! We agree with other feminist scholars that weakening boundaries between the personal versus professional and play versus work can help to sustain feminist work (Abel et al., 1983; Ahmed, 2017). To become transformational feminist psychologists, we need to push back on noncollegial aspects of academic culture (Bagilhole & Goode, 2001; Stewart, 2016), and we need to teach students to do this too.

We seek to model collegial behavior as faculty. For example, advancing the idea that when one of us "wins" we all win, we encourage showing up to support other lab members when they are presenting their work at a conference or research event. This behavior conveys an investment in the work and success of others. Other examples of how we model supporting and celebrating the work of others include tweeting about recent publications or awards of our colleagues, attending colleagues' talks and events, and sharing information about resources or opportunities that are a good fit for others in our network. In addition to recognizing academic accomplishments, Natalie celebrates nonresearch-related life events with her lab, such as a student adopting a new pet. Appreciating people's lives outside of the lab strengthens relationships and helps model work–life balance, and both contribute to sustained collegiality.

Modeling how to handle feedback is also important to the lab's environment. Rejection and criticism happen, and the lab can provide crucial space for learning how to process it. When a manuscript rejection included comments from an exceptionally critical reviewer, Jes discussed with student coauthors how it felt to receive that tone of review and used rejection as an opportunity to discuss how to give feedback. Students agreed that the tone was distracting and not as useful as constructive criticism (this observation is good to remember when providing feedback to undergraduate and graduate advisees). In our experience of giving feedback within our labs, constructive criticism works best when it balances positive and negative observations, avoids assumptions, is presented with care, and provides actionable ideas and suggestions.

Central to building collegiality is also encouraging noncompetitiveness in the lab. It is important for you to proactively address competition and retroactively lessen it if it occurs. For example, we encourage lab members to consider how the overlap of ideas and sharing of authorship within the lab can be mutually beneficial. We promote the idea that it is exciting and promising, rather than threatening, to have multiple people interested in similar inquiries. Staking claim in work can undermine the feminist foundation of a lab if it reproduces the ego and "building your brand" messaging so often encouraged of academics; moreover, being territorial about research can block productivity as it lessens possibilities for collaborations to succeed.

The faculty mentor within a lab plays a big role in shaping students' confidence and security, especially given our relative position of power for establishing norms. We can enhance confidence and lessen competition by celebrating accomplishments for the lab as a collective (advocating for a shared group identity), reflecting on how social comparison feels and why it is not helpful, and providing positive feedback to students.

Within a lab, all people should be made to feel valued, but they do not need to be valued for the same reasons. Promote the idea that everyone has something to offer. Encouraging lab members to focus on what they specifically have to offer can help to reduce insecurities—an important aspect of student motivation (Alon, 2010). It is easy to do this in everyday forms of interaction, such as using microvalidations to communicate students' strengths through small messages of praise and affirmation. For example, telling a student that you value the perspective they are bringing to the work or telling another student that you appreciate how they mentor undergraduate students might offset invalidations that they receive elsewhere. Knowing when students need validation is also important. Jes believes that an effective part of her mentorship involves sensing when students might be in most need of validation to push forward. When a student feels discouraged or is struggling to finish a challenging writing task, Jes reminds them of their strengths and praises their growth. Validations can be motivating.

Finally, we emphasize that faculty should not only model collegial behavior but *reward* it. Positively reinforce collegial behavior in the lab when it occurs. We can do this by nominating highly collegial students for awards, emphasizing the usefulness of students' collegiality in letters of recommendation, and publicly thanking or recognizing their efforts (e.g., in lab-wide communications). Show students that good people serve as the best of colleagues!

Collaboration

Strong collaborations, whether that be with graduate students, undergraduate students, or other faculty, is a cornerstone to a thriving lab. Cultivating collaborations with students and other faculty who are supportive, whom you enjoy spending time with, and whose vision is similar can contribute to your quality of life and to long-lasting collaborations. Though faculty–student collaborations within the lab have an inherent power dynamic built into them and often occur in the context of mentoring, they function similarly as any collaboration and raise the same questions of when to start a collaboration and how to maintain it. A good reason for starting a new collaboration with a graduate student, for example, may be because they posed an interesting research question in a class you taught. With your guidance, the student could develop that idea into a successful project, and perhaps all it takes is a little encouragement from you for the idea to get the ball rolling. Or maybe you have an idea or already lead a project that could use a spark. Folding a graduate or undergraduate student into the project could reignite your progress and provide an opportunity for training and mentorship. Natalie also has built collaborations with graduate students in other departments by offering data as the basis for the collaboration around a shared interest. For example, she collected cortisol data as part of a larger project on women's health but had not yet analyzed the data. A graduate student wanted to learn this analysis, which led to an ongoing collaboration. Sharing information about your research and data both within and across departments can foster collaborations.

A common problem with collaborations, even those occurring within a lab, is that people might have different levels of investment in the work and different schedules for completing the work. Their behavior can interfere with your goals and delay your progress, which can feel stressful. Consider discussing the timeline (and returning to this discussion throughout a project) to avoid frustration and stalled projects that may be critical to your own research trajectory for promotion. Nevertheless, some collaborators may miss deadlines, be difficult to contact, or delay progress in other ways. We have both had this happen and have learned that the only way to resolve the problem is to address it directly. Handling difficult conversations is a skill that helps us to become good communicators and team members in other spaces we occupy. Think about what needs to happen for a collaboration to succeed, and either write an email or request a brief "check-in" meeting. Plan for what you need to say and focus on the outcomes you're hoping to achieve. For example, restate expectations, set dates together, and ask them how they are doing as there may be serious reasons for not meeting expectations (e.g., health, other work demands). Prepare yourself with talking points, which can make the exchange feel less nerve-wracking and scattered, and take time to work through emotions prior to having a difficult conversation, as that can help to keep communication collegial. If working with a collaborator who isn't responding, another strategy is to email them with language such as, "If I don't hear from you by X date, then I'll move forward with the proposed plan." In some cases, you may choose to discontinue the collaboration, revisit it at a later date, or choose not to work with this person on future projects. Working through the challenging moments of collaboration can also be a great topic to be discussed within a peer mentoring group.

Ultimately, your collaborative behavior sets an example for others to follow, which will strengthen dynamics within the lab if everyone upholds best practices for collaboration. For example, on various occasions with students, we have demonstrated that it is simple but effective to admit when we have missed something or messed up, and how not responding in a collaboration is worse than a quick response. We emphasize how allowing room for collaborators and nurturing our relationships with them improves our work and well-being.

Sustainability

In academia, burnout is common, and it has been exacerbated by the added physical and psychological demands of the COVID-19 pandemic. Burnout (i.e., prolonged stress and exhaustion) can be a barrier to building a thriving lab for the long-term; therefore, we need a *sustainable* approach to success. We put forward two questions to guide a sustainability plan: (a) How will you approach research, mentoring, and collaboration in ways that are sustainable? (b) How will you evaluate and course correct as you determine which strategies work for you?

How to Create a Plan for Sustainable Research

We encourage all faculty and students to engage in documentation and experimentation to develop a sustainable plan. What constitutes a sustainable research plan will be specific to your preferences (e.g., What time of day do you do your best thinking and writing? How do you best communicate with collaborators?), the demands on your time (e.g., Do you have commitments to groups or people outside of work? Are you a parent, a partner, or part of a friend group that requires time and mental energy? Are you managing health issues or caregiving?), and the expectations for your position (e.g., What must you do to achieve tenure and to continue a satisfying and productive career post-tenure?). For your lab's research to be sustainable, it must integrate your nonwork life as part of the plan, not as an afterthought. We believe that taking good care of ourselves is part of the job and our responsibility to the lab.

Learn to Lean Into the Ebb and Flow of Your Semester

To get started, it is helpful to note or track the ebb and flow of the academic term and *work with this instead of against it*. Create a calendar that allows you to see the scope of the semester or year; bullet journals can be used to customize this approach. After trying many planners over the years, Natalie found that a bullet journal she creates herself works best for both short- and long-term planning. She uses a blank journal that is divided into sections that are easy to flip between. The first section houses ongoing to-do lists that are carried over from week to week. The second section has monthly calendars that lay out all deadlines and important dates. The third section tracks each project she's working on and notes the status and next steps so that there's room to organize and document any notes or details in one place. Bullet journals are customizable, so testing out different sections, layouts, or systems may be of interest. Jes uses a similar planning process as Natalie but prefers to work electronically via an application called Evernote that syncs across devices (e.g., phone, computer). Across our approaches, a common theme is that we know what we will be working on and when. There is no right or wrong way to organize and plan for work, but organization is instrumental to our success and well-being. Planning frees space in our minds to focus on the tasks at hand because we trust our process will tell us what is next.

When it comes to organizing your schedule, it is key to look ahead and make note of upcoming deadlines. For example, when are conference proposal deadlines? Are there any upcoming deadlines for journal articles? When are larger assignments or exams due for classes that you may need to grade? Do you want to block off time for friends and family and self-care (e.g., doctors' appointments)? Visualizing how commitments unfold across your semester can illuminate how full your time is. For example, grading often is not factored into planning, but recognizing that you need to grade 30 papers in the 6th week of the semester can help you form realistic plans. Know which weeks will require the most time or energy for service, teaching, and advising. Anticipating these and planning for them helps you adjust or plan ahead for research expectations when needed, which can reduce feelings of guilt or disappointment.

Set Limits on What You Agree to Do for Others

We recommend balancing your own projects (e.g., first-authored projects) with projects that you support for others, and the balance between these may shift depending on the criteria for your promotion. It can be helpful to revisit the list of your major projects that serve your vision before filling in what you can offer others. Convey to others when you have reached the maximum you can handle, which will take some trial and error to determine. Natalie uses her writing accountability group spreadsheet to track her tasks and identify when she's at capacity. In the spreadsheet, she tracks how many writing days she has each month (e.g., weekdays when she has childcare) and notes how much time she spends on different types of tasks. By tracking this over time, it became clear what amount of work she can reasonably accomplish with regard to her research depending on prior commitments, teaching, and service. Knowing where you stand in terms of current short- and long-term commitments will make it much clearer whether you have the capacity to take on new projects and when to say no.

Start or Maintain a Weekly Check-In With Yourself

This can be as detailed or broad as suits you, but you should articulate what you aim to move forward within the lab each week. At the most basic level, this can be kept short and may simply require listing active projects versus those that are on hold. Be sure to loop in students and collaborators periodically so that everyone is working from the same understanding. A more granular approach to your check-in could identify specific tasks that will fit into your schedule in the upcoming week. We recommend taking 10–15 minutes per week to engage in this process; this can even be factored into your planning for the ebb and flow of the semester. Another way to approach the weekly check-in is to consider it a brain dump. Your check-in need not be strictly limited to research. In fact, documenting other tasks and commitments you have in a week can help you to be realistic about your time, what will fit into your calendar, and when you are at your limit.

Work in Short Bursts

Small bits of work add up! If you spend 10 minutes per day moving a project forward, at the end of a week you have put in nearly an hour on a project that may not have happened otherwise. Although some tasks may seem as though they require large blocks of uninterrupted time to be executed, experiment with what tasks you can do to prepare for the larger task (i.e., prework). For example, for a daunting data analysis session, using 10–15 minutes ahead of time to open the data, open the codebook, and identify your variables can be your prework and a big help in setting up an effective work session later. When preparing to write a section of a manuscript, your prework may require you to gather material you need to read or review for the section. Getting organized before doing the larger task sets yourself up to (a) actually complete the task, (b) not feel overwhelmed, and (c) effectively use time in your day to make progress on a project. Relatedly, you do not need to wait for motivation to get your work done; rather, motivation might often follow small bursts of work.

Choose When to Focus

Our attention is pulled in a hundred different directions, yet the most important research toward tenure will require deep focus. Choose a short, finite amount of time each week and keep your focus squarely on the task at hand by closing email or notifications, disconnecting from the internet, using noise-canceling headphones, closing your office door, blocking time on your calendar, putting your phone in another room, or using a timer. Your attention is your most powerful tool. Learning how to wield and control it feels like a superpower. We recommend the book by Cal Newport (2016) on working through distractions, titled *Deep Work: Rules for Focused Success in a Distracted World* (see Resources).

Track Your Energy, Not Just Your Time

Not all time is created equal. Learn when to work on tasks in relation to your energy levels. Of course, this may be compromised by the demands that other people put on your time. Noticing how and when your energy affects your ability to focus and to complete your work will help you begin to plan to protect your energy. You are the steward of your energy, your time, and your focus.

How to Create Sustainable Life–Work Integration

Integrating work and aspects of your life in your sustainability plan is critical for building a lab and research career for the long-term. Incorporating nonwork aspects of your life into your plans can produce less friction in both areas and can benefit your productivity overall. For example, designating time for nonwork tasks, such as exercise, time with friends, food prep, reading, or other activities in our weekly schedule—even during typical "work" hours—can help provide a break from work and increase feeling restored. One suggestion is to put these activities in your calendar at your weekly check-in and to protect it the same way that you would for work commitments. It is okay to be unavailable because you've already committed to something that sustains you. We endorse the idea that taking care of ourselves, physically and mentally, helps us best take care of the students and collaborators with whom we work too. We suggest that you encourage your students to follow these guidelines as well.

Figuring out what works best for you is key, even when this seems to contradict the external expectations that academia seems to convey. Identify when you are getting diminished returns and when you would benefit from a different approach. Feeling tired, having trouble with focusing, or finding that work is progressing more slowly than usual can be indicators of diminished returns. The assumption in academia is that faculty and students "push through" to produce. However, noticing when a break would serve you better than continuing to work can alleviate overwork and can open up experimentation with ways to take breaks (even short breaks) that help you return refreshed and ready to work. One example of this is that when you don't get enough sleep, your brain works less efficiently, so prioritizing sleep (or taking a nap instead of continuing to work) is a good strategy to reduce diminished returns. Similarly, taking time to prepare or purchase nourishing foods that you enjoy and that fuel you is a worthwhile task. When your body is signaling that you need a break, listen to it. Reframing productivity as encompassing elements beyond work is key for unlearning mainstream pressures of academia. To learn more, we recommend Hillary McBride's (2021) book, *The Wisdom of Your Body: Finding Healing, Wholeness, and Connection through Embodied Living* (see Resources).

Rest can encompass any activity that gives you energy or sustains you. Engaging in restorative and enjoyable physically active time that is not focused on work can contribute to rest. For example, Natalie loves to quilt and regularly takes breaks from academic work to sew. The time spent using her hands and creating a tactile object fuels creativity and brings a sense of accomplishment unrelated to academic work, and she's noticed that when working with her hands her mind is freer to process information and make connections. Although her goal is never to intentionally engage in academic work while crafting, taking time away from academic work lends itself to making progress in thinking about complex ideas or solutions to work-related challenges. To learn more about the value of rest, we recommend Alex Soojung-Kim Pang's (2016) book, *Rest: Why You Get More Done When You Work Less* (see Resources).

Finally, facing resistance you may hold around both work and time spent on your own needs is a powerful way to change long-standing patterns that are not serving you. Most of us have internalized scripts around what we think we need to do to be "successful" as an academic (or a partner, parent, or in other roles we embody), but the needs we actually *need* to meet are our own. Enacting some of the choices needed to build a sustainable research program may not serve everyone else yet are valuable characteristics of the feminist psychologist who endures.

Conclusion

Establishing your lab while on the tenure track is an exciting opportunity, but it will present challenges that you have likely not yet encountered. We encourage you to leverage your network of feminist psychologists to provide you with support as you embark on this new academic task. Be patient with your progress. It may take a few years before you see the impact of your efforts, but we strongly promote the idea that planting the seeds now will help everyone within your lab to blossom later. Your lab can become a hub for your work toward tenure, the enactment of your vision, and a mechanism toward institutional transformation for the next generation of scholars. We hope you cherish the opportunity to build a lab that reflects your feminist values and nurtures the growth of feminist psychology.

Suggested Resources

McBride, H. L. (2021). *The wisdom of your body: Finding healing, wholeness, and connection through embodied living.* Brazos Press.

Newport, C. (2016). *Deep work: Rules for focused success in a distracted world.* Grand Central.

Pang, A. S-K. (2016). *Rest: Why you get more done when you work less.* Hachette Book Group.

Sustainable Academic website: www.sustainableacademic.com

References

Abel, E., Hirsch, M., & Langland, E. (1983). "They shared a laboratory together": Feminist collaboration in the academy. *Women's Studies International Forum*, *6*(2), 165–167.

Ahmed, S. (2017). *Living a feminist life*. Duke University Press.

Alon, U. (2010). How to build a motivated research group. *Molecular Cell*, *37*(2), 151–152. https://doi.org/10.1016/j.molcel.2010.01.011

Bagilhole, B., & Goode, J. (2001). The contradiction of the myth of individual merit, and the reality of a patriarchal support system in academic careers: A feminist investigation. *European Journal of Women's Studies*, *8*(2), 161–180. https://doi.org/10.1177/135050680100800203

Matsick, J. L., Kruk, M., Oswald, F., & Palmer, L. (2021). Bridging feminist psychology with open science: Feminist tools and shared values inform best practices for science reform. *Psychology of Women Quarterly*, *45*(4), 412–429. https://doi.org/10.1177/03616843211026564

Posselt, J. R. (2016). *Inside graduate admissions: Merit, diversity, and faculty gatekeeping*. Harvard University Press.

Settles, I. H., Warner, L. R., Buchanan, N. T., & Jones, M. K. (2020). Understanding psychology's resistance to intersectionality theory using a framework of epistemic exclusion and invisibility. *Journal of Social Issues*, *76*(4), 796–813. https://doi.org/10.1111/josi.12403

Stewart, A. J. (2016). Feminist psychologists and institutional change in universities. In T-A. Roberts, N. Curtin, L. E. Duncan, & L. M. Cortina (Eds.), *Feminist perspectives on building a better psychological science of gender* (pp. 319–332). Springer.

CHAPTER 9

Securing Grants

- **Danielle Dickens**
  Spelman College

- **Katie M. Edwards**
  University of Nebraska-Lincoln

Why Feminists Should Secure Grants

For many feminist academics, securing external funding is critical to maintaining and expanding one's program of social justice–oriented research and may be an expectation for promotion and tenure. Feminist scholars may also strive to obtain grants to fund research that amplifies the voices of those who are often silenced and minoritized. Feminist research is critical to addressing societal issues and grants permit well-supported research that allows for the needed time and resources to effectively fulfill project goals and objectives. With the ever-increasing demands of academic life, academics are expected to do more and more. Specifically, many academic feminists may be juggling more social justice–centered teaching and service, which requires more time to engage and inspire change. Receiving grant support may create space and time to have more balance with teaching, service, and research.

Despite the importance of obtaining grant funding for feminist scholarship, many feminist academics receive little to no formal training in grant writing and management and can find the process daunting and even discouraging. Indeed, some people may even ask themselves, "Can I do this?" The answer is, yes you can! The key to writing a winning grant grounded in feminist approaches is to make a compelling case for how the theories and methods you propose will lead to meaningful outcomes for science, practice, and policy. Though this may feel like a daunting task, in this chapter, we provide tips and tools to help secure that grant. We consider questions that we are often asked about finding, writing, and managing research grants. We share our own experiences and advice that we have received from other successful feminist scholars, reflect on our own successes and failures, and provide resources you may find useful.

Positionality

It is important for us to discuss our social identities and relevant experiences, because they shape our approach to research and grant writing. Therefore, before getting into the details of grant writing, we start by describing our positionality.

Danielle Dickens

I am a Black heterosexual cisgender woman and Black feminist social psychologist. My research focuses on the identity development and identity formation of Black women and how they navigate the world. I use qualitative and quantitative methodologies to examine the intersection of multiple identities, specifically race, gender, age, and class identities, with an emphasis on Black women in the workplace, higher education, and STEM. I took a grant writing course while in graduate school, but that was my only formal grant writing training. To date, I have secured over $11 million in external funding from the National Science Foundation (NSF), United Negro College Fund, and American Psychological Foundation. As a professor at a Black women's liberal arts college that emphasizes undergraduate teaching and a curriculum centered on liberal arts and the sciences, I learned about grant funding from serving on grant review panels, reviewing copies of awarded grant proposals, and getting feedback from program officers.

Katie Edwards

I am a white, non-Latinx queer cisgender woman. I am a midcareer scholar at a research-intensive institution with expectation of high grant activity. As a tenured associate professor, I am committed to developing and evaluating interpersonal violence prevention and response efforts among minoritized populations. I believe that interpersonal violence and other related public health and safety issues must be understood within a sociopolitical and historical lens, that community-based participatory action research (CBPAR) is the most effective and ethical way to prevent and respond to interpersonal violence, and that researchers' power and privilege, including white privilege, must be acknowledged and dismantled through reflexivity and a commitment to antiracism work. Despite little formal training in grant writing as a graduate student and assistant professor, over the past 10 years I have secured over $12 million in external funding from the National Institutes of Health (NIH), Centers for Disease Control and Prevention (CDC), NSF, and Department of Justice (DOJ). Much of my success has been self-taught (e.g., reading books, asking questions of successful scholars, reading, and studying successful proposals) and based on lessons learned from failures (e.g., reading reviews from unfunded grants, recognizing omissions from grant budgets).

How to Start: Writing Your First Grant

Before sharing specific details about the components of a grant proposal and how to craft a strong proposal, we offer some tips for getting started as a new grant-writer.

Start Small and Then Grow

A great strategy is to start small and then build your grant-funded research portfolio over time. This allows you to get your feet wet and gain some grant-writing skills without the significant investment of time required for a large grant proposal. You might apply for small grants from your institution (e.g., faculty development awards), or small grants from foundations, professional societies, or federal funding agencies. You can often expand these projects into larger awards later, sometimes using the data you collect as pilot data for a larger grant proposal. Even when not funded, these small proposals can provide valuable experience. For example, I (Danielle) originally submitted a foundation grant proposal for $15,000 to fund a study of Black women's coping in the face of discrimination. My proposal was not funded; however, it gave me practice writing a research grant proposal. I learned to provide clear details of my research design (e.g., clear definition of the methods), ensure the proposed projects were theoretically grounded, and have someone who has successfully received grant funding review my proposal. Roughly 2 years later, I expanded that proposal to a funded half million-dollar research grant. If you find that a weakness identified in your grant proposal is a skill set you need to enhance, seek that out. For example, if you receive feedback that you need more experience doing a specific type of methodology, see if you can get experience partnering with someone in the field doing that type of research, seek a small pot of money to attend a training, and so forth. Another way to learn grant writing is to collaborate on a proposal with more senior individuals in the field. The experience will advance your skill development and confidence and, in turn, you can offer your expertise to the project.

Deciding on a Project

Often academics have multiple ideas for a grant submission and have to decide what topics and projects to prioritize. Although some academics can manage simultaneously writing multiple grants, this is often a challenge, especially for more junior academics who are still learning the ropes. Thus, early in your grant-writing career, you may want to focus on leading one grant proposal at a time. That said, you might be asked to take a smaller role (e.g., co-investigator [Co-I], consultant) on a grant proposal someone else is leading; this may be manageable to do while leading on writing your main grant, and the collaboration may help you gain skills, fund some of your work, obtain course releases, or obtain additional funds for summer salary.

Find a balance between an idea that excites and an idea that is fundable (but is still related to your program of research and area of expertise). It is important that as a feminist you look for grants that fit your idea, not the other way around. I (Danielle) select topics based on my current program of research since I have limited time to develop new research areas. My first grant research proposal was an extension of my dissertation work on identity shifting (a coping strategy that involves altering how one talks and behaves, one's appearance and perspectives) among early career Black women. My grant proposal extended my dissertation topic to the STEM context and also proposed to utilize a daily diary methodology; this innovative method and the novel context helped to distinguish the proposed research from my earlier work and build my program of research.

Similarly, I (Katie) have been successful in obtaining funding from the National Institute on Alcohol Abuse and Alcoholism (NIAAA) given the intersections of violence and alcohol misuse. The way I frame the grant for an agency like NIAAA, however, is different than how I frame a grant for another agency, such as the CDC. However, the core ideas and outcomes are still very similar. The point is to be flexible but not compromise the integrity of your idea or veer too far astray from your program of research and true passions.

Study Funded Grants

The best way to learn how to write a grant proposal is to get examples of previously funded grants that are as close to what you are applying for as possible. If you do not know a colleague personally, it is okay to email a scholar you do not know and ask to review their funded proposal. Explain to them that you are new to writing grants and that you would love to learn from their experience and success. Ensure that you will keep their grant confidential. The worst case is that they say no. You can also find summaries of previously funded grants via most government and foundation websites. NIH Matchmaker is a great way to find similar NIH proposals to yours, for example.

Who Can Help?

If you are new to grant writing and submission, we recommend that you reach out to someone who can assist you. Reaching out to a seasoned colleague at your institution or another institution is a great start. You may also want to meet with staff at your university who oversee grants and fellowships. For example, your university may have an Office of Institutional Advancement (or something similar) that manages foundation grants and an Office of

Sponsored Programs (OSP) for all other grants (e.g., federal grants). Staff working in these offices are knowledgeable about different funding agencies and programs, and thus they can free up a lot of time you would otherwise spend searching websites. Those offices may even have access to funded grants proposals that they have permission to share with others, including you. There might also be a center on your campus that focuses on a topic related to your research area (e.g., gender-focused center or institute); they may have staff who can help with various aspects of grant writing. If you are not sure where to start on your campus, ask other colleagues, especially those in leadership roles and/or individuals who write and submit grants.

At some funding agencies, you can reach out to a program officer *prior* to preparing your grant. The program officer's role is to manage grant proposal review (gathering external reviews from scholars in the area), make recommendations to award or decline each proposal to the division director, and oversee funded grants. However, before the review process, the program officer (if allowed) can also provide feedback on whether the project you have in mind is a good fit for their agency and specific funding program. To set up this meeting, you typically will draft a one-page project summary of your proposal idea, email it to the program officer, and request a follow-up phone or Zoom meeting to discuss it (some program officers may prefer to provide you with feedback via email). The purpose of that meeting is to get their initial thoughts on your idea, and you can ask them to point out aspects of your project that might be problematic during the review process. We have found their feedback to be thorough and helpful in narrowing down the focus of the project, in terms of feasibility of research design and study population of interest.

In our experience, most NIH and NSF program officers are very willing to discuss potential proposals, but other federal agencies like the CDC and the DOJ are unable to do so because of their institutional policies. If you are unsure whether this meeting request is allowed, there is no harm in reaching out to the program officer or checking with your OSP or a colleague with experience with that funding agency first. Generally, the program officer you reach out to is listed in the specific funding announcements; you can also find them by searching Institutes (at NIH) and Directorates (at NSF).

There are a number of ways to find grants via websites (e.g., NIH Reporter), listservs (e.g., federal funding agencies, professional organizations), books, journal articles, internal university postings, and word of mouth. The reference list provided at the end of this chapter has a number of resources that cover these topics in depth. One strategy for finding appropriate funding programs is noticing the funding sources noted in published journal articles in your research area of interest. Since authors are required to disclose funding sources in their publication acknowledgements, you can see which agency is funding grants on topics similar to the idea you seek to have funded. You can also review specific funding announcements to understand if the program is a good fit for your project. These announcements are often filled with jargon and administrative considerations; try to look past that to the description of the types of research they plan to fund. Ask a mentor, senior colleague, or OSP staff person to review the announcement with you. Some funding agencies even host an informational session for specific funding announcements where they walk through the entire solicitation and answer questions. Understanding whether the funding program is a good fit for your project is a critical first step and will save you from writing grants unlikely to be funded because of poor fit, not because of a poor idea.

What's in a Grant Proposal? Understanding the Components of a Grant

Once you've identified a terrific funding program, you can start writing the grant. But what are the components of a grant application? Some funding agencies or program announcements will provide detailed information of what to include in each section of the grant, and some funding agencies, like NSF and NIH, have a guide for proposal writing that you can find on their website. Be sure to first determine what components are required for your application. Always adhere to all guidelines in the solicitation regarding page restrictions as some agencies will not send your application out for review if you do not follow the instructions (or are late—never submit your grant proposal late!). At many institutions, the principal investigator (PI) is not the one who officially submits the application. Rather, it is an authorized representative/official of the institution. Early in the process, check to see if there are internal university deadlines you must meet and administrative approvals (e.g., department chair, dean or provost) needed to ensure you meet the funding agency's deadline.

Specific Aims or Project Summary

Almost all grants will request a summary of your specific aims or project. This section (ranging from a half a page to a page, depending on the funding agency) includes your specific goals and objectives and contains a concise, comprehensive overview of the entire project, including background, gaps in the field (that the project will presumably address), research questions/hypotheses, research designs, and often specific statements regarding the proposal's alignment with the funding agencies' priorities and, if applicable, public health/broader impact. It is recommended that you do not start writing anything else until the aims/project summary is done and refined, since it is the roadmap for your entire proposal.

Project Narrative

After you write your specific aims/project summary, you will often focus on the main narrative (NIJ terminology), research strategy (CDC and NIH terminology), or similar section of the application; this is essentially the component of the proposal where you include the background information for your project as well as a detailed methodology. This section, which can range from a few pages to over 20 (depending on the solicitation and agency), likely includes the background literature (including your theoretical framework) and research plan (e.g., design and methods, such as objectives, research participants, design, measures and procedures, and analysis plan). In addition, in this component you may be required to include a timeline, project evaluation plan, summary of prior research funded by the agency, and information about the project investigators. Relatedly, it's ideal if you can present pilot data in your proposal. Even for funding programs that say pilot data is not required, it can still help. Presenting results from pilot data shows that you have begun the work and are not starting from scratch. You may collect qualitative or quantitative data specifically for this purpose, or you may be able to use data that you previously collected and/or published.

Other Components and Considerations

In addition, researchers may be required to provide documentation of institutional resources and research space to ensure that they have the capacity to carry out the proposed project. In the "Facilities, Equipment, and Other Resources" document, you should include research space available on campus, computer/computer supplies, office space (e.g., for PIs, postdoctoral research associates), and administrative assistance, to name a few things. If you do not have a lot of institutional resources, you may want to partner with a collaborator at another institution to enhance your grant proposal. This also speaks to the importance of getting collaborators that can help strengthen your grant proposal, but also can be advantageous for career advancement. Ideally, it would be great to find collaborators who have successfully received grant funding or individuals who have any expertise that you may be lacking to illustrate you can collectively carry out this project. Be aware that some grant agencies will not release funds until you have IRB approval, so be realistic in the proposed start date.

Budget

The budget is one of the most important parts of your application, yet for many the budget is the most daunting part of the proposal. At many institutions, you are required to have an appropriate staff person (e.g., grant manager) approve your budget before you can submit the grant application. If not, make sure someone with relevant expertise reviews your budget to make sure you did not miss any major budget items. If you plan well, you are less likely to find that in your funded project you have run out of money for a specific budget category (but this still occurs even among the most seasoned grant writers); otherwise, you may have to reallocate funds from another budget category (this may require funder approval), seek other funding (e.g., internal grant), or pay out of pocket (e.g., food for participants). Further, most agencies allow for what is called a no-cost extension, which means you can carry unspent funds forward into an additional year of funding; this is a great safety net for completing your project, but your proposal should not figure in this additional time.

In your grant proposal, you will have to include a budget, along with a budget justification. The budget should align with the project aims and objectives. The budget justification is a separate document that includes a narrative explanation of each of the components of the budget to justify the cost of the proposed work. This may include justification for senior personnel (course release and/or summer salaries for PIs), other personal (graduate research assistant, program manager/coordinator, or postdoctoral fellow), fringe benefits (you can get this information from your office of budget and contracts), travel (funds requested for travel to a data collection site, conference travel), participant support costs, and other direct costs (e.g., materials and supplies, computers/tablets, software, sub-award to another partnering institution, like where a Co-I is located).

One of the most critical pieces to running a successful grant-funded projects is communication. If the budget allows for it, have a solid project manager who can help you with the day-to-day coordination and administrative pieces of the grant so that you can focus on the parts most exciting to you and relevant to your scholarship. As a feminist psychologist, it is important to advocate for yourself and your time, so include sufficient funding for yourself (e.g., ample course releases, summer salary). Also, be willing to be transparent with team members about the budget (e.g., where funds are being directed and why).

Timeline: Planning and Organizing Writing

A helpful strategy in grant writing is to create a timeline and try to stay on it, but do not be too hard on yourself if things get delayed. Make sure to block time off and really protect it for grant writing. If you get writer's block, take a break and come back to it or reschedule writing time. I (Katie) often get the best ideas when I step away. During this time of not working on the grant or thinking about it, sometimes ideas will come to me, and I will quickly jot down what comes to mind in a notebook or on my phone (in an email to myself) so that I can integrate it when I return to grant writing. Also, you may want to consider creating a writing accountability group with other colleagues who are also writing grant proposals. Some institutions may also have these writing groups already established. If not, you can always start one!

When preparing your grant, we recommend focusing first on your specific aims/project summary and then the main narrative/research strategy; focus on the supplemental pieces later as they tend to be shorter, often less challenging to write, and boilerplate (to some extent). For parts of the grant that require other people (e.g., letters of support for partnering agencies, statistician to run power analyses to determine your sample size), you should solicit materials sooner rather than later to account for unanticipated delays. Some of your pieces (e.g., budget to pay a statistician) also may depend on these individuals' work (e.g., sample size produced from power analyses). There are a lot of moving pieces that go into grant writing, but as you gain more experience, it will become more second nature.

Writing a Strong Grant Proposal

You can increase your chances of having your grant proposal funded with some additional knowledge of the review process. We have found it helpful to understand who reviews grants and the criteria they use to do so. With this knowledge in hand, we have been able to craft proposals in which it is easy for reviewers to find the information they need for their evaluation.

Know Your Audience: Grant Reviewers

A panel of grant reviewers will be invited by the funding agency to read and review your grant proposal. They are your audience. To the extent possible, we advise you to learn who your reviewers will be, since writing to your audience is important. Reviewers are scholars who have different expertise relative to research topic, methodology, content, and statistical analyses; they may be academics or nonacademics (e.g., practitioners, service members for a Department of Defense grant) depending on the funding agency and specific solicitation. The structure of reviewing is different across agencies (e.g., some agencies may have individuals review without discussion with one another, whereas other agencies may have reviewers come together in person or virtually to discuss applications), but regardless, you must keep the variability of your reviewers in mind—you cannot assume they will be experts in all the areas relevant to your proposal. As a result, you should justify all theoretical, methodological, programmatic, and analytical decisions in your grant and why you decided to do what you are proposing rather than an alternative approach. Never assume that reviewers will "just get it."

It can be tricky to know who your reviewers are likely to be. NIH publishes rosters for review panels, and a lot of the members are standing members; in this case, you can assume the standing members will review your proposal. For foundations, you can try to get a sense of who they normally invite to review by asking colleagues or your institution's OSP or Office of Institutional Advancement. If the reviewers are known to you and they work in the subject area of your proposal, get familiar with their work, and cite it if it is relevant.

Know the Review Criteria

Reviewers will be given a set of criteria to use to evaluate your proposal. Often, those criteria are stated as part of the funding announcement or on the funding agency's website. It is important to make sure your proposal is strong in each of those areas. And although they vary between agencies, there are some common criteria you can expect your proposal to be reviewed on. One criterion is alignment with the funding announcement and/or agency mission. Make it clear how your project aligns with both the funding announcement and the larger mission of the funding agency. It is helpful to mirror language used in the funding announcement in your proposal so that it's easy for reviewers to see the alignment.

You will also be reviewed on feasibility—whether you can carry out the proposed project within the timeframe and budget of the grant. It is important to find the balance between over-proposing (proposing to do more than is feasible) versus under-proposing (proposing to do too little in relation to the timeframe). You will likely be dinged by reviewers if you put an unrealistic amount of time to accomplish all of this in your grant application. For instance, if you are submitting a proposal for a 3-year grant, you want to make sure you realistically think about what you can get done within that time. You may spend the first couple of months getting funds released, hiring a research team (e.g., postdoctoral research associate and graduate/undergraduate research assistants), getting IRB approvals (which are required by some agencies to release funds), and/or getting a research lab set up, so you may want to factor in that time to the 3-year grant.

Grant proposals are also evaluated on the team's ability to do the work. A big piece of this is based on the PI, so it's critical that you do not sell yourself short and emphasize your relevant expertise pertinent to the project (e.g., scholarly and methodological expertise, leadership experience). You should have a record of publications in the research area of your proposed project; these are viewed as evidence that you have the expertise to do the work you are proposing. If there are areas of your project in which you lack expertise, bring on a Co-I. For example, in all of my grants, I (Katie) budget for a methodologist and statistician. I also have a Co-I on my NIAAA grants whose sole expertise is in alcohol misuse prevention. When I (Danielle) submitted my first grant, I collaborated with a more senior colleague for a collaborative grant proposal; their greater experience may have helped secure funding for the grant by reassuring reviewers that the project was likely to succeed. While you want to make sure that all areas of expertise are covered, you do not want to duplicate roles. In other words, having two investigators with identical or similar expertise may lead to criticisms that will impact your evaluation. Finally, some reviewers and funding agencies like to see a successful history of collaboration (e.g., publishing together prior to submitting your grant). Make a case for how you both have successfully collaborated with each other and have formed a strong working relationship in writing the grant.

Make It Easy to Read

When writing your grants, make it as easy as possible for your reviewers. Often reviewers are assigned multiple grants totaling hundreds or thousands of pages. The reality is that reviewers do not always read every word of every grant. But there are ways to make the experience more pleasant for reviewers and increase the likelihood that the parts they do read are the most important pieces of your proposal. As reviewers, we appreciate it when there is some blank space (but not too much), paragraphs are short, the most important sentence or sentences of a paragraph are bolded, and there is a good mix of text, tables, and figures. If you number the sections in your grant, you can refer back to earlier text (e.g., "As reviewed in Section A.8, …"). That said, if something is critical to your project and there is space, saying it more than once is not a bad thing, as reviewers will sometimes overlook important things in your grant. Therefore, bolding and some repetition is good!

To ease the writing task, you can pull from papers you have previously published and/or are currently working on. It is okay to use text from other documents you have written if you vary the language/wording. It's also important to be aware that writing grants is different than writing scientific papers. For example, in a grant, you typically will have limited space for a literature review (and less than in a manuscript) because focusing on your approach and methods is often the most important part. Grants are often not written with the same flow as a manuscript. As an example, because grants often have clearly defined sections, subsections, and so forth, you can be less concerned about traditional paragraph structure and smooth transitions. However, a common feature of manuscript and grant writing is the need to be clear and concise and have logical flow.

Get Feedback on Your Proposal

When possible, have others read your grant, especially other academics with a history of successfully receiving funding from the agency to which you are submitting. Whenever possible, solicit feedback from trusted colleagues and from your OSP. At some institutions, OSP staff will review and provide feedback on your grant proposals before submission. If they do not have time to read the entire proposal, ask them to read your specific aims/project abstract page since this is the most important part of your grant application and serves as a roadmap for everything else in your proposal. Some institutions may even pay external reviewers who are experts in the field to review your proposal, but this often requires that you have a full draft 4 to 6 weeks in advance of the deadline. Another thing that is very helpful in writing successful grant proposals is to volunteer as a grant reviewer (email a program officer with your CV and express that you are interested in serving as a grant reviewer).

Managing Rejection and Staying Motivated

Just like with manuscript submissions, getting rejections from grant proposals can sting but is a part of the process. The quality differences between funded grants and unfunded ones are often small. Thus, try not to get discouraged if you don't get funded as it doesn't mean that your ideas aren't good. Most people get poorly evaluated on their approach (i.e., research methods and design). If you receive reviews, they will help you understand why your grant proposal was rejected. To understand the reviews, you can ask senior mentors to read the reviews and give feedback, and if additional clarity is needed, it may be helpful to talk to the program officer (if allowed), especially if the reviews seem unfair (i.e., reviewers stated a component was missing that was actually in the proposal). Many grant-funding agencies have an appeal process if you believe that you were unfairly judged. However, before you reach out to the program officer to potentially discuss an appeal, speak to your OSP staff to get their thoughts on how to navigate your situation. They may be able to advocate on your behalf.

Do not just sit with your rejected grant proposal, resubmit! When revising and resubmitting your grant, the same individuals may review it again, so be sure to address every single reviewer critique with a change in the proposal or through a strong theoretical and/or empirical justification for why you did not make the change. Program officers, if allowed, can often be helpful in addressing reviewer critiques, as can senior mentors and scholars in the field. Try not to get too discouraged by reviewer critiques. In our experience, many of our grants were not funded on the first submission, and even those with harsh critiques were ultimately funded.

Just because your proposal was rejected does not mean it can't count toward tenure and promotion. On your CV, you can list all the grants that you submitted, whether funded or not; include where it was submitted, the proposed grant amount, and your potential role (e.g., PI or Co-PI). You may want to ask senior mentors, especially at your institution, about this practice, as in some departments listing unfunded proposals may be viewed negatively. In your narrative statements, highlight the strengths noted in your proposal reviews as well as your future plans for (re)submitting grant proposals. It shows that even though you did not successfully receive funding, you will continue to submit grant proposals (with the hope that they will begin to get funded).

Managing Grants

Congratulations—you got the grant! Now what? Notify your project partners and then take time to celebrate and honor your achievements! A number of great resources exist on managing grants (see next section), but we want to emphasize a few things that we have found especially helpful. As the PI, you cannot do everything, especially as an academic because you have multiple other responsibilities. We approach this from a feminist perspective by including the research and professional development training of scholars (e.g., postdoctoral fellows, project managers/coordinators, and research assistants) from underrepresented backgrounds (e.g., people of color, women, and community-based staff). Next, note that project-related delays are common. Having a senior mentor on the grant can help a lot with project-related setbacks both in terms of overcoming them, coping with them, and communicating them to your program officers. Lastly, plan for ample time at the end of a grant for data analyses and dissemination efforts. The dissemination of your project findings as journal manuscripts, conference presentations, and through community engagement are important criteria. In conclusion, we hope that we have provided some normalization to the unpleasant feelings often associated with grant writing, fostered a sense of confidence in your ability to embark on grant writing, and equipped you with some useful skills to do so. Best of luck and in solidarity, Danielle and Katie.

Recommended Resources

Clarke, C. A. (2009). *Storytelling for grantseekers: A guide to creative nonprofit fundraising* (2nd ed.). Jossey-Bass.

Gerin, W., Kinkade, C. K., & Page, N. L. (2017). *Writing the NIH grant proposal*. SAGE.

Kienholz, M., L. & Berg, J. M. (2013). *How the NIH can help you get funded: An insider's guide to grant strategy*. Oxford University Press.

National Institutes of Health. (2021). *NIH regional seminars on program funding and grants administration*. https://grants.nih.gov/news/contact-in-person/seminars.htm

Robertson, J. D., Russell, S., W., & Morrison, D.C. (2021). *The grant application writer's workbook—National Institutes of Health Version 12.21*. Grant Writers' Seminars and Workshops. https://www.grantcentral.com/workbooks/national-institutes-of-health/

Smith, N., & Works, E. (2012). *The complete book of grant writing: Learn to write grants like a professional* (2nd ed.). Sourcebooks.

CHAPTER 10

Intersectional and Antiracist Pedagogy

Teaching as the Soul's Work

- **Kim A. Case**
  Virginia Commonwealth University

- **S. Brooke Vick**
  Muhlenberg College

Over the last 3 decades since intersectionality entered the academic lexicon (Crenshaw, 1989), intersectional pedagogy has grown and expanded, sometimes for better and sometimes for worse. Buzzword use of intersectional theory spread like wildfire across disciplines in the 1990s and 2000s, resulting in watered-down application and surface-level use that mimicked the same old additive and categorical models (Berger & Guidroz, 2009; Davis, 2008). For example, feminist scholars continue to apply an additive approach, squeezing in small bites of diversity to break up the over-representation of the "mythical norm" (Lorde, 1994).

At the same time, the systems in place to evaluate teaching and pedagogical applications beyond the traditional idea of the "classroom" are severely broken and overly dependent on biased likability measures. We want to clearly state that the brokenness rests with the systems, not in you as an individual. You do not need to squish yourself into a ball to fit the structures. Those structures were built for the most privileged and to maintain systemic oppression. With that in mind, our offer of advice and insight in this chapter are not meant to indicate that individual faculty need to be fixed. As we all collectively organize to transform the broken systems, we aim to empower individual feminist scholars and pedagogues.

Teaching as the Soul's Work

A couple of months ago, I (Kim) interviewed Brooke for my *Enough Y'all* podcast season focusing on antiracist pedagogy. Our conversation took us into a sort of flow state of co-discovery. We meandered down the path to institutional barriers to antiracist pedagogy, running the continuum from implied discouragement to intentional gaslighting, to bullying attempts to remove us from the academy. In describing her own teaching and the national mentoring she does with BIPOC faculty, Brooke noted how institutions often ask us to deny our own humanity when we teach from expertise steeped in lived experiences, historical accuracy, family, culture, and deeply held core values. Entering the classroom as feminist scholars and educators, our families, our histories, and the ever-present urgency for justice walk with us. Brooke put words to what I have always felt: For some of us, teaching from an intersectional, antiracist, feminist pedagogy frame is not a choice. Our intersectional pedagogies cannot be turned off like some mythical, convenient light switch. In other words, teaching is the soul's work. As Rockquemore and Laszloffy (2008) pointed out in their famous book for Black academics, "losing your soul" refers to losing the ability to uphold your own integrity and stay true to your core self. When well-intentioned colleagues advised us to turn down, limit, pull back on our feminist, antiracist, and intersectional teaching, they might as well have been telling us to slice off a limb. We must teach this way. For the most part, those advising me intended to protect me, but the outcome was that they reinforced oppressive systems by urging me to stay silent and avoid any possibility of disrupting power and privilege. You may experience similar advice warning you to pull back on your infusion of intersectional pedagogy.

What We Mean by "Feminist Scholar"

In our view, if you identify as any form of feminist scholar, you also identify as a feminist educator. You may even locate yourself at the academically unconventional intersection as a feminist teacher-scholar-activist. And we love you for it. As a feminist educator, we know your drive for supporting marginalized students and teaching from a critical pedagogy perspective comes from within. This drive to bring liberation and justice to your students originated deep within you. That is why we view our *teaching as the soul's work*.

Before we dig into that, we want to complicate and clarify how we are defining "feminist scholar." The popularity of the term *white feminism* represents valid critiques of decades of mainstream feminism silencing the voices of women of color and failing to address systemic racism. Even today, many white women claim the label feminist without any reflective work on their own whiteness or any action to dismantle white supremacy. We do not view this as feminism. Heterosexual or lesbian women may identify as feminists while quietly or loudly discriminating against trans sisters and gender-fluid siblings in movements for justice. We firmly locate their behavior outside of feminism. These are not "forms" of feminism. They are not feminism at all. We unapologetically state that you cannot be a feminist scholar without intersectionality and antiracism at the core of your work.

As a Black woman and a white woman in alliance, we write this chapter intentionally applying the complex definition of an intersectional, explicitly antiracist, feminist scholar. To allow for a loose definition would be to deny our core values. We first met at one of Brooke's conference presentations. I (Kim) snuck in the back and then stayed during the break to thank Brooke for her work. That was our first conversation many years ago, but that was enough for me (Kim) to know Brooke is one of my people. Fast-forward to now, we both made career moves into academic administration at the same time. Despite a white supremacist culture that strives to separate us, our honest conversations about intersectionality, antiracism, social class, and more support our soul's work and our ability to keep making moves for justice. For further reflections on unlikely alliances across race, see Rios and Case (2020).

Our Intersectional Identities and Impact on Teaching

One of the fundamental commitments we make as educators and scholars dedicated to intersectional, antiracist work is consistently acknowledging our complex social identities and reflecting on our location with hierarchies of power, privilege, and oppression. Doing so reminds us to practice cultural humility in all of our work and reminds the reader that our perspectives are necessarily informed and influenced by our identities and experiences.

Kim's Social Location

My privileged group memberships, although all co-constructed by the full intersectional picture, include being white, heterosexual, able-bodied, systemic gender-conforming or cisgender, a citizen of the United States from birth, an English speaker as my first language. According to the Pew Foundation calculation based on income, I am also now a member of the "upper middle class." Typing that sentence made my skin crawl because my family background and identity contrast sharply with this. The power and privilege bestowed upon me by systemic oppressions protected me when my marginalized identities might have presented great barriers.

In terms of marginalized identities, I am a working-class (culturally and psychologically) woman from East Tennessee. I am talking Dollywood, Gatlinburg, and a previously thick southern accent (Case, 2017a). Classism, sexism, and marginalization as a religious minority have been my major obstacles. When I am in my teaching zone, my great-grandmother Nellie, Mamaw Betty, Aunt Brenda, Aunt Mamie, Momma Ann, even Dolly Parton and more powerful women of Appalachia that never had these educational opportunities, walk with me in the classroom. Much like I write for them, I teach for them first and foremost. My soul's work is to harness education as the practice of freedom (Freire, 1970; hooks, 1994).

Brooke's Social Location

Though I acknowledge ways in which my identities intersect to represent both privilege and disadvantage, I recognize my sources of privilege as a straight, cisgender, relatively able-bodied, U.S. citizen from birth and first-language English speaker. I also acknowledge that, although I identify as a Black woman, I am light-skinned and therefore benefit from legacies of colorism. As someone with multiple advanced degrees, I also hold the power and privilege that comes with education and location within the upper-middle class (like Kim, this is markedly different from the class of my upbringing).

As a biracial Black woman who grew up in lower–middle class circumstances with a single mother and frequent experiences of insufficient resources and instability, my experiences of oppression are located within my race, gender, and class identities. Raised in predominantly white educational and neighborhood spaces, I was frequently one of the only Black children (or people) in any given environment. I was not taught by a Black teacher or professor until I was a sophomore in college. These tokenistic experiences challenged my sense of identity and belonging, and I struggled to find my place, my confidence, and my voice. I teach for all of those students who share my experience in higher education, to show them that it need not be this way and they should expect better. I strive to be someone I wish I had at a much younger age in my educational journey, someone who not only removes barriers to belonging and inclusion in education, but someone who challenges the foundation upon which those barriers stand.

Our Intersectional Pedagogy Journeys

My (Kim's) first full-time teaching gig was at a primarily white, rural Kentucky state university. White students told me they chose this state university to avoid the urban University of Cincinnati because it was "too Black." My early efforts included teaching psychology of race and gender courses by adding perspectives beyond Black and white, infusing readings from an array of intersectional social location perspectives, and focusing on systemic oppression and privilege. Unfortunately, I still managed to teach this course very categorically, due to my additive model approach, dividing the schedule into 7 weeks on gender and 7 on race (Case, 2013). This artificial separation reinforced categorical thinking. My next attempt to bring intersectional pedagogy into my actual practice meant fundamentally rewriting learning goals.

On the tenure track in Texas, my master's comprehensive state university served a high rate of first-generation, working-class, transfer, nontraditional/returning, students of color. In my 14 years there, we earned the label "Hispanic-Serving Institution." I dove in hard on teaching privilege awareness using feminist, critical race, intersectional, and queer pedagogies. I began to trust that students can be exceptional co-creators. For example, my students and I co-developed an intersectionality-focused graduate course and a careers course to expose the hidden curriculum for students (e.g., Case et al., 2014). We also co-designed and launched a new Applied Social Issues graduate concentration all about social justice and applying science to public policy. I had to unlearn my disciplinary "sage on the stage" training and realize that controlling the classroom was counter, even harmful, to student learning. The less I controlled and the less I dominated the time by speaking, the more we learned together.

My (Brooke's) first full-time teaching position was on the tenure track at an elite liberal arts college and predominantly white institution (PWI) serving mostly 18–22-year-old upper–middle class students (similar to the type of undergraduate institution I attended). Being in such a traditional and "elite" educational environment as a new professor, and the only Black woman or Person of Color who had ever taught full-time in the history of my department, I was initially focused more on proving myself and disconfirming stereotypes than I was my desire to teach in transformative ways. I was a young Black woman teaching courses on the psychology of prejudice and social stigma and was aware of all the ways that others could justify dismissing my expertise. I, therefore, taught in ways that I was led to believe were rigorous, rigidly upholding high standards and engaging only with quantitative data that came from experimental work. I expressly rejected personal narratives and lived experiences of my students as irrelevant and out of place in a serious intellectual space (whew, that is embarrassing to admit now).

After some time, it became obvious that I wasn't serving those students who embody targeted and systematically excluded identities, who were seeing themselves (or not) in the data. Clarity on this point came to me rather suddenly at the end of a social stigma class meeting during which I described a recent and painful personal experience with stereotype threat. Immediately after class, there was a line of Black and Latinx students, women, and first-generation students waiting to talk to me, thanking me for sharing my story, expressing anger for those who led me to doubt myself, and sharing how much it meant to them to hear how I moved through those moments successfully. I realized then that rather than making space for and honoring the very thing that might be drawing historically excluded students to my courses—an interest in self-exploration, understanding their own experiences, and gaining tools to make change—I was dismissing it. The longer

I taught, the more I realized that ignoring emotions and lived experiences in these courses was reifying the hierarchical systems of the academy that I purportedly wanted to change, privileging ways of knowing rooted in colonialism and white supremacy. I then shifted my pedagogy quite a bit to include space for intergroup dialogue and self-reflection, empowering students to lead and incorporating qualitative research, nonfiction narratives, and even fiction into the curriculum. I learned that students' personal connections to their learning is fertile ground for the growth we seek in our students.

Feminist Pedagogy Means Intersectional and Antiracist Pedagogy

We stand firm that feminist pedagogy must be intertwined with both intersectional and antiracist pedagogy. Although feminist teachers may in fact center antiracism and intersectional theory at the very foundations of their pedagogy and mentoring, not all feminist teachers do (Case, 2017b; Grande, 2003). Given the increased conference discussions, publications, resources, and general awareness around the lack of intersectionality and antiracism within feminism, our collective prioritization of both is past due (Buchanan et al., 2020; Dill & Zambrana, 2009; Shields, 2008). Our main piece of advice to feminist teacher-scholars is to move away from the temptation to add and stir. Going back through a course you already developed and sprinkling in data or narratives by women of color, people living with disabilities, or gender nonbinary lived experiences will improve the inclusion factor. However, quality intersectional and antiracist pedagogy may require us to take a more foundational approach to course structure (Case, 2017b). Intersectional and antiracist pedagogies must be intentionally and thoughtfully baked into the core foundation of a course.

Growing Your Intersectional Pedagogy Skills

Before we cover suggestions for sharpening your pedagogical skills, we want to encourage you to embrace pedagogical humility as well as intersectional cultural humility (Buchanan et al., 2020; Case et al., 2021) throughout your lifelong growth process. Through pedagogical humility (Case et al., 2021), educators not only embrace the uncertainty of designing an effective learning experience, but also share openly with peers and students that the pedagogical process is one of discovery. Guess what? We do not always know how to proceed in difficult moments. We do not always know how to precisely choose readings, activities, and assignments that guarantee learning. Opening up to new ideas and ways to radically alter the fundamentals of our teaching can feel overwhelming or even threatening to the ego.

Academia teaches us that we should be brilliant educators just because we finished the terminal degree or were born natural teachers. Pedagogical humility provides the gift of letting that all go. As feminist scholars, we may be more open to learning and growth than the average academic. And yet that very truth may cause us to be more closed off to being challenged in the areas where we were taught not to see (McIntosh, 1988). Intersectional theory presents a direct challenge to socialization within the U.S. context of individualism, belief in meritocracy, and categorical assumptions about social identity. Antiracism asks us to unlearn everything we thought we knew about justice, whiteness, power, and systems.

Growth in these areas can be painful from any intersectional social location. Our privileged identities require more humility and willingness to engage with unsettling discomforts. These forms of humility will also support your openness to input from your students on their own learning, including co-construction of knowledge and co-development of courses. No matter how much of an ally I (Kim) strive to be, no doubt my whiteness and able-bodied experiences result in course design and assignments that miss the intersectional mark. Outside the classroom, whether recruiting students into my research group or contributing to a curriculum committee, my privilege may work against my ability to incorporate intersectional theory into my praxis.

So where to start? If you are new to exploration of intersectional pedagogy, we recommend my (Kim's) *Intersectional Pedagogy* (Case, 2017b) edited book full of innovative contributions from exceptional teacher-scholars. In the first chapter, I (Kim) provided a 10-point model for intersectional pedagogy that can be used as a self-reflective tool. To expand on that model, the core tenets also apply to intersectional work beyond the classroom, such as in service to the community or university policy change. Feminist teachers have shared with both of us that they go back to this model to find new ideas for enhancing their own teaching of intersectional theory and praxis. Find ways to read two or three articles on intersectional pedagogy each semester, perhaps before you prep your next set of courses, both within and outside your own discipline. Commit to choosing textbooks, readings, videos, images, and other course materials that rise to the challenge of recognizing complexity and co-construction of systems of power. For example, incorporating Crenshaw's Say Her Name campaign builds content and critical questions about power, co-construction of systemic oppression, and how public policy and institutional gendered racism impact Black women. This must be your intentional practice as an educator because our defaults will likely result in texts and course materials that miss the mark. Identify the teacher-scholars in your field who are known for moving the intersectional needle forward.

One thing that will be essential to your ongoing learning and enhancement of intersectional pedagogy is to break out of pedagogical isolation

(Case et al., 2021). Many of us struggle and suffer for years as we try to reinvent the wheel when others may have already come up with amazing ideas. At your favorite conferences, find ways to attend the workshops and talks on intersectionality and antiracist scholarship, especially those focused on teaching. Even though none of us feel like we have the time, we must make this a priority as lifelong learners for continuous improvements. If your go-to research conference does not offer anything on intersectionality, no doubt there is a professional association section, division, group, or even a more specific conference within your discipline that focuses on this work.

Inclusive Practices Do Not Equal Intersectionality

We must note here that intersectional theory and critical race theory, which serve as the foundations for these critical pedagogies so integral to feminist teaching, get distorted, watered down, and conflated with inclusive teaching practices (Berger & Guidroz, 2009; Collins & Bilge, 2020; Dill & Zambrana, 2009). Some of the resources you review may claim an intersectional approach but actually present inclusive teaching approaches that fail to incorporate intersectionality. For example, content focusing on voices from African American, queer, and deaf communities without discussion of power, systems, and policy would not necessarily integrate the foundational tenets of intersectional theory. Likewise, diversity and inclusion approaches, such as adding a reading about racial identity, may qualify as an advancement toward inclusion. And yet, without instruction to address systemic racism or white supremacy, that reading alone would not move the curriculum into the space of antiracist pedagogy (for examples of inclusion versus antiracist pedagogy, see www.drkimcase.com/essays).

Feminist teachers working to intentionally build intersectional pedagogy into the construction process of their teaching often have not read the most influential scholarship by Black women scholars and others. We recommend some fundamental resources to enhance your own background knowledge (see Anzaldua, 1987; Collins, 1990; Crenshaw, 1989; Gunn Allen, 1986; Lorde, 1984). This practice is essential to credit and honor the work of marginalized feminist and womanist scholars whose work gets erased, rendered invisible, credited to others, and not cited as highlighted by the #CiteBlackWomen campaign (Alexander-Floyd, 2012).

Critical Pedagogies and Your Career Journey

Academia is nothing if not traditional—it lifts up and rewards a narrow set of pedagogies, methodologies, and practices, many of which are borne of and remain steeped in white, patriarchal, and colonial ways of producing and disseminating knowledge (e.g., rewarding strictly quantitative, biased metrics of teaching ability). Intersectional, antiracist, and other critical pedagogies directly challenge these traditions and threaten status-quo academic practices, reward structures, and individuals who benefit most from these traditions. As decades of social psychological research demonstrates, when deeply held beliefs are threatened, any number of vigorous defenses will follow in order to keep those beliefs or practices in place, particularly when those beliefs reflect on the self (Sherman & Cohen, 2006). As educators committed to intersectional teaching for social justice, it benefits us to be aware of the shape these defenses can take, understand the kind of challenges and opportunities they create for careers, and work together to navigate them while maintaining our pedagogical commitments and well-being.

Individuals threatened by intersectional pedagogy may respond by belittling your work. Senior colleagues, particularly at research-intensive institutions, may say that you are spending too much time on your teaching when it matters little for your tenure review. Powerful colleagues at a teaching-focused college may critique your pedagogy as spending too much time on diversity or antiracism content as opposed to more "mainstream" content in your field. Other colleagues may take a more reductive approach, framing your pedagogy as a "soap box" you use to advance a political ideology. Naive colleagues may accuse you of male bashing because you teach about systemic sexism and genderism, for example. Others can try to steer you away from developing your intersectional practice early in your career, warning you about student resistance that could hurt your evaluations or reminding you that it is best to simply "go along to get along" until tenure by replicating what everyone else does.

To combat gaslighting, we found it critical to seek out the perspectives of those with similar pedagogical and scholarly commitments to our own, either within or outside of our institutions, or even from texts like this one when we doubted ourselves. The experience of attributional ambiguity in these situations can be especially taxing, so checking in with someone else who can validate or confirm your suspicions will be helpful. When colleagues express concern about the way you are spending your professional time or the content of your courses, you can avoid meeting their defenses with defensiveness by practicing openness about your pedagogy. Invite them to come to class, offer to share your syllabi, or share your course evaluations. To be clear, we are not suggesting that you need to defend your pedagogy to colleagues who oppose your methods. However, it can benefit you, particularly with senior colleagues who are in a position to evaluate you, to demonstrate confidence and transparency in your approach. Admittedly, this practice will not convince the most committed detractors, but we were able to use these practices to draw them into conversation that increased their appreciation for what we do.

Strengthening Your Case for Promotion and Tenure

To strengthen your case for tenure and promotion, you want to make sure that those evaluating you clearly recognize the alignment between your teaching and their stated priorities. In my (Kim's) 1st year, I met with as many senior faculty as possible, asked for and read as many recent promotion and tenure narratives I could get my hands on, and created organized folders to document my work. I took note of what the policy and my colleagues interpreting that policy said they value and collected my evidence based on those criteria. In other words, documentation of my work aligned with the written policy *and* the evaluation practices of those with power.

When putting together a tenure file, start with a thorough review of the evaluation criteria that will be applied to your work. How does your institution define the standards for excellence in teaching? What are they looking for to determine if you are an effective educator? Though these specific criteria will differ across institutions, many characteristics of evidence-based teaching excellence will be consistent. By and large, effective educators demonstrate a commitment to continually developing their pedagogy and expertise, practice intentional course design to achieve clear learning objectives, cultivate inclusive learning environments that spark students' curiosity and promote intellectual growth, create meaningful assessments that align with learning goals, and contribute to the development of critically and socially aware students (Addy et al., 2021). As an intersectional, antiracist, feminist educator, you are doing this work. However, it is not enough to simply label yourself a feminist teacher-scholar and assume your evaluators will understand. Some evaluators may even be resistant to your work based on their own privilege or unconscious threats to their identities. Your case will benefit from the additional (invisible) labor of educating others about your pedagogical practice, helping them to connect the dots between their criteria and your approach.

As we described, intersectional pedagogy is complex, difficult to master, and easy to get wrong. Developing your own thinking beyond an additive understanding of marginalized perspectives, guiding students away from understanding identities as individual and monolithic toward systems-level thinking, and helping them apply their understanding in meaningful ways is a deeply challenging pedagogical project. You can strengthen your case for promotion and tenure by educating your evaluators on intersectional, antiracist, feminist pedagogy, documenting your efforts to master it, and outlining them for your review. Document time invested in different scholarly and pedagogical projects.

Reflective questions:

- Did you attend any professional development workshops on critical pedagogies? List those workshops in your file.

- Did you do research to better understand feminist pedagogical practices? Cite those sources.

Student outcomes are another indicator of effective teaching. Peer review committees want to see evidence that you are contributing to their broader mission and goals to develop intellectually curious, critical, socially aware students who are prepared for meaningful civic engagement. As you educate your evaluators on intersectional pedagogy, we advise providing evidence from the research literature and your own teaching to show that intersectional approaches result in precisely the learning outcomes that they value. Research on intersectional pedagogy demonstrates that raising students' intersectional consciousness is associated with increased openness to experience, perspective taking, and intentions to contribute to social change as well as heightened awareness of privilege and acknowledgement of racism (for summary, see Case, 2017b). All of these characteristics align with most institutional goals to develop lifelong learners who are prepared to lead in diverse environments. Evidence for desired outcomes may come from a variety of sources: formal course evaluations, student narratives within evaluations or other assessments (essays, presentations), and student work that directly reflects valued learning outcomes (e.g., community-engaged projects).

Recognizing institution-mandated student evaluations may not fully capture the goals and values that are central to your teaching practice, consider developing customized ways of assessing learning outcomes that speak more to your soul's work, perhaps measuring systems-level thinking, complex understanding of privilege, and commitment to social justice work. Addressing student outcomes provides an opportunity to highlight the learning opportunities, assignments, and projects you developed as a result of your intersectional and antiracist work.

Reflective questions:

- How have you altered your assignments as you have developed your feminist practice?

- Have you seen student learning change as a result? Perhaps you have noticed that students are asking different questions or developing different types of projects as you have evolved your pedagogy. Be sure to document and highlight those changes as additional evidence of your effectiveness.

Addressing Student Dissatisfaction

We would be remiss if we didn't also note that student resistance, discomfort, and dissatisfaction can also show up in these intersectional learning spaces. In her work on pedagogy of discomfort, Megan Boler noted that the emotions that result from acknowledging and confronting systemic injustice can provide valuable insights into students' beliefs and help them interrogate their resistance to learning (Boler, 1999; hooks, 1994). However productive student discomfort can be expressed as dissatisfaction in course evaluations that are referenced during tenure and promotion review. This is especially likely if the instructor embodies a marginalized identity. If this is the case in your file, rather than apologizing or deflecting attention, the best approach is to engage this feedback directly in your narrative statement. Continue to educate your evaluators on resistance and discomfort as a common response to intersectional pedagogy and discuss the ways you address student discomfort in your classes. For example, I (Kim) developed a community-building activity that I use in week 1–2 of each course to explicitly address myths about what learning should feel like. Students brainstorm possible emotions or reactions they may have to studying challenging topics. We then process those possibilities as a group and identify ways students can intentionally choose to stay in the learning, such as asking for support if they begin to feel frustrated or tempted to withdraw.

Reflective questions:

- Is a pedagogy of discomfort central to your approach to teaching? Explain the benefits.

- Do you intentionally structure your learning spaces to anticipate and respond to discomfort? Describe how. Not all negativity or dissatisfaction expressed in course evaluations merits attention or invalidates your pedagogical expertise. Help your evaluators recognize and understand the difference.

Intersectional Pedagogy Is Inclusive

As of this writing in early 2022, we can nearly guarantee that your institution has something in their mission statements or strategic plans about diversity and inclusion. Many institutions state specific goals with respect to recruitment and retention of historically marginalized (or "underrepresented") student populations. Many also state the critical importance of developing an inclusive campus climate for learning or highlight the importance of achieving a sense of belonging for everyone within the campus community. You can strengthen your case for promotion and tenure by addressing how your work as an educator embodies and advances these stated values of the institution. We suggest formally connecting the dots for your evaluators between (a) what you do with your students in the classroom every day, the learning environment you create, and the diversity of perspectives you honor as worthy of intellectual inquiry and (b) the ability to recruit and retain minoritized students, expand their sense of belonging, and build an inclusive campus community.

In my (Brooke's) administrative role leading DEI work, I have written numerous colleague letters for tenure and promotion, highlighting syllabus statements and learning goals that promote awareness of systemic biases in their field, course content that meaningfully centers minoritized experiences, and culturally relevant learning opportunities that affirm the value of diverse students' experiences as practices that improve sense of belonging and, therefore, the likelihood of retention. In his talks addressing inclusion and equity, Shaun Harper of the USC Center for Race and Equity cites climate data showing that university classrooms are the least inclusive spaces on campus (Harper & Davis, 2016). Your intersectional pedagogy is working to change that. Be sure to let them know.

Curating Your Community

We recommend that you develop a village of like-minded educators who can provide support and validation and serve as mentors as you develop your pedagogical practice. Given the extreme levels of exhaustion and burnout that can occur, building a solid community you can depend on could make all the difference in maintaining hope and sustainability. Your network can include senior colleagues inside or outside of your department, peer educators who share your pedagogical commitments to intersectional antiracist work, and colleagues outside of your institution who are engaged in these practices (Flores Niemann et al., 2020; Gutiérrez y Muhs et al., 2012; Chapter 4, this volume). Knowing that there may be those who seek to devalue the work that you do along the way, building a community of sponsors—those who will speak up for you when you are not in the room—is a preemptive step you can take to build a safety net against threats to your career progression (Rockquemore & Laszloffy, 2008). Consider ways to be strategic about who might serve on your tenure committee and connect early on with colleagues who you suspect will support your work. If you are at an institution where your teaching is directly observed by colleagues, talk with your observers about your pedagogical intentions and commitments. Seek out connections with like-minded colleagues across academia as you attend conferences. Invite other feminist scholars to meet-ups (virtual or in person) as a way to connect and sustain each other. Don't be shy about reaching out to intersectional teacher-scholars to share resources and ideas and get feedback in times of crisis.

Bottom line: Practicing intersectional, antiracist, feminist pedagogy can be lonely, but we can break out of pedagogical isolation (Case et al., 2021). Having a strong case by the time you get to your tenure and promotion review, and making it to that point in your career with your health and well-being intact, may depend on actions you take much earlier in your professional journey. The work to develop intersectional feminist pedagogy, as with true liberatory education, should be a collective endeavor.

References

Addy, T. M., Dube, D., Mitchell, K. A., & SoRelle, M. (2021). *What inclusive instructors do: Principles and practices for excellence in college teaching.* Stylus.

Alexander-Floyd, N. G. (2012). Disappearing acts: Reclaiming intersectionality in the social sciences in a post-Black feminist era. *Feminist Formations, 24*(1), 1–25. https://doi.org/10.1353/ff.2012.0003

Anzaldua, G. (1987). *Borderlands/La frontera.* Aunt Lute Books.

Berger, M. T., & Guidroz, K. (Eds.). (2009). *The intersectional approach: Transforming the academy through race, class, and gender.* University of North Carolina Press.

Boler, M. (1999). *Feeling power: Emotions and education.* Routledge.

Buchanan, N., Rios, D., & Case. K. (2020). Intersectional cultural humility: Aligning critical inquiry with critical praxis in psychology. *Women and Therapy, 43*, 235–243. https://doi.org/10.1080/02703149.2020.1729469

Case, K. (Ed.). (2013). *Deconstructing privilege: Teaching and learning as allies in the classroom.* Routledge.

Case, K. (2017a). Insider without: Journey across the working-class academic arc. *Journal of Working-Class Studies, 2*, 16–35.

Case, K. (2017b). *Intersectional pedagogy: Complicating identity and social justice.* Routledge.

Case, K., Kite, M., & Williams, W. R. (2021). Pedagogical humility and peer mentoring for social justice education. In M. Kite, K. Case, & W. R. Williams (Eds.), *Navigating difficult moments in teaching diversity and social justice* (pp. 3–16). American Psychological Association.

Case, K., Miller, A., Hensley, R., & Jackson, S. (2014). Careers in Psychology: Creating customized learning to expose the invisible curriculum. *Psychology of Learning and Teaching, 13*, 32–37. http://dx.doi.org/10.2304/plat.2014.13.1.32

Collins, P. H. (1990). *Black feminist thought: Knowledge, consciousness, and the politics of empowerment.* Routledge.

Collins, P. H., & Blige, S. (2020). *Intersectionality,* 2nd ed. Wiley.

Crenshaw, K. (1989). Demarginalizing the intersection of race and sex: A Black feminist critique of antidiscrimination doctrine, feminist theory, and antiracist politics. *University of Chicago Legal Forum, 1989*, 139–167.

Davis, K. (2008). Intersectionality as buzzword: A sociology of science perspective on what makes a feminist theory successful. *Feminist Theory, 9*(1), 67–85. https://doi.org/10.1177/1464700108086364

Dill, B. T., & Zambrana, R. E. (Eds.). (2009). *Emerging intersections: Race, class, and gender in theory, policy, and practice.* Rutgers University Press.

Flores Niemann, Y., Gutierrez y Muhs, G., & Gonzalez, C. (Eds.). (2020). *Presumed incompetent* (Vol. 2). Utah State University Press.

Freire, P. (1970). *Pedagogy of the oppressed.* Bloomsbury.

Grande, S. (2003). Whitestream feminism and the colonialist project: A review of contemporary feminist pedagogy and praxis. *Educational Theory, 53*(3), 329–346.

Gunn Allen, P. (1986). *The sacred hoop: Recovering the feminine in American Indian traditions*. Beacon Press.

Gutiérrez y Muhs, G., Flores Niemann, Y., González, C., & Harris, A. (Eds.). (2012). *Presumed incompetent*. Utah State University Press.

Harper, S. R., & Davis, C. H. (2016). Eight actions to reduce racism in college classrooms. *Academe, 102*(6), 30–34.

hooks, b. (1994). *Feminist theory: From margin to center*. South End Press.

Lorde, A. (1984). *Sister outsider*. Crossing Press.

McIntosh, P. (1988). *White privilege and male privilege: A personal account of coming to see correspondences through work in women's studies* [Working Paper No. 189]. Wellesley Centers for Women.

Rios, D., & Case, K. A. (2020). Unlikely alliances from Appalachia to East L.A.: Insider without and outsider within. In Y. Flores Niemann, G. Gutierrez y Muhs, & C. G. Gonzalez (Eds.), *Presumed incompetent* (Vol. 2, pp. 131–142). Utah State University Press.

Rios, D., Case, K. A., Brody, S., & Rivera, D. (2021). When faculty experience stereotype threat. In M. Kite, K. Case, & W. R. Williams (Eds.), *Navigating difficult moments in teaching diversity and social justice* (pp. 59–74). American Psychological Association Press.

Rockquemore, K., & Laszloffy. T. (2008). *The Black academic's guide to winning tenure without losing your soul*. Lynne Reinner.

Sherman, D. K., & Cohen, G. L. (2006). The psychology of self-defense: Self-affirmation theory. *Advances in Experimental Social Psychology, 38*, 183–242.

Shields, S. A. (2008). Gender: An intersectionality perspective. *Sex Roles, 59*(5–6), 301–311. https://doi.org/10.1007/s11199-008-9501-8

CHAPTER 11

Resetting Dysfunctional Education Ecologies
Dealing With Marginalization in the Classroom

- **Kat Klement**
  Bemidji State University

- **Jill Fish**
  Minneapolis Veterans Affairs Health Care System

- **Sarah Cronin**
  Bemidji State University

Securing a tenure-track position is a daunting prospect, with disappearing budget lines, exhausting application and interview procedures, and hidden pitfalls. For the lucky scholars who receive an offer, life can seem suddenly easier. However, there are still obstacles to face, particularly if you're a feminist and/or womanist faculty who belongs to one or more historically marginalized groups. For those of us who are People of Color, Indigenous, 2SLGBTQ+, disabled, and/or first-generation or low-income, doing the job of teaching presents unique challenges. Thus, we're here to discuss the challenges facing untenured feminist and womanist faculty inside and outside of the classroom. While we recognize and embrace feminist allies who only belong to dominant social groups, in this chapter we focus on those issues encountered by feminist and womanist faculty who have at least one marginalized identity. We discuss challenges we face both inside the classroom and outside it. We detail how oppressive structures are reproduced in the classroom to affect marginalized faculty and students, particularly what Annamma and Morrison (2018) termed "dysfunctional education ecologies" (p. 70). Throughout, we give examples of how we've encountered obstacles and ways that we've resisted them.

Our Positionality

We are three instructors at varying points toward tenure; one just submitted their application (Sarah, third author), one is a year away from submission (Kat, first author), and one is working as contingent faculty while completing a research fellowship (Jill, second author). We have a range of doctoral training, conduct both applied and basic research, and have a variety of teaching experience from community colleges to regional public universities, to R1 research institutions.

The first author (Kat) is a middle-class, fat, atheist, white, queer, and transmasculine nonbinary person whose background is in social psychology and women's studies. Their pedagogical philosophy of liberation psychology and intersectional feminism is infused in their course policies, content, and delivery. The second author (Jill) is from the Tuscarora Nation of the Haudenosaunee Confederacy of Western New York; her lineage is through her father, who is an enrolled member of the nation. She is a cisgender, pansexual, able-bodied woman. She is primarily concerned with empowering and liberating Native American and Indigenous peoples across various contexts. The third author (Sarah) is a white, middle-class, genderqueer, pansexual, able-bodied, secular Buddhist, non-monogamous person with a background in counseling psychology. She is on the journey of infusing culturally responsive pedagogy and liberation psychology throughout her work with special consideration for how her privilege shapes assumptions, norms, and relationships in these settings. For each author, their positionality informs their clinical practice (Jill, Sarah), teaching, and research.

Coping With Dysfunctional Education Ecologies

As a feminist and/or womanist faculty, you face increasing threats in your teaching, including spillover from conservative backlashes against teaching about systems of oppression (e.g., Baker & Rodrigues-Sherley, 2021; Diaz, 2022), challenges from students in the physical and virtual classroom (Pittman, 2010), and biased student evaluations (Esarey & Valdes, 2020), particularly in the switch to remote learning (Ayllón, 2021), all of which may impact your ability to secure tenure. Though we are in the midst of promising racial justice and labor rights movements, feminist and womanist faculty, especially those of us who have multiple marginalized identities, continue to experience negative outcomes as a result of how others perceive us and our teaching.

Feminist pedagogy is a broad umbrella of perspectives, techniques, and principles that you might use to create inclusive classrooms and meaningful learning experiences for students (Hayden & Crockett, 2020). You may also work to incorporate more diverse content into your courses, relying on cross-cultural scholarship rather than that produced exclusively in North America and Western Europe. Feminist pedagogy and instruction veer away from the expected norms of academia: that the professor is always the expert, the students are always subordinate, and that assessment in the classroom is a high-stakes endeavor to reinforce a hierarchy of intelligence. Instead, we seek to draw students in to connect their own lived experiences with the content they are learning, in a safe and compassionate climate that holds space for difficult conversations (Webb et al., 2002). These are pedagogical choices that the three of us intentionally make and have even been thanked for by students. However, regardless of whether you intentionally engage in feminist pedagogy, any faculty who is part of a marginalized group can encounter obstacles in the classroom and academic systems.

Embracing Our Identities

Being a marginalized instructor can be fraught and exhausting, as we discussed. For many of us, there is no option to hide our membership in a racial or gender group; others, such as queer faculty or faculty with invisible disabilities, can make the decision to share their identities and experiences in the classroom. There isn't a lot of research on instructor self-disclosure, but what there is indicates it's a mixed bag (Hill et al., 2021). Our students' perceptions of us can change based on what we reveal. My (Kat) 1st year at my current position (right out of my PhD), I was teaching Human Sexuality and unsure how open to be about my identity. I was out as queer, but not quite comfortable discussing it with my students. I relied on the invisibility of my identity and largely taught the class as it might be expected: from a cis-heteronormative lens. It was 2 years later, in the middle of questioning my gender identity, when one student asked me what my pronouns were. I hesitated to answer, because I wasn't sure myself and didn't know how much I wanted to share. That question was a turning point for me. In the moment, I panicked—not knowing the student's motivation for asking, I was afraid of regretting a candid response. I took a while after that to consider whether I wanted to be out in the classroom about my gender. Strangely, the emergency remote teaching due to COVID-19 gave me space to make a final decision; by fall of 2020, I decided to officially change my pronouns in class. I realized that by being open about both my queer and trans identities, I could be an access point for my cisgender and straight students to learn about being queer and being trans, and I could represent future possibilities for my queer and trans students. I'm glad I waited to come out to my students, though. Being sure of myself and already having the support of my department meant that I could count on being supported if I did face backlash.

Another reason I (Kat) decided to bring my identities with me into the classroom was that being a queer and trans faculty means that I can see what's missing in the curriculum; for example, what do safer sex practices look like for trans men? Whose anatomy are students most likely to see represented? Intentionally centering queer/trans voices and experiences, particularly those of Black, Indigenous, and other People of Color, reveals to my students a richer array of human sexuality and spotlights voices often left out of the conversation. With that being said, owning our identities in the classroom brings a degree of risk, too. Next, we discuss the extra lab or of regularly monitoring and responding to this risk to ensure the classroom is safe for us and our students.

Making the Classroom Safe for Us and Our Students

In contrast with professors who belong to only dominant social groups, marginalized faculty may be more likely to use *identity safety cues*, or signals that communicate the faculty values and supports students in minority groups (Kruk & Matsick, 2021). These cues can take the shape of minority representation, classroom policies that emphasize accessibility and flexibility, and counter-stereotypical information. Identity safety cues can also impact students across multiple marginalized identities (e.g., Chaney et al., 2020). For example, I (Kat) give my pronouns on my syllabus and provide a content note about my pedagogical lens so that my students all know to expect discussions highlighting the impact of systems of oppression on the course content. Whether marginalized or not, you can utilize identity safety cues in your classrooms and policies to support your marginalized students.

An additional way that belonging to a marginalized group can be beneficial for faculty is that our "outsider" perspective can allow us to highlight identities and experiences frequently missing in the classroom. As with most areas of psychology, the textbooks and curriculum are usually developed by scholars belonging to dominant groups. Texts and instructor materials may touch on racial, gender, or cultural groups, but often in short sections or through a deficit lens. Supplementing traditional textbooks or using open educational resources (OER) can help faculty design more inclusive materials and decenter dominant perspectives. When I (Jill) was handed down the past course curriculum for the Cultural Psychology course I was going to start teaching, I noticed that it lacked Indigenous perspectives on common topics. Given my positionality and program of research, I knew I could address this gap, but how? Over several semesters, I figured out how to balance my lived experiences with the course content, but it wasn't always easy. The extent to which I anchored myself to my various identities varied each time I taught the course. At first, I was excited to share with students that I'm Tuscarora, which gave way to trepidation when I received a particular comment on my student evaluations of teaching (SETs): "She's clearly biased towards Native Americans." Seeing a negative comment like this gave me pause because I knew it was common to share SETs as a part of faculty application materials. Although the job market was still far away for me, I was already thinking about how SETs could affect my chances of securing a tenure-track position.

Despite this, I continued to teach Indigenous perspectives on topics like development—one of my areas of expertise. I even started sharing my TEDxTalk with students, which includes vulnerable information about my life (e.g., self-harm) and how it has informed my commitment to centering Indigenous voices in psychology. I knew that narratives like mine could help Indigenous students and Students of Color imagine a future in which they, too, champion changes in mainstream psychology. After seeing students feel connected to me and material that is often omitted from their psychology courses, I created an assignment so that students could connect with more psychologists from historically marginalized identities (see the Interview with a Psychologist project; Fish, 2021). However, as some of you are likely aware, there is a cost associated with taking such an approach.

The Burden of Extra Labor

When you incorporate your identities and lived experiences into your teaching, it can help students to connect with course materials and themselves. However, there will likely be times when you are the object of or a witness to macroaggressions or microaggressions. In this section, we detail approaches that you can take to respond to oppression in these forms. Macroaggressions are overt actions that cause tangible harm (Williams, 2019), while microaggressions are "brief and commonplace daily verbal, behavioral, and environmental indignities, whether intentional or unintentional, which communicate hostile, derogatory, or negative slights, invalidations, and insults to an individual or group because of their marginalized status in society" (Sue, 2014). Microaggressions are inevitable in our classrooms yet are unique because the classroom is an environment set up for learning (Berk, 2017). Being prepared for how to respond and cope is key to have good responses that promote student learning and well-being for both you and your students.

Responding to Macroaggressions

Perhaps the most clear-cut circumstances to be prepared for are instances of verbal macroaggressions. For those of us who have experienced macroaggressions, we likely have phrases we have turned to that help establish our boundaries. With the power we have as instructors in the classroom, we can clearly lay out what will not be tolerated. Naming specific behaviors that will result in being asked to leave class or be reported can be included in your syllabus as a notice for students about your expectations. When a student says or does something that is overtly harmful toward an individual or specific group of people, we can say things such as, "I do not accept that language in my classroom. If I hear language like that again you will be asked to leave" or "That is a hurtful thing to say. This learning community does not tolerate harmful speech."

Because I (Jill) had little guidance when I first started teaching, most of my phrases were developed in response to students inflicting harm on myself or others, phrases that I was able to hone by consulting with colleagues or through reflection. Once when I was a graduate instructor, a white, male student berated me in my office, including standing over me when I was seated and cursing at me. I fumbled to get the words "You cannot speak to me like that and need to leave now." I was able to process my experience with the faculty advisor for the course and chart a path for how I can respond in the future. Now, I co-create classroom expectations and responses to breaking them, including specific phrases, with students at the beginning of the semester, making sure we're all on the same page. If you're fortunate enough to read this chapter before you begin teaching, having some phrases beforehand can be incredibly helpful. Saying a phrase aloud can help you remember it and use it in the future; practicing what to say in the mirror or with a friend or colleague can help to reinforce its use and allow you to respond quickly with a firm and confident tone.

Responding to Microaggressions

Microaggressions can be more complicated to respond to than macroaggressions. They aren't as obvious and take persistence to stay mindful of what may occur around you (Berk, 2017). Our hope is that your institution's policies and administrators protect marginalized students, faculty, and staff through an affirming atmosphere and campus climate; however, since many spaces are not close to that sort of leadership, our actions as faculty are still critical in impacting the campus climate (Byers et al., 2019).

You may feel uncertainty and caution when responding to macro- and microaggressions in your classroom. Imposter syndrome can be common for us, especially if you have multiple marginalized identities (Edwards, 2019), but first consider how what you are experiencing might be a result of systemic oppression and not individualized feelings of being an imposter (Edwards, 2019). For me (Sarah), being open with safe colleagues about my feelings about my work has helped me reflect and figure out what might be a result of sexism or homophobia I experience versus what might be my own personal lack of confidence. There is no clear line distinguishing these, but reflective conversation helps me maintain self-compassion. I use questions such as "What might be behind my imposter feelings and thoughts? What messaging I have received from society or genuine lack of knowledge or experience related to the professional setting?" More often than not, my imposter feelings are from internalized messages about what it means to appear feminine or be queer in a professional space. Our hope for you is that you can unpack internalized beliefs about your abilities that are rooted in oppression.

Like the first author (Kat), I (Sarah) have evolved how I present myself in the classroom. I heavily closeted myself in my early teaching positions. I was at an institution known for past homophobic policies. The largest reason for my comfort being out now is because I am in a department that has a clear commitment to equity, antiracism, and inclusion. Working in this setting is another privilege that many are not afforded. Now, I share my identities when introducing myself to my courses and use myself in examples throughout the semester. Students started coming to me during office hours to ask for help about coming out or experiencing discrimination. I have not experienced backlash on my SETs, and students have not challenged my classroom approach as much as I anticipated (probably a result of the privilege I carry).

Sometimes students have made statements that challenged my (Sarah) teaching of intersectionality, privilege, and power in undergraduate counseling courses. I have found that leaning into the opposition from students in turn helps the entire class understand them more deeply. For example, when I was using gender and racial pay gaps as an example for introducing intersectionality, a cisgender, white, male student raised his hand and told me that the gaps are not an accurate reflection of reality because they only exist for salaried positions. He had a tone that communicated pride in challenging the concept as if he were proving me wrong. I was able to reply to this comment by using it to strengthen my teaching. I told the class he brought up a great point, we could add intersectionality of economic privilege and consider that most salaried employees make more than hourly positions. I have applied for tenure with some confidence that this approach will be well received (again, likely because of the many privileges I carry).

My courses increasingly center historically marginalized groups. This takes many forms such as ensuring the resources I am using are from Black, Indigenous, or People of Color (BIPOC) psychologists and using a liberation psychology lens to interpret research and theory taught in class. In my counseling skills course, I take time every class period to discuss how microaggressions might play into the day's case studies. Toward the end of each class, we reflect on stereotypes and assumptions students had about the case. Maybe they assumed something about the person's pronouns, gender of their dating partner(s), socioeconomic status, or something else. We normalize that our brains automatically jump to these assumptions as a result of implicit bias and how the systems around us are designed for some groups to maintain social dominance (Williams, 2019), yet we also have the power to contribute to change both the systems and ourselves.

This practice helps to set up the classroom environment as safe and supportive as we learn to do better. When I call out microaggressions that happen during class, there is already a norm of using those moments to learn and improve rather than feel shame. Students have in turn held me accountable when I have materials or statements that contain microaggressions. Being called out by students helps me maintain my cultural humility and normalize that we are all on a growth journey, even me as a tenure-track faculty member. Building in frequent class time on antiracism and understanding systems of oppression has normalized within my counseling skills class that these topics are important, and we are all working to improve. It set my learning environment up so that students and I are empowered to respond and correct others in creating an inclusive classroom environment.

Setting Healthy Boundaries

Boundaries are a great tool to cope with both macro- and microaggressions. Just like there are different types of support, there are also different types of boundaries. How you were socialized has great impact on your boundaries. For example, we are socialized that women should have fewer boundaries and carry emotional labor for others, and there are notable distinctions between these messages for Women of Color and white women (Gonzales, 2017). These can be small things, like setting *and following through on* designated times for academic writing, responding to emails, or holding office hours, to bigger things, like turning down requests to do diversity, equity, and inclusion, or DEI-related work or being a token minority member on a committee or taskforce. To those of you reading this who can establish boundaries with little to no social backlash: Take responsibility to call out others when they do not respect BIPOC colleagues who set boundaries for themselves. Not that your BIPOC colleagues cannot do this for themselves, but the more we all work toward resisting systemic racism and fighting stereotypes, the better off we will all be. For instance, in the same example I (Jill) referenced with the white, male student lambasting me in my office, I asserted a boundary regarding how students speak to me. However, the student did not immediately leave my office when I asked, but only did so when my colleague (a fellow graduate instructor and a white woman) heard him continue to yell and came to my office to ask if I needed assistance. Despite setting a clear boundary in this instance, it was the support of my colleague that helped me feel seen and heard in a moment where I desperately needed it.

Boundaried generosity is a concept in counseling psychology. It refers to the idea of sharing yourself while still having some sort of separation and boundaries (Skovholt & Trotter-Mathison, 2016). As instructors, we share our knowledge, personhood, and care with our students, yet we also need to preserve ourselves so that we can contribute to our field and communities throughout our career with minimal burnout. We give of ourselves to our students and institutions, often doing much emotional and intellectual labor given our societal position as marginalized peoples, yet need to strive for a separation or boundary that gives us room to care for ourselves. One example that I (Sarah) have been working on is my boundaried generosity with students who drop in to my office when it is not my open office hours. In my first years of teaching, I would drop whatever I was doing to help a student who came to my office, even if it wasn't my open office hours. Over the years, I've learned how to empathetically say, "I'm so glad you found my office. I would love to answer your questions. Right now is my time to focus on research tasks, and I have some deadlines coming up. Take a look at my office hour schedule posted on my door; is there a time that works for you to come back within those hours?" It has been a good lesson for students to learn about the many tasks faculty have that are not just teaching, and it has helped me protect my energy and time. In my experience, students have been respectful of such statements even if they were disappointed I couldn't immediately help them.

Being Perceived as an Expert

Within the classroom, there are well-established structures in place that disproportionately impact marginalized feminist and womanist faculty. For example, SETs are unfair regardless of whether they are reliable and valid, as they produce an exceptionally high error rate (Esarey & Valdes, 2020). Despite this, SETs continue to play a role in major decisions (e.g., hiring, tenure), which is something that I (Kat) am particularly cognizant of as I begin to prepare my tenure narrative. My evaluations for my fall 2021 Human Sexuality section were lower than usual. One qualitative comment that stood out was the perception of a student who thought I had failed at creating a truly inclusive class environment. This semester was the first time I had explicitly taught content related to the contemporary impacts of events like colonization and enslavement. I am open about my progressive politics, and my sarcastic personality sometimes leads me to make deadpan asides about the harms done to marginalized communities. This student's comment and the lower quantitative ratings remind me that there is true diversity of thought in my classroom. It also shows me that if I want to get higher evaluation numbers, I might need to ease back on my anti-oppression stance; this is a situation that many feminist and womanist faculty face: whether to speak the truth or try to be palatable for students who belong to dominant social groups. This calculus is part of the additional burden feminist and womanist faculty carry into the classroom.

In addition to student expectations and evaluations, we are also faced with unrealistic expectations from departmental and university officials.

We not only have to prepare new courses, we have significantly more service commitments than other faculty, and are often tasked with "diversity work" (Settles et al., 2019, p. 5). Even as a contingent faculty member and postdoctoral fellow, I (Jill) have been asked to be on DEI-related committees for two separate APA divisions, one of which was to "represent" Native American peoples. At the time of this writing, I've also been asked to give approximately 10 talks in the past month (often at no cost), some of which are only peripherally related to my area of research, but all broadly concern Native American peoples. Even as we are tokenized for DEI initiatives, we are excluded from others. For example, Faculty of Color report being excluded socially and professionally in their departments, lacking access to valuable mentoring opportunities (Settles et al., 2019). Feminist and womanist faculty also face epistemic exclusion, in which our scholarship is rejected due to our methods or topic area (Settles et al., 2020). On several occasions, my (Jill) work using digital stories as a research method has been likened to an "art project" or referred to as "non-traditional" for psychological science. Indeed, it is not uncommon for us to endure unrealistic expectations with little institutional support before entering or while navigating the tenure track.

The Challenges We Face Outside of the Classroom and Strategies for Coping

With growing campaigns against liberal education and critical theories in the classroom, we can also face attacks and challenges outside of the classroom. This section discusses some of these threats along with ways we can support each other through them.

Being a Target

In addition to encountering marginalization in the classroom, we are increasingly experiencing oppression through forces outside of it. The website Rate My Professors (RMP; www.ratemyprofessors.com/) is a common method students use to provide anonymous peer evaluations of faculty at over 7,000 schools, though it is biased against faculty with marginalized identities. Although there are positive reviews on RMP, the potential for bias is evident in my (Jill) anticipation each time I check to see if a profile has been created for me—one hasn't been, which I'm grateful for as I've seen how unfair and uncalled for comments affect my colleagues. Faculty of Color and non-native English speakers receive more negative evaluations from students than white faculty (e.g., Baker, 2019; Subtirelu, 2015), just as male faculty fare better than female faculty. I (Kat) admit to always being curious about my RMP reviews, so I check them every few months. While I haven't had any majorly negative comments, at least one review has misgendered me since I came out as trans.

Since 2016, another platform has emerged known as the Professor Watchlist (PW; https://professorwatchlist.org/), which is hosted by the conservative organization Turning Point USA. The PW does not provide student rankings of faculty, but rather is intended for the general public to "unmask radical professors." Through an obscure process, faculty are added to the PW, which is considered a major threat to academic freedom and a form of intimidation with real-life consequences. It is not uncommon for faculty members on the PW to receive death threats and verbal abuse, whether by email, via social media, or even to university officials (Kamenetz, 2018). To date, the three of us are not on the PW, though we know of other psychologists who are. Consequently, not only do we have to contend with biased student evaluations, but we must also endure massive pressure and threats of violence by broader society.

Building Supportive Networks

As educators, much of our energy and thought process is likely on our students, not ourselves. However, our ability to care for ourselves has implications for our own well-being (Hou & Skovholt, 2020), especially when we have marginalized identities. When we care for ourselves, we also have a positive impact on our students (O'Neal et al., 2017). Finding ways to cope with this reality can protect or lessen the impact microaggressions can have on your well-being (Miller et al., 2017). The rest of this section will discuss the importance of connections as ways of coping with macro- and microaggressions.

Connecting with others is a great way to cope and get support. Since each relationship we have may give us a different sort of support, consider how your relationships vary. The greater variety of authentic and trusting connections you can have, the better supported you will be (Hou & Skovholt, 2020). While this might sound like a lot to maintain, the intention is not to check in frequently with all these people, but instead to strive toward trusting relationships in a variety of places. Your support network can be a place where you can share your own experiences with microaggressions and hear from others about how they cope with them, too. Even if you are isolated as one of a few marginalized professionals in your community or at your institution, knowing that there are other people going through the same thing can reduce the negative effects of the persistent marginalization (Kivlighan, 2021). Together you can navigate resisting oppressive structures, promote legitimacy of each other's experiences and work, reduce burnout, and validate each other (Miller et al., 2017).

We can also find support in unexpected places. When I (Kat) was on the job market a few years ago, I had a campus interview for a job I did not end up getting. While there, I met a colleague with whom I've become friends and collaborated with several times. Even in such a fraught and awkward experience as an academic interview, I found someone who supports me and who I support both personally and professionally. Coincidentally, this is how the relationship among all three authors began. While the second author (Jill) and third author (Sarah) knew each other since graduate school, Jill came to interview for a position at my (Kat) and Sarah's institution. Although Jill decided on a different path, we have continued to collaborate ever since Jill asked me to participate in her Cultural Psychology class interview project, and she has returned to our institution to give talks and visit with Indigenous students on campus. As a result, when I was approached to write this chapter by the editors, I knew I wanted Jill and Sarah as coauthors for the project. I thought of Jill first, to bring a critical Indigenous perspective to an institution founded in settler-colonialism. I also invited Sarah to bring another valuable counseling perspective based in culturally responsive pedagogy. Even though we do not all operate out of the same institution, we continue to deepen and build our supportive network; we encourage you to do the same.

Within your support networks, consider finding people who formally or informally agree to advising you on your path. Again, having diversity in mentorship can be helpful. For example, I (Sarah) have identified three mentors: one in my department, one at the same institution outside of my department, and one within my field but not at my institution. Each mentor brings different perspectives and strengths. Together, there is a great team that is ready to uplift me as I work to serve my communities and accomplish my goals. I (Jill) similarly have mentors of various backgrounds and positions to give me a wide range of opinions and different feedback, which has been crucial as I begin to take my next steps beyond being a contingent faculty member and postdoctoral fellow. On the flip side, I (Kat) appreciate being someone others can turn to for mentorship, whether they are students or tenured colleagues. The many perspectives on who we are, where we are going, and how to navigate the world can come together to shape us into the strong professionals we are.

Challenging Oppressive Structures in Academia

Given structural inequities to entering and persisting in psychology from the undergraduate to graduate level and, finally, to the professoriate and tenure, inclusive education ecologies are of paramount importance. While we have no doubt that oppressive structures are (re)produced in and outside of the classroom, we're also finding innovative ways to challenge such systems and remain on the tenure track (or remain feeling encouraged to enter it). Of course, remaining on the tenure track is not the only or best option; stepping off might be the only and best option for you because of the factors we've described here. Therefore, we write this for those of you who wish to remain on the tenure track in need of additional insight on how to effectively do so.

As we mentioned earlier, finding mentors and supportive networks is important, but when it comes to challenging oppressive structures, leveraging that community is just as crucial. For instance, your fellow faculty members can advocate for you during the tenure review process, garner additional support from the department, and point you to valuable resources throughout the tenure track (Harris & Lee, 2019). Most universities have policies against faculty, staff, and students bullying and demeaning faculty, as well as recommendations for pursuing disciplinary action. Additional resources that can help you challenge oppressive structures include offices for equity and diversity, which may include conflict-resolution services, information about filing reports related to discrimination and harassment, and staff to consult with. However, given higher education's well-documented tendency to (re)produce systems of oppression, using the resources provided by departments and universities may prove to be inadequate.

It is critical that you have a much broader community who is willing to push back against universities on your behalf. Take, for example, faculty who have been denied tenure or who have been targets of racist attacks. In the well-known case of Nikole Hannah-Jones, who was denied a tenured position at the University of North Carolina (UNC) due to conservative opposition, hundreds of academics, journalists, and the like published a letter supporting her and condemning the university (see Coates et al., 2021). Eventually, UNC reversed their decision, but Hannah-Jones had already sought out a more supportive environment. As another example, Dr. Brittney Cooper has received hate mail and violent threats as an associate professor of Africana and Women's, Gender, and Sexuality Studies at Rutgers University. Rutgers' newly established Black, Indigenous, and People of Color Faculty Caucus wrote a letter to the university to denounce such acts and to ask for the university to do the same. With the help of preexisting or newly created communities, you should be able to tackle the indignities associated with being marginalized on the tenure track at your university, or at least give 'em hell with your friends in tow. Should the three of us ever need support at our various institutions, you can guess who we'll turn to.

Conclusions

Academia, like so many other institutions, was built to privilege and prioritize the experiences and voices of dominant social groups. Because of this, feminist and womanist faculty, particularly those of us with multiple marginalized identities, face challenges from students, colleagues, and administrations related to our course content, teaching style, and classroom management. In this chapter, we described many of these challenges and provided suggestions for ways that you can push back and cope with them. We also extend a call to action for our white and otherwise privileged readers: Keep in mind your/our role in making culture change in the academy to end oppression. Creating coalitions and working with diverse others is an essential part of social justice (Adams & Bell, 2016), and solidarity is the only way we can move toward a more inclusive academy.

Resources

Byers, D. S., McInroy, L. B., Craig, S. L., Slates, S., & Kattari, S. K. (2020). Naming and addressing homophobic and transphobic microaggressions in social work classrooms. *Journal of Social Work Education*, 56(3), 484–495. https://doi.org/10.1080/10437797.2019.1656688

Johnson, V. E., Nadal, K. L., Sissoko, D. R. G., & King, R. (2021). "It's not in your head": Gaslighting, 'splaining, victim blaming, and other harmful reactions to microaggressions. *Perspectives on Psychological Science*, 16(5), 1024–1036. https://doi.org/10.1177/17456916211011963

Willoughby, B. (2018). *Speak up at school: How to respond to everyday prejudice, bias, and stereotypes*. Teaching Tolerance. https://www.learningforjustice.org/sites/default/files/2019-04/TT-Speak-Up-Guide.pdf

References

Adams, M., & Bell, L.A. (2016). Theoretical foundations for social justice education. In M. Adams & L. A. Bell (Eds.), *Teaching for Diversity and Social Justice* (3rd ed., pp. 3–26). Routledge.

Annamma, S., & Morrison, D. (2018). DisCrit classroom ecology: Using praxis to dismantle dysfunctional education ecologies. *Teaching and Teacher Education*, 73, 70–80. https://doi.org/10.1016/j.tate.2018.03.008

Ayllón, S. (2021). *Online teaching and gender bias*. (Research Report No. 14787). IZA Institute of Labor Economics. https://docs.iza.org/dp14787.pdf

Baker, C. A. (2019). A quantcrit approach: Using critical race theory as a means to evaluate if Rate My Professor assessments are racially biased. *Journal of Underrepresented & Minority Progress*, 3, 1–22. https://doi.org/10.32674/jump.v3i1.1012

Baker, C. N., & Rodrigues-Sherley, M. (2021, August 11). Critical race theory bans target feminist professors: "This is Censorship." *Ms. Magazine*. https://msmagazine.com/2021/08/11/critical-race-theory-feminist-teachers-women-gender-studies/

Berk, R. A. (2017). Microaggressions trilogy: Part 3. Microaggressions in the classroom. *Journal of Faculty Development*, 31(3), 95–110.

Byers, D.S., McInroy, L.B., Craig, S.L., Slates, S., & Kattari, S.K. (2020). Naming and addressing homophobic and transphobic microaggressions in social work classrooms. *Journal of Social Work Education,* 56(3), 484–495. https://doi.org/10.1080/10437797.2019.1656688

Chaney, K. E., Sanchez, D. T., & Remedios, J. D. (2020). Dual threats: Women of color experience both gender and racial stigma in the face of a single identity threat. *Invited for Revision and Resubmission.*

Coates, T., Gilmore, G. E., & Jones, M. S. (2021, May 25). We stand in solidarity with Nikole Hannah-Jones. *The Root*. Retrieved from https://www.theroot.com/we-stand-in-solidarity-with-nikole-hannah-jones-1846956586

Diaz, J. (2022, March 8). *Florida's governor signs controversial law opponents dubbed "Don't say gay."* NPR. https://www.npr.org/2022/03/28/1089221657/dont-say-gay-florida-desantis

Edwards, C. W. (2019). Overcoming imposter syndrome and stereotype threat: Reconceptualizing the definition of a scholar. *Taboo: The Journal of Culture and Education*, *18*(1), 18–34. https://doi.org/10.31390/taboo.18.1.03

Esarey, J., & Valdes, N. (2020). Unbiased, reliable, and valid student evaluations can still be unfair. *Assessment & Evaluation in Higher Education*, *45*, 1106–1120. https://doi.org/10.1080/02602938.2020.1724875

Fish, J. (2021). *Interview with a Psychologist: Representing marginalized psychologists and diversity science in psychology coursework*. PsyArXiv. https://doi.org/10.31234/osf.io/v29uh

Gonzales, L. D. (2017). Subverting and minding boundaries: The intellectual work of women. *Journal of Higher Education*, *89*(5), 677–701. https://doi.org.10.1080/00221546.2018.1434278

Harris, T. M., & Lee, C. N. (2019). Advocate-mentoring: A communicative response to diversity in higher education. *Communication Education*, *68*(1), 103–113. https://doi.org/10.1080/03634523.2018.1536272

Hayden, S. C. W., & Crockett, J. E. (2020). Applying feminist pedagogy to teaching counselor advocacy. *Journal of Creativity in Mental Health*, *15*, 509–521. https://doi.org/10.1080/15401383.2020.1733723

Hill, K. G., Martischewsky, M. J., & Erickson, C. A. (2021). Information type influences students' perceptions of faculty self-disclosures. *Teaching of Psychology*, *48*(3), 215–220. https://doi.org/10.1177/0098628320952408

Hou, J. M., & Skovholt, T. M. (2020). Characteristics of highly resilient therapists. *Journal of Counseling Psychology*, *67*(3), 386–400. https://doi.org/10.1037/cou0000401

Kamenetz, A. (2018, April 4). *Professors are targets in online culture wars; some fight back*. NPR. https://www.npr.org/sections/ed/2018/04/04/590928008/professor-harassment

Kivlighan, D. M. III, Swancy, A. G., Smith, E., & Brennaman, C. (2021). Examining racial microaggressions in group therapy and the buffering role of members' perceptions of their group's multicultural orientation. *Journal of Counseling Psychology*, *68*(5), 621–628. https://doi.org/10.1037/cou0000531

Kruk, M., & Matsick, J. L. (2021). A taxonomy of identity safety cues based on gender and race: From a promising past to an intersectional and translational future. *Translational Issues in Psychological Science*, *7*(4), 487–510. https://doi.org/10.1037/tps0000304

Miller, R. A., Jones, V. A., Reddick, R. J., Lowe, T., Flunder, B. F., Hogan, K., & Rosal, A. I. (2017). Educating through microaggressions: Self-care for diversity educators. *Innovation in Research and Scholarship Feature*, *55*(1), 14–26. https://doi.org/10.1080/19496591.2017.1358634

O'Neal, C. R., Gosnell, N. M., Ng, W. S., & Ong, E. (2017). Refugee-teacher-train-refugee-teacher intervention research in Malaysia: Promoting classroom management and teacher self-care. *Journal of Educational and Psychological Consultation*, *28*(1), 43–69. https://doi.org.10.1080/10474412.2017.1287576

Pittman, C. T. (2010). Race and gender oppression in the classroom: The experiences of women faculty of color with white male students. *Teaching Sociology*, *38*(3), 183–196. https://doi.org/10.1177/0092055X10370120

Settles, I. H., Buchanan, N. T., & Dotson, K. (2019). Scrutinized but not recognized: (In)visibility and hypervisibility experiences of faculty of color. *Journal of Vocational Behavior*, *113*, 62–74. https://doi.org/10.1016/j.jvb.2018.06.003

Settles, I. H., Warner, L. R., Buchanan, N. T., & Jones, M. K. (2020). Understanding psychology's resistance to intersectionality theory using a framework of epistemic exclusion and invisibility. *Journal of Social Issues*, 76(4), 796–813. https://doi.org/10.1111/josi.12403

Skovholt, T. M., & Trotter-Mathison, M. (2016). *The resilient practitioner: Burnout and compassion fatigue prevention and self-care strategies for the helping professions*. Routledge.

Subtirelu, N. C. (2015). "She does have an accent but ...": Race and language ideology in students' evaluations of mathematics instructors on RateMyProfessors.com. *Language in Society*, 44(1), 35–62. https://doi.org/10.1017/S0047404514000736

Sue, D.W. (2014, September 16). *Microaggressions and marginality: Manifestation, dynamics, and impact* [Speech]. Penn State University, State College, PA.

Webb, L. M., Allen, M. W., & Walker, K. L. (2002). Feminist pedagogy: Identifying basic principles. *Academic Exchange Quarterly*, 6, 67–72.

Williams, M. T. (2019). Microaggressions: Clarification, evidence, and impact. *Perspectives on Psychological Science*, 15(1), 3–26. https://doi.org/10.1177/1745691619827499

CHAPTER 12

Movidas, Rage, and Last Chances on the Road to Achieving Tenure With Community-Based Research

Desdamona Rios
University of Houston–Clear Lake

My inspiration for doing community-based work (i.e., applied research) is based on where I come from, my formal training, and my goals as a feminist psychologist. I grew up in a Mexican immigrant/Mexican American working-class neighborhood in Los Angeles, the oldest of two daughters to a single mother. We struggled financially for most of our lives, with my mother sometimes working two jobs to support us. In high school, an academic counselor once said to my mother that I would never amount to anything, essentially reinscribing a stereotype attributed to working-class Chicanx people. No one in my peer group had plans to go to college, and I had no idea what steps were necessary to get there. Through a series of events, mentors, encouraging friends, and the steady support of my mother, I eventually did go to college at the age of 28, and then onto a doctoral program at the University of Michigan.

I preface this chapter with my personal experiences because many negative stereotypes about Latinx people, education, and intelligence persist. As a feminist social psychologist, the persistence of these stereotypes motivates my community-based work, which involves challenging myths about the Latinx community, addressing internalized stereotypes about the potential of the Latinx community, and promoting Mexican American studies (among other area studies) as often as possible. It is from this standpoint that I share pragmatic steps for building community partnerships[1] and how those can result in products valued by the academy

---

1. I would like to acknowledge my community-based mentors, Patricia Cabrera, Beatrice Garza, and Margaret Rodriguez, for their generosity and brilliant *movidas*. I would also like to thank the

(and thus tenure), as well as how community-based work is congruent with social justice priorities valued by academic feminist psychologists.

Learning From Our Elders

Community psychologists have argued that conventional scientific constraints can impede scientific innovation (Rappaport, 2005), and yet we have many examples of how scientific dogma can replicate itself. Like others before me, I sought a doctoral degree to gain knowledge and skills I could use to serve my community of origin. And like others before me, I experienced the tension between "real" research that is valued by academia and applied community-based research with marginalized communities. In her 1998 memoir, Sandra Bem described how she was denied tenure in the 1970s at Stanford because of her feminist-focused research. Luckily for the field, Bem went on to have a fabulous career and was later appointed director of Women's Studies at Cornell University. In a similar vein, bell hooks (2003) recounts in her book, *Teaching Community,* the challenges she faced as a professor who deviated from status quo teaching norms. hooks argued that academia is simultaneously "limited in scope" and offers the potential of "creating spaces where teaching and learning could be practiced outside the norm" (p. 23), although the latter is not always valued when measured against demands for uniformity within the academy.

Michelle Fine (2016) argued for divergent or less commonly practiced methods of teaching and research, including community-based participatory action research, and especially during these "revolting times" in which we live. Although community-based projects require time, patience, and building trust with community partners, the work matters for building collaborations that enrich science, education, and community for both privileged and oppressed stakeholders. However, because community-based work should be directed by the needs of the community with whom we wish to collaborate, the timeline may not align with academia's tenure clock which demands productivity regardless of real-world barriers. In my experience, it is challenging but possible to engage in meaningful community-based research and achieve tenure.

Overcoming Structural Barriers: The Role of *Movidas* and Rage

Almost all advice about achieving tenure involves the mechanics of the process and baseline criteria such as minimum number of publications to earn tenure, all of which is useful. What is less common are discussions about the

---

students who gave so much of their time and game-changing insights to our work: Jacqueline Harris, Meghan Johnson, Brittany Hiett, Beth Rainey, Jazmin Orozco, Taylor Langford, Cindy Rios, and Luetta Walker.

emotional and psychological toll of the tenure process, especially for underrepresented groups such as Black, Indigenous, and people of color (BIPOC), working-class academics, and other underrepresented groups. A basic human motive is a sense of belonging (Fiske, 2018), and in academia, belongingness requires a lot of conformity and can be threatened if there is perceived competition, resulting in exclusion from the in-group. My own experience in academia has been at times a lonely journey, with well-intentioned colleagues not fully understanding my work but offering platitudes nonetheless (e.g. "social justice work is so important to our society"), whereas other colleagues have evaluated my work as less rigorous based on their limited knowledge about community-based work and its significance to the field of psychology (Fine, 2012; Rappaport, 2005). I have also experienced self-doubt about my intuitions and direction of research. Deviating from group norms (i.e., basic research) requires a lot of confidence to stay purposeful and committed to community work. Even worse, community-based work that receives accolades (e.g., national awards, media coverage) may elicit jealousy and a sense of competitiveness among colleagues.

It is therefore necessary to engage in *movida*, defined by Espinoza et al. (2018) as "multiple kinds of 'moves,' from those undertaken in games and on dance floors to those that take more subversive forms like forbidden social encounters, underground economies, and political maneuvers" (p. 2). In the context of achieving tenure while doing community-based research, *movidas* are necessary for securing support from colleagues who will evaluate your tenure portfolio, which may also involve translating the importance of this work. For example, a *movida* may be subtly guiding some colleagues through a process of self-persuasion that shifts them away from privileging basic research over applied. *Movidas* require strategy and planning, and I know this all seems laborious and exhausting up front. However, there is evidence that self-persuasion is highly effective for changing attitudes and may be especially effective for people who have low confidence in their attitude to begin with (Abeywickrama & Laham, 2020). In my experience, attitudes about community-based work are strong but uninformed. Once the negative attitude has shifted, allies will preach the value of your work in your absence.

For scholars from underrepresented groups (e.g., BIPOC, LGBTQ+, working class) who are using their privilege as members of the academy to collaborate with underserved communities, the burden of convincing colleagues of the *scientific* value of your work is quite daunting. The erasure and/or devaluation of the work of women of color in the academy is well documented (see *Presumed Incompetent*, volumes 1 and 2 for a broad range of issues faced by women in the academy) and evidenced in who is represented in the tenured professoriate (see NCES [2020] report for tenured faculty by race/ethnicity and gender). Brittany Cooper (2018) describes how her "eloquent rage" is informed by the many racist and/or sexist instances she experienced across her own life span, including in the academy. The common use of jargon about diversity, equity, and inclusion by colleagues may not hold up in practice, especially when colleagues (un)consciously review tenure materials through the lens of White supremacist patriarchal standards. As Cooper (2018) argues, rage *can* be sublimated into meaningful work that serves the community, and *movidas* are necessary to navigate the demands of a traditional academy's criteria for tenure.

To be clear, I am not promoting individuals blindly rage against the machine, but rather imagine how rage is the manifestation of pain resulting from the absence of love in one's academic community. The idea of love in academia is absurd on its face, but consider the alternative of competitiveness, arrogance, relational aggression, and other forms of antisocial behavior so prevalent in our workplace (Cortina et al., 2019; Petersen & Pearson, 2020). hooks (2018) explained that love is important for all meaningful relationships, not just romantic ones. As feminist psychologists, many of us are motivated to improve our communities because we *love* our communities, and rage about social injustices can be a motivator to realize that love. Admittedly, I have felt rage in my workplace, and notably, it was guided and assuaged by the love given to me by my academic feminist community.

Context

Community-based work takes time, patience, and humility, and offers innumerable opportunities for professional and personal growth. Below I outline my process in identifying an opportunity to be of service to the community, and the many lessons I learned along the way.

When a "Last Chance" Becomes a First Chance

I was able to sublimate rage into community-based research and make *movidas* when an opportunity came up during my second semester as a tenure-track faculty member. It was then when a master's-level student, named Victoria, enrolled in one of my courses. Over the semester, she and I talked after class about our common interests in educational disparities, especially for Latinx students. It turned out that Victoria worked for a charter school that was opened in the early 1990s by a nonprofit organization whose mission was to address various inequalities faced by the Mexican community in Houston (the focus has shifted as the community has diversified to include various Latinx ethnic groups). The charter school was initially established to address the low high school graduation rates of Mexican Americans in Houston and is known as a "last chance" high school for students who had been expelled from other high schools or who were referred by the juvenile justice system.

Although the high school is considered a "last chance" for many students enrolled, the opportunity to collaborate with the charter school offered me my "first chance" to do community-based research. An unforeseen outcome was the opportunity to share with my non-Latinx colleagues about a high school hidden in plain sight and where many stereotypes about Latinx people would be dispelled. What I mean by "plain sight" is that the high school can be seen from the main highway that cuts through Houston, and yet many of my colleagues and students had no knowledge of it or noticed it while driving north on the highway.

Before I continue, I want to stress that the students who participated in this research were eager to learn, and those who had lived fairly privileged lives understood their standpoints to be limited to their White, middle-class upbringing. For Latinx students who participated in this research, they had the opportunity to apply their lived experiences and knowledge to the overall project, including collaborating with their White peers who were less knowledgeable about the context. For example, several students were apprehensive about doing on-site research because the charter school was attended by "bad students" and located in a "bad neighborhood." One poignant memory is one of our first visits to the charter school where one of the boy students held the front door open for the entire research team. One student commented about how polite he was, and that his behavior was unexpected. Her comment opened space for us to talk about negative stereotypes about Latinx people and the working poor, as well as Latinx cultural norms that include *respeto* ("respect"), and even the basics of operant conditioning to understand how charter school students who were transitioning from schools where they were regularly punished for behaviors were experiencing a nurturing environment where they were rewarded for good behavior.

Developing a Trusting Relationship

Developing a trusting relationship takes time and sometimes requires an introduction from a trusted insider. In my case, it was Victoria. She facilitated a meeting with the CEO of the nonprofit that funds the charter school, the school's superintendent, the director of the Adult Education program, and several other key administrators. The meeting included a tour of the school, along with a brief history of the funding organization and school, and an overview of current initiatives. The administrators asked me *a lot* of questions about myself, including where I grew up (not Houston), where I went to graduate school (also not Houston), and why I was interested in their charter school. I was anxious about explaining why I might be suitable for working with them. I explained that my feminist training included looking for "what has been left out" (Stewart, 1998) and identifying the "presence of an absence" (Fine, 2002), including the voices of parents and students in educational policy or Latinx people in educational curriculum more generally. I also shared that my feminist psychologist training involved the practice of self-reflexivity (Hurtado, 1996) and recognizing my insider/outsider status (Collins, 1986), meaning although I shared some experiences as a Latinx person with both students and administrators, I was not from Texas and no longer working class. Honestly, I debated sharing my feminist training because I (incorrectly) assumed the administrators to hold conservative views because of their Texas origins and because of internalized stereotypes of Latinx people as grounded in traditional gender roles. Long story short, they welcomed me into their Houston feminist circle, and we have attended many feminist professional meetings together.

After the initial meeting, I was invited to sit in on classes and meet with teachers and counselors where I took notes on teaching style and curriculum, and later asked questions of each person to learn more. There were several one-on-ones, where they continued to ask questions and share their vision. Eventually, I was invited to attend leadership meetings where I was asked for my perspective on key issues, including grant writing, framing of initiatives, implicit bias training, curriculum development, and after-school programming. By the way, I do not consider myself an expert in most of these areas at the K–12 level; I include this information to describe the collaborative environment I experienced working with them and the self-efficacy I felt in offering my insight from a fresh (reframed from "outsider") perspective. I was later invited to commencements, graduations, and awards ceremonies where I began meeting other members of the core group of Latinx leaders in Houston from whom I gained a better understanding of the key issues and players in the Houston Latinx community.

After a full year of demonstrating my commitment to learning about their model of education, my pilot study was approved for implementation. It may seem like a long time to nurture a relationship, but the administrators, teachers, and staff explained their protective stance was informed by experiences with exploitative researchers whose goals were to "study" the children without any long-term commitment to the school or larger community. In the meantime, I worked on other lines of research and scholarship with several colleagues both at my institution and nationally to ensure I met tenure requirements within the academic clock.

The "protectiveness" of vulnerable populations is something we as researchers should take seriously and is a worthwhile inconvenience that does not align with the academic tenure clock. I was mindful about including researchers (students and colleagues alike) who would exhibit cultural humility (Buchanan et al., 2020), meaning having some sense that outsiders can never be experts on someone else's culture but are committed to lifelong learning. Community-based work can be rewarding but sometimes requires difficult decision-making in the best interest of community well-being.

For example, I invited a colleague to join me in a meeting with administrators because I believed their skills would come in handy. I made no promises about a research collaboration, but instead suggested they might be interested in knowing more about the charter school. My colleague was neither Latinx nor from the working class but seemed well intentioned based on my professional interactions with them. However, during our meeting with the charter school administrators, they dominated the discussion with opinions and recommendations for a research plan and asked few questions about the community with whom they had little to no prior experience. They made statements based on stereotypes about Latinx families, albeit out of a sense of paternalistic concern for the education of Latinx children (e.g., Why don't Latinx parents care more about education?), which triggered memories about my own experiences with teachers and school counselors who knew little about the financial and social constraints experienced by Latinx parents.

Nonverbal communication from administrators during the meeting and later polite reminders of their priority of building a community of respect for the students meant that I needed to find a researcher who was in alignment with the goals and vision of the charter school. Culturally insensitive mistakes, foot-in-the-mouth statements, or other behaviors that harm vulnerable communities should be recognized, discussed, and followed with a clear plan for amendment and/or growth. My colleague is not alone in missing an opportunity for learning and collaboration; I have said or done things I wish I hadn't (more on that later). Rather than give up, I educated myself, sought mentorship, and asked for forgiveness and the opportunity to correct for my error.

(Re)Socialization From the Academy to the Community. And Back

The term *resocialization* is typically used to describe formerly incarcerated person's reentry into general society, but there is a certain amount of resocialization needed out of the academy and into the community. What "counts" as science and "rigorous" evidence are measured by the standards of a "science of banal dispossession" (Fine, 2011, p. 4) where adherence to conventional goals of psychological science (e.g., replicability, generalizability) can be misaligned with actual community needs and ignore oppressive social structures (Rappaport, 2005). To be honest, I had my own ideas of research topics I wanted to explore at the charter school, and the administration was agreeable to allowing me to conduct some pilot studies with their students and theoretically, I believed I had developed the skills to listen with intent and allow the research questions to emerge based on community feedback.

However, I found it difficult to codeswitch from working in the community and fitting into academic norms among colleagues (Rios & Case, 2019; for an overview of challenges of community-based research, see Sandwick et al., 2018). For example (and not unlike my colleague I mentioned earlier), I had a lot of advice to give based on "empirical evidence" and the like. In some cases basing recommendations on empirically based best practices is ideal; however, in community-based work where people's lives are complex and informed by social forces outside their control, empirically based references may not be most useful and may seem more like know-it-all positioning. I had only been out of grad school 3 years at this point and was still operating from a perspective of proving myself as worthy to be in the room with brilliant people. Lucky for me, the charter school administrators were patient and identified with my anxieties since they each had also been the first in their families to attend college, graduate school, and hold professional leadership positions.

(Im)Practical Outcomes

Experiencing our work beyond quantifiable products to earn tenure, such as number of publications or scores on teaching evaluations, is possible in community-based work where we have opportunities to teach beyond the classroom, apply the tools of our trade, and build relationships that are reciprocally beneficial for the well-being of the community and ourselves.

Social Support While on the Tenure Track

Social support is one of the most studied constructs in community psychology because of the correlation between helping behavior and well-being (Barrera, 2000); however, I find there is less discussion about the importance of social support during the tenure track process, and even less discussion about social support *outside* of academia during this process. In my process of building my relationships with community partners, I have been fortunate to meet many nonacademic mentors, and now friends, who reminded me of the value of my working-class Chicana values. Conventional wisdom dictates the necessity to network within one's own profession and/or organization for career success, so intuitively academics would network with other academics. This is good advice generally, but for people who are perceived as outsiders (e.g., underrepresented groups of people), certain opportunities will be unavailable because they are less likely to be invited to informal networking events. In addition to family and existing friends, support from these new mentors helped me maintain my psychological health by reminding me that (a) there is a world outside of academia that is simultaneously more and less serious; (b) I am competent and my skills are valuable and helpful toward building better communities; (c) there are many collaborative spaces working toward building a better society; and (d) my identity should be more than my job title.

Additionally, nonconventional methods and approaches to psychological research may further marginalize a community-focused scholar. To be accurate, I did have some support within my department, but it was palatable that the general opinion of my colleagues was that my research was less rigorous and not "scientific" enough. My professional relationships with my students who introduced me to the administrators at the charter school, as well as the administrators themselves, eventually evolved into mentorships and friendships. This process took a couple of years and included frequent meetings, lunches, professional gatherings where we grew to know each other, and where they offered social support in different professional contexts. Their support really helped me focus on my goals as a researcher because they explicitly valued my expertise and commitment to doing right by the community.

Classroom Without Borders

In her book *Teaching Community*, bell hooks (2003) describes her own experiences as a burned-out teacher, with one source being the psychological and emotional toll as a result of well-meaning colleagues who did not fully understand race and racism and had internalized the belief that it was acceptable to "teach down" to meet their students of color where they were (or so they imagined). hooks pushed back and challenged her students to grow through unconventional teaching methods that assumed the students could rise to the challenge. Although my pedagogy is intersectional across classes (see Rios et al., 2017, for an overview), textbook learning is not sufficient for students to understand the structural barriers experienced by various marginalized groups. As I mentioned above, in my community-based work, my students have witnessed firsthand the challenges faced by Latinx students who faced all sorts of structural barriers. It has been during community-based work when students can contextualize the lessons we covered in my courses taught on a college campus.

bell hooks also notes how teaching at a state school shifted how she identified excellent students. Like hooks, my first job out of grad school was at an elite private institution. And like hooks, my next job was/is at a public state institution where I observed first-generation college students with great potential doubt themselves, unlike what I witnessed in students at the private university, who were for the most part not first-generation students. My students at the public university had also experienced many of the issues faced by the charter school students; like in the aforementioned opportunity created by the boy who held the door for the research team, together we made connections between their experiences with language and theory, and then through our community-based work my college students began to see themselves as agents of change, with many going on to work in community-based agencies that serve some of the most vulnerable populations in Houston.

I have conducted a couple of studies at the charter school, but the pilot study on Latinx history has been the most impactful for the high school students, college students, and me. The project was a collaborative one and took another year to develop interview protocols, curriculum development, and lesson plans, and implement with frequent check-ins with school administrators to approve lesson plans, recruiting students to participate and teach the supplementary material. I had hoped that the high school students would appreciate the lessons and be inspired to do well in school. What I did not expect was for students to tell their friends about the study, to ask parents and grandparents about historical events and people, ask for an additional post-study, post-semester interview to keep talking about the history, and talk about how inspired they were to finish high school! Students on the research team gained a deeper understanding of intersectionality and how social institutions work differently for groups of people at the intersection of race/ethnicity, social class, and immigration status (e.g., education, immigration) to create barriers or facilitate success for groups of people.

Back to *Movidas*

The bottom line is that the immaterial, warm, fuzzy stuff will not get you tenure. In her critique of the uncritical demands for evidence-based research, Michelle Fine (2011) gives several real-life instances of whose evidence is (il)legitimate and cautions about the "too familiar intimate dynamics of privilege, blame, and violence" (p. 9). Her examples include domestic and sexual violence against women, but the parallel I want to make here is that these examples are about systemic bias. Tenure evaluations are a systemic example of who gets to stay in the academy. I abbreviate the *movidas* I mention throughout this chapter for ensuring your community-based work is recognized as worthy of tenure:

- Relationships with community partners take time to develop. While you are establishing those relationships, identify other opportunities for research and publishing.
- Publish. You don't have to wait for the project to be "completed" to publish. Publishing on process, community-based teaching, or preliminary results is important to share with the academic community.

- Many of your colleagues may not know about the value of community-based research. Discuss as often as you can with your colleagues to normalize this type of research in formal settings (monthly meetings) and informal settings (ask someone to lunch).

- Identify champions to serve on your tenure committee. If possible, identify established scholars/senior faculty who can explain to the rest of your tenure committee the importance and rigor of community-based research. Once you have tenure, do the same for others and/or encourage colleagues to advocate for colleagues at their institutions.

- For teaching institutions, field research can be viewed as an extension of teaching. Document the number of hours you are spending in the field with students and detail the activities you engage in with your students.

- Also for teaching institutions, student presentations at regional and national conferences are generally evaluated favorably and "count" toward teaching achievements.

- Something that I am not great at but I see the benefits of is this: Advertise your work and accept invitations to speak about your community-based work. Document those "invited addresses" on your curriculum vitae and dossier. An easy place to start is Facebook; join topic-specific groups (e.g., Institute for Academic Feminist Psychologists; Society for the Teaching of Psychology) and post your upcoming talk. While in the community, start asking around about where you might present your research or offer workshops on your expertise.

- For service, note any publications written in collaboration with your community partner. These may be a report written for internal use, a report for boards of directors, presentations for other stakeholders (e.g., parents, donors, etc.), or op-ed pieces.

- Apply for awards that recognize community-based or participatory action research and teaching. For me, receiving national teaching awards at the junior level expanded the overall evaluation of my teaching evaluations. If you are unsure about your qualifications, discuss with trusted colleagues, and if they agree you are competitive, ask them to nominate you. Be sure to supply organized materials to minimize their work since the process can sometimes be lengthy.

Final Reflections

I did earn tenure doing community-based research, but I also engaged in other research projects that I was able to complete according to the tenure clock. My teaching evaluations were in line with tenure standards, but the field research conducted with teams of students were recognized at the national level from several societies within the American Psychological Association. Just as important, there have been immeasurable experiences that have illuminated the possibilities of academia, including celebrating my tenure with students who worked with me on these community-based projects and several women who worked at the charter school. My "win" turned into a collective win! Academia is full of overachievers, and our achievements may be minimized because of the bounty of accolades among us. Colleagues may not recognize the relevance or impact of your work because it is beyond their knowledge base, expertise, or interest. My community-based mentors reminded me of my worth and mentored me in new areas not always valued in academia, such as recognizing "ways of knowing" in the academy that may also represent so many ways of not knowing in other domains. Community-based work can remind us of our worth—that our expertise is valuable and that we are competent.

A final unexpected outcome of my work with the charter school is the many opportunities that have manifested, including invitations to sit on several advisory boards and collaborations on research and community development initiatives with Latinx community leaders. Additionally, community partnerships have resulted in several of my students finding professional positions in organizations that serve some of the most vulnerable populations in Houston. What is satisfying about these placements is watching a new generation of feminist activists/scholars do community-based work. And as a tenured professor, I am able to mentor many more feminist activist/scholars in community-based efforts.

References

Abeywickrama, R. S., & Laham, S. M. (2020). Meta-cognition predicts attitude depolarization and intentions to engage with the opposition following pro-attitudinal advocacy. *Social Psychology*, *51*(6), 408–421. https://doi.org//10.1027/1864-9335/a000424

Barrera, J. (2000). Social support research in community psychology. In J. Rappaport & E. Seidman (Eds.), *Handbook of community psychology* (pp. 215–245). Kluwer Academics/Plenum.

Bem, S. (1998). *An unconventional life*. Yale University Press.

Buchanan, Rios, D., & Case, K. A. (2020). Intersectional cultural humility: Aligning critical inquiry with critical praxis in psychology. *Women & Therapy*, *43*(3–4), 235–243. https://doi.org/10.1080/02703149.2020.1729469

Collins, P. H. (1986). Learning from the Outsider Within: The Sociological Significance of Black Feminist Thought. *Social Problems*, *33*(6), S14–S32. https://doi.org/10.2307/800672

Cortina, L. M., Cortina, M. G., & Cortina, J. M. (2019). Regulating rude: Tensions between free speech and civility in academic employment. *Industrial and Organizational Psychology: Perspectives on Science and Practice, 12*(4), 357–375. https://doi.org/10.1017/iop.2019.63

Espinoza, D., Cotera, M. E., & Blackwell, M. (2018). *Chicana movidas: New narratives of activism and feminism in the movement era.* University of Austin Press.

Fine, M. (2002). 2001 Carolyn Sherif Award address: The presence of an absence. *Psychology of Women Quarterly, 26*(1), 9–24. https://doi-org.uhcl.idm.oclc.org/10.1111/1471-6402.00039

Fine, M. (2012). Troubling calls for evidence: A critical race, class and gender analysis of whose evidence counts. *Feminism & Psychology, 22*(1), 3–19. https://doi.org/10.1177/0959353511435475

Fiske, S. T. (2018). Stereotype content: Warmth and competence endure. *Current directions in psychological science, 27*(2), 67–73. https://doi.org/10.1177/0963721417738825

hooks, b. (2003). *Teaching community: A pedagogy of hope.* Routledge.

hooks, b. (2018). *All about love: New visions.* William Morrow.

Hurtado, A. (1996). *The color of privilege.* Michigan University Press.

National Center for Educational Statistics. (2020). *Table 315.20. Full-time faculty in degree-granting postsecondary institutions, by race/ethnicity, sex, and academic rank: Fall 2015, fall 2017, and fall 2018.* https://nces.ed.gov/programs/digest/d19/tables/dt19_315.20.asp

Petersen, N. J., & Pearson, R. L. (2020). Mobbability: Understanding how a vulnerable academia can be healthier. In C. M. Crawford (Ed.), *Confronting academic mobbing in higher education: Personal accounts and administrative action* (pp. 104–131). IGI Global.

Rappaport, J. (2005). Community psychology is (thank God) more than science. *American Journal of Community Psychology, 35*(3/4), 231–238. https://doi.org/10.1007/s10464-005-3402-6

Rios, D., Bowling, M. J., & Harris, J. (2017). Decentering student "uniqueness" in lessons about intersectionality. In K. A. Case (Ed.), *Intersectional pedagogy: Complicating identity and social justice* (pp. 194–213). Routledge.

Rios, D., & Case, K. A. (2020). Unlikely alliances from Appalachia to east L.A.: Insider without and outsider within. In *Presumed Incompetent II* (pp. 131–142). Utah State University Press.

Sandwick, T., Fine, M., Greene, A. C., Stoudt, B. G., Torre, M. E., & Patel, L. (2018). Promise and provocation: Humble reflections on critical participatory action research for social policy. *Urban Education, 53*(4), 473–502. https://doi.org/10.1177/0042085918763513

Stewart, A. J. (1998). Doing personality research: How can feminist theories help? In B. Clinchy & J. Norem (Eds.), *The gender and psychology reader* (pp. 54–68). New York University Press.

CHAPTER 13

Value-Driven Service and the Right to Say No

- **NiCole T. Buchanan**
  Michigan State University

- **Martinque K. Jones**
  University of North Texas

No. It is a simple, two-letter word with great power. Its simplicity masks the complexity it embodies and the challenges many face when attempting to set boundaries and live in accordance with their values. Saying no and concretizing your values are important to success in academia. Saying no allows you to say yes to endeavors that reflect your values, gives you agency, and contributes to your personal and professional well-being. However, not all of us have equal capacity to say no. Those of us with less social power (e.g., women and people of color) are expected to do more service, unpaid labor, and undervalued tasks and are more harshly punished when we do not comply with these demands. This is no less true in academia, where women, Black, Indigenous, and people of color (BIPOC), and especially BIPOC women faculty, are expected to willingly engage in higher levels of mentoring, service related to justice, equity, diversity, and inclusion (JEDI), and a host of invisible and unrewarded labor activities (Guarino & Borden, 2017; Hanasono et al., 2019; Kiyama & Gonzales, 2019; O'Meara et al., 2017; Pyke, 2015). These demands will not change without systemic institutional efforts and collective action. In this chapter, we offer strategies to feminist scholars aiming to resist disparate service demands and use a values-based no to your advantage.

Author's Values and Positionality to This Work

As academics and authors of this chapter, our identities are central to the experiences we have and inform the writing of this chapter. I (NiCole) identify as a Black cisgender woman (she/her pronouns), and I am a licensed psychologist and tenured full professor at a research-intensive predominantly white institution (PWI), where I have worked for 20 years. My research examines the ways in which social identities intersect to inform victimization experiences (e.g., racialized sexual harassment; Buchanan et al., 2018) and barriers to JEDI in higher education (e.g., epistemic exclusion of JEDI-related research; Settles et al., 2019, 2021). The values that guide my work are *justice, equity, diversity*, and *inclusion*; *privilege investment* (using one's privilege to actively agitate for socially just changes in society; Case, 2013); and *solidarity* across minoritized groups. I am intentional about using my privilege and power as a tenured full professor to address inequities in academia, clinical research, training, and practice. I have written about the challenges I have faced in academia and strategies I use to navigate them (Buchanan, 2020), critiques of the field (psychology and other STEM disciplines), exclusionary research practices, and strategies to promote inclusion within and outside of academia (Buchanan et al., 2021). I align myself with the needs and values of minoritized populations and work in solidarity across identity groups to ensure equitable access, practice, and utility of academic research and clinical practice, and, perhaps most important, to reduce the burden of inequitable practices on vulnerable populations.

I (Marti) self-identify as a Black cisgender woman (she/her pronouns), and I am a licensed psychologist and assistant professor of psychology at an emerging research-intensive minority-serving institution (MSI). My research centers on how Black women self-define their Black womanhood (i.e., gendered racial identity; Jones & Day, 2018), how Black women's gendered racial identity and stereotypical portrayals of their group impact their mental health (e.g., Jones et al., 2021), and counseling interventions with Black women (e.g., Jones & Pritchett-Johnson, 2018). The primary values guiding my work include *authenticity, belonging, connection*, and *liberation*. These values are represented in my research and service, which center on elevating the voices of women of color (voices that are too often misconstrued through the perpetuation of race-gender stereotypes), the creation and facilitation of spaces that contribute to identity affirmation and connection, and the dissemination of research findings useful in moving toward liberation for marginalized, and specifically Black, communities. We draw on our expertise as Black women scholars and positionality as informants to our discussion of value-driven service.

Service and the Raced-Gendered Context of the Ivory Tower

Historically, institutions of higher education were designed for white men and openly excluded BIPOC scholars and women academics (Fox Tree & Vaid, 2022; Thelin et al., 2021). BIPOC and women scholars continue to be underrepresented in faculty roles, which is exacerbated at higher ranks and in faculty leadership (Griffin, 2019), and their service obligations differ significantly from those of white men. A nationwide study of over 20,000 faculty across 140 institutions showed that women provide a large range of service activities and spend more hours a week on service, particularly institutional service that is low in prestige and high in emotional labor (Guarino & Borden, 2017). Similarly, faculty representing BIPOC, queer, and working-class backgrounds reported four times the amount of service as white faculty (Social Sciences Feminist Network Research Interest Group [SSFNRIG], 2017). These service activities were essential to the institution's functioning, but were also devalued, and included activities such as serving on task forces to improve institutional climate, invisible mentoring and advising activities (e.g., writing recommendation letters, reading drafts, providing career advice), and cultural taxation activities, such as promoting equity initiatives, chairing diversity committees, and giving lectures on JEDI (Griffin, 2013, 2019).

Risk of Not Enacting Your Values

The values endemic to academia are frequently at odds with those of feminist scholars. For instance, the academy values a specific type of scholarly productivity, like high numbers of academic publications, whereas feminist scholars may determine their productivity based on service activities, like community building and enacting social change, both of which may reap fewer traditional scholarly products. And we, as feminist scholars ourselves, have experienced firsthand how service of any kind, though rewarding, may come at personal and professional costs. A growing number of service roles can lead to exhaustion and disengagement, in other words burnout, which has a negative impact on scholarly productivity, and ultimately promotion, tenure, and merit (Carter-Sowell et al., 2019; Griffin, 2013; SSFNRIG, 2017). Prioritizing service that aligns with our core values can counter this cycle of overwork and burnout.

Our values serve as a guide, directing us toward service that is fulfilling and minimizes the drain on our energy. Aligning service with our values helps us avoid saying yes to tasks that do not advance our career or contribute to our sense of accomplishment and belonging. Not aligning service with our values risks taking service assignments to please others and taking on more service obligations than we can healthfully sustain, personally and professionally. These compounding and occasionally unfulfilling service roles are in addition to invisible service (e.g., informal student mentoring and JEDI work that is not formalized through committee work), which is typically essential for the institution but devalued and unrewarded (SSFNRIG, 2017). Women and other marginalized faculty often engage in invisible service because it aligns with their values (Griffin, 2013; Kiyama & Gonzales,

2019)—for many it is rewarding to mentor underrepresented students or to support students processing racialized college experiences because they value *diversity*, *connection*, and *growth*. In other instances, we (women, people of color, and other marginalized scholars) take on these tasks because we have been socialized to be agreeable within a precarious academic context. Nevertheless, a conundrum emerges when these value-congruent activities undermine our professional and personal well-being. We assert that engaging in value-driven service is a feminist act, thereby fostering equity in academic contexts (e.g., balancing service workloads across *all faculty* and not just a few), enhancing faculty professional and personal well-being, as well as creating opportunities for future feminist scholars. In the sections that follow, we reflect on our own experiences as feminist scholars navigating value-congruent service responsibilities.

Value Driven or Not: Narratives From Black Women Faculty

In the section that follows, we reflect on our own experiences as feminist scholars navigating value-congruent service responsibilities. First, Marti describes how she used support from a senior mentor to deliver a value-driven no to a service request in order to better honor her mental health and wellness throughout the pandemics. Then, NiCole recounts how she began to say no after realizing how her engagement in diversity-related service obscured the need for her institution to bring in other faculty who share her passion and expertise.

Marti's Story: "Congratulations, You've Been Elected to Serve on the Diversity Committee!"

The spring and summer months of 2020 were difficult. The COVID-19 global pandemic persisted, and the racial pandemic intensified with the police murders of Breonna Taylor and George Floyd. I was grieving alongside many others in the Black community. At the same time, my academic responsibilities as a pre-tenure faculty member did not stop, but rather intensified. I felt a great need to support students in processing their emotional reactions to various racialized events, and this contributed to longer advising and lab meetings; I felt it was necessary to disseminate statements denouncing racism, which lead to additional hours on the computer carefully crafting emails; and I also found it ever so important to continue my scholarship on identity-based mistreatment and this, too, contributed to a pressure to publish in a way I had never experienced before. I was doing a lot and I could feel it: Writing became more laborious, and I had lost the energy to do anything pleasurable (e.g., take a long run). That said, in August, when

I was elected by my department to serve on the newly formed diversity committee, I immediately wanted to respond, "No. No, thank you. … I am tiiirrrred."

However, saying no would be difficult. I value *diversity* and recognize that under my leadership the department could grow. Moreover, as a pre-tenure faculty member it seemed almost impossible to say no to the faculty who had elected me to this role. At the same time, I value *authenticity* and realize that my election to the committee (as the only Black woman tenure-track faculty member) was simply cosmetic, and much more work was needed to achieve the department's goals for diversity and inclusion. And, once again, I was just tiiired!

I shared these sentiments with my mentor, the only woman of color full professor (Yolanda Flores-Niemann) in our department, and she supported me in strategically navigating, and subsequently declining, this service request. We decided that during a faculty meeting she would ask the faculty to revisit the departmental bylaws, and specifically the rules pertaining to the diversity committee. Then, she would suggest that pre-tenure faculty be protected from service, including serving on the diversity committee. The faculty agreed with her proposal, and I was excused from this role.

As I reflect on this experience, I applaud myself for recognizing my limits and the signs of burnout, as well as being vulnerable with my mentor, who used her status and power to contribute to meaningful change. I also know that there are factors in this example that lead to this successful outcome. First, my mentor and I strategized with how to go forward and get buy-in from other faculty. Then, my mentor had the faculty review their established practices and values as a department (that pre-tenure faculty are protected from service), which helped them come to the conclusion that I should not be asked to serve on the committee. In essence, reflecting on *their* values drove them to tell me no to taking on this additional service. As a result, I am in a better position to engage in service that aligns with my wellness and my values.

But I also wondered: *What would have happened if I did not have such an excellent mentor?* The answer is I am not sure. As a pre-tenure faculty member who cares deeply about diversity and inclusion, I felt a strong pressure to take on this service role, but at the same time I was not in a position professionally, nor personally, to do so. That said, it was critical for me to strategize a way to ultimately decline this service role. One potential solution would be to inform the department of my current service obligations and compare my current responsibilities to what is expected of me based on my workload; this would alert my department as to how additional service may be misaligned with my workload or even provide me with an opportunity to directly ask that some service be reassigned so that time can be dedicated to this new service task. Other solutions may include reminding the department of my pre-tenure status and the necessity of research productivity for promotion and tenure or expressing great interest in this service role and a willingness to serve in the future—post-tenure. These are also strategies that help the department reflect on their values (e.g., *productivity*), and in turn make decisions that ultimately align with my own.

NiCole's Story: "If I Don't Do It, Who Will? I Am the Only One Here …"

I spent 20 years being the only Black woman in the Clinical Science program at a research-intensive PWI. I developed diversity programming and trainings, established the first diversity committee, created a graduate course on social justice and diversity in psychology, chaired diversity hiring and admissions committees, and on and on and on. My efforts aligned with my values of *justice*, *equity*, *diversity*, and *inclusion* and were aimed at training clinical scientists to conduct research and serve those subjected to systemic marginalization (e.g., BIPOC, queer, and impoverished communities). I often did service that was diversity related but outside my expertise, which added to a workload that was unsustainable and filled with work that was not rewarded and largely unrecognized in my department's tenure, promotion, and merit considerations (e.g., developing in-house JEDI trainings for the clinical science program). I fulfilled every request to "come and be Black for me" (Smith, 2019), as well as the requests that generalized to come be female, be Brown, be not white and male for me.

A dear friend and peer mentor noted that as long as I kept doing all of the diversity work there would never be a reason for people in my department, who were mostly white, to learn how to do it. This advice was simple, yet ground-breaking. I realized that each time I accepted diversity service obligations, I contributed to the problem by obscuring the true problem. Structurally, there were too few people to do this work, and me filling the gaping hole allowed the institution to ignore these unmet needs in the department. For others to recognize that we do not have enough people with JEDI expertise in the department and to potentially expand their own knowledge in these areas, I needed to stop doing this work for them.

When I do it all, they—the institution, my department, my colleagues—never experience the discomfort necessary to foster change. So I stopped saying yes just because I was the only one in the group who could. I started letting everyone grapple with the fact that there were too few of us with JEDI expertise; I stopped filling in gaps in the training and let them sit in the fact that students wanted training that they could not provide. However, this came with risks, such as others not recognizing the value of this work or seeing the need to bring in more people to do it. Nevertheless, I had to accept that their devaluing of diversity and inclusion should not change my value-driven no that prioritized my well-being and sustainability.

Six Tips for Prioritizing and Enacting Your Values

As you work to identify your values, you can begin to actualize these values for yourself. When we act in value-congruent ways we attract people who do the same, share similar values, and support us in acting in ways that align with our values.

1. **Prioritize your mental health and well-being.** First and foremost, enacting your values involves prioritizing your mental health and wellness. By prioritizing your wellness you will be better able to identify values and service activities that are of most importance to you. Prioritizing your wellness truly means valuing yourself (your emotions and energy) more than your academic responsibilities (see Marti's example); and recognizing that your ability to honor your own emotional needs contributes to you being a better scholar—one who is energized about the work ahead, clearly and creatively thinking, and best positioned to support your students and colleagues. But you may be thinking, "Well, what does this *look* like?" Prioritizing your wellness looks different for every scholar, but examples may include the following:

    - Saying yes to service responsibilities that energize you

    - Limiting your total number of service responsibilities, including invisible service, to ensure you have the personal time to dedicate to your well-being

    - Setting aside time to find and receive mentorship and support from other scholars—no matter your rank

    Extra tip: Identify mentors by connecting and fostering relationships with senior faculty outside of your department or institution by attending college-specific events and conferences in your field or joining an online group specific to women in academia; each will provide you access to individuals who may support you in navigating issues and concerns specific to academia. In fact, we encourage you to have a circle of mentors, preferably with a mix of people at your institution within and outside of your department, as well as those outside of your institution, but within academia. Together, these mentors will be able to provide varying degrees of department-, institution- and field-specific mentorship that fosters discretion and promotes broad opportunities for you in the field.

- Participating in faculty skill-building opportunities such as those offered by the National Center for Faculty Diversity and Development (see Resources)
- Finding a culturally responsive therapist
- Maintaining relationships with friends and family outside of academia

2. **Identify and clarify your values.** Values refer to one's principles or what they believe is important in life, such as authenticity, change, diversity, equity, freedom, openness, respect, and security (financial and otherwise). Our values often dictate our behaviors and vice versa. For instance, a scholar may value *connection*, so they participate in collaborative projects. Another scholar may value *diversity* and seeks to recruit diverse colleagues and students to their institution.

   To identify your values we encourage you to review lists of common core values and consider what is most important to you. As appropriate, include financial freedom, building wealth, and having leisure time and comfort if they are important to you. During this process, take a close look at your current service activities—departmental committees, mentoring, invited talks and presentations, national service—as well as broader community services. Then, ask yourself, "What activities do I enjoy the most and why?" This will further reveal your values. For instance, I (NiCole) am often eager to serve on our department's promotion and tenure committee because it aligns with my commitment to promote equity.

   Consider your values for the present and the long-term. Journal about how they show up in your day-to-day interactions and choices. How do you want them reflected in your life over the next 3 to 5 years? For example, if you value your health and well-being, how are they reflected in your life currently? What would you need to do to best align your life with this value? If you are successfully aligned, what do you expect it to look like 5 years from now?

3. **Make value-congruent decisions.** Once you identify your values and what it would look like for you to be in alignment with your values, you can align them with your decisions about service responsibilities. The goal is to accept only those responsibilities that closely align with your values and respond using a value-driven no to anything that does not align. For example, if you are asked to serve as ombudsman for your department, you may weigh this service request against your values. If you value *advocacy*, you may be eager and excited to serve, but if this is not one of your primary values you may respond with a

value-driven no. In another scenario you may be asked to give a keynote to an established health center in your community. If you value *wellness* and *financial stability*, you may respond with excitement, while asking about the honorarium or sending them a contract with your standard speaking rate.

Decline (or, in other words, deliver a value-driven no) service responsibilities that do not align with your values. Declining these service activities will prevent you from becoming overburdened with service and give you the space and energy to engage in more fulfilling service activities in the future. In essence, you are saying no to say yes. Remember that you are considering these requests within a full range of your values, including those for wellness and balance. This may mean that you also need to say no to activities that may align with some of your values but conflict with others. In one instance you may say no to a request to be on a student committee because you are already at capacity for committees and mentoring. Despite being difficult, explaining to students why you cannot be on their committee and discussing the need to balance these responsibilities can be powerful in shaping their ability to say no and achieve work–life balance in the future. We also encourage you to recognize these as opportunities not only for you to have balance, but to also open opportunities for others and even future opportunities for yourself. For example, you might choose to decline a speaking request that you would normally want to do but saying yes would overload your schedule and increase your stress. You could use this as an opportunity to suggest other faculty who would benefit from such an opportunity. This not only maintains your balance, but also allows you to support a colleague's career, and leaves the door open for you to secure future value-congruent speaking engagements.

There are also times when you might be unable or unwilling to decline a service request. When this is the case, you can try to restrict the scope of work, goals, and expectations for the task to ensure that it does not become overwhelming. Break down the task into modest goals for the project so that you are likely to successfully complete the task. We encourage you to *under*promise and *over*perform, meaning set easily achievable goals with a generous timeline to completion. Then if you accomplish those goals earlier and do more than promised, you have now *over*performed.

4. **Track your progress.** Keep track of your service responsibilities and roles. You can do this by keeping a running list of service roles on a Word document, notebook, or spreadsheet. We encourage you

to use this list as a space to document the time it took to execute the task and the various types of work it took to complete it (e.g., being a guest speaker for a student organization includes time to prepare the presentation, travel, and deliver the talk). Additionally, document the time you spend working on service in your calendar and immediately add service activities to your CV. Track *all* of your sort-of-service roles and requests, like participating in an ad hoc committee or informally mentoring a junior scholar. These tasks are part of the "invisible service" that is often unrecognized and under-rewarded. If you have these documented, you can better advocate for yourself and illuminate these undervalued areas of service. For example, I (NiCole) added categories to my annual review document that included unofficial peer mentoring with other faculty and informal mentoring with graduate students that were not my direct mentees. The sheer volume of names and time commitments listed in these categories highlight that the service I provide in this area is unique and surpasses that of my colleagues. Keep track of the requests that you decline as well. These are important because you may be able to use this information for annual reviews and because they give you data that you can reflect on as you are strengthening your commitment to align your service with your values. Review this list and ask, "Did I lose anything by declining this request? Would it have added additional stress if I had said yes to it?"

Keeping track of your service responsibilities, roles, and requests can be helpful for several additional reasons. First, this information may help you (and your department administrators) consider equitable workloads and demonstrate whether the amount of service you are doing aligns with what is expected of you; with this information in hand, you may be able to negotiate a workload adjustment that aligns with your values and your institution's values, and you may be able to report this service, including invisible service, so that it may be counted in your annual review. Second, tracking your service roles, responsibilities, and requests allows you to analyze this data—taking into account what types of activities you have accepted, declined, or been asked to do, the number of roles and responsibilities you have taken on, as well as the time you have dedicated. With this data, you can reassess and clarify your values accordingly. To do this you may ask yourself, "Is what I am doing (or being asked to do) aligned with my values?" and "Am I satisfied with the number of service roles and responsibilities I have and the time I am spending on service?" If you discover that what you are doing does not align with your values or the time you have to spend, then adjust: Ask to be removed from committees, excuse yourself from other responsibilities, and definitely do not take on any other roles that do not align with your values. Third, keeping track of your service requests can illuminate how others perceive your values and what they value in you. For example, students may see you as student focused and therefore ask you to speak at their organizational meetings. Similarly, individuals may see you as valuing equity and frequently request that you serve on various diversity and inclusion committees; with this example, we also encourage you to consider if you are being subjected to tokenism and how that might impact your decisions going forward.

5. **Reflect on your experiences.** Beyond tracking your service roles and responsibilities, it is equally important for you to *reflect* on these experiences, with intentional consideration of the time spent on the activity with its benefits, the value congruency of the task, and the extent to which the activity aligned with your institutional merit standards. Perhaps using the same tracking sheet, ask yourself, "Did the time spent equate with the personal and professional gains I experienced doing this work?" or "Did this activity bring an unexpected benefit or live up to the benefit I anticipated?" and "How did I feel while I was doing, or anticipating doing, the work?" This last question could be especially important for identifying tasks that were more stressful or personally taxing than expected and may not be worth the perceived benefit from doing them. In considering your values, ask, "Which of my values did I expect this activity to fulfill? Did the task ultimately align with any of my values?" Finally, it is critical to consider, especially for pre-tenure faculty, the extent to which the task is aligned with the guidelines for what is considered meritorious and valued for promotion and tenure. With this in mind, ask, "Did this activity 'count' for my annual review, promotion and tenure? Did this activity contribute to me achieving my promotion, tenure, and merit goals?"

6. **Set boundaries.** Once you have mastered the ability to deliver a value-congruent no and are only committed to service roles that best align with your values, there is still more work to do. As you start operating in value-congruent ways, you will begin to attract more service requests that align with your values (e.g., being known as someone who values diversity leads to requests that you attend or speak at every diversity event on campus or serve on the diversity committee, like Marti described). Navigating these requests can be even more difficult than turning down service that does not align with your values and will require that you set strong boundaries.

Consider setting a limit for how many service activities you participate in each semester (e.g., three to four activities per semester or one to two activities per month) or place a limit on how much time you can devote to each activity and have that time set aside on your calendar (do not forget to include your preparation time!). By setting boundaries, you can ensure that you are doing the service you enjoy while being well and energized doing it!

Tips and Tricks for Saying No

- **Identify your values before others define them for you.** This is perhaps most crucial for pre-tenure and early career faculty, but applies to anyone who has not fully aligned their service with their values-driven yes or no. There is never a wrong time to reset your service expectations to align with your values.

- **Set a time to review your values and your service obligations at least once a semester.** Consider using the journaling prompts we provided. As you find discrepancies between your values and your service obligations, adjust accordingly.

- **Never answer a service request right away.** Institute a mandatory 24-hour consideration period where you allow yourself to think about how the request makes you feel, how it aligns with your values, and what time and energy you are willing to give to the task. Let others know that this is your process with a reply such as, "Thank you, I am honored that you thought of me. I need some time to consider the opportunity with my current workload. I will email you back on Tuesday (within 48 hours with my reply)." You can always come back to answer sooner, but it is important that people learn that you will not rush to accept service requests. If you decide to decline the request, you can send a brief email stating, "Thank you once again for thinking of me. I carefully considered my current tasks and the timeline. Unfortunately, I cannot accept at this time." Notice that we did not offer a reason for declining and do not invite them to negotiate further about the opportunity. Doing either will invite further attempts to get you to say yes, which can tempt you to agree to something you already decided was not in your best interest. Another benefit to this strategy is, over time, people are more selective about what they ask you to do. Making it your standard process not to reply immediately is especially important when influential people, like your department chair or college dean, approach you with a service request. You can appeal to this as your established process and create some space to consider the request in private and in consultation with your mentors.

- **Defer to your annual review committee.** This is most applicable to pre-tenure faculty who are actively being reviewed on a regular basis and may be most helpful when you receive a request that you do not want to take. Talk to your annual review committee about the requests you receive and be honest about your concerns or desires to serve in that capacity as they will have useful advice about how a particular service task will be evaluated and contribute (or not) to your review for promotion. Often, they will give you their suggestion to decline, especially in instances when you both agree the activity is not aligned with your values and long-term professional goals. When this happens, it is easy to reply to the request with "Thank you for considering me. I consulted with my review committee, and they have strongly recommended that I not take on additional service at this time (or that I not take a service request such as this one at this point in my career)." It is wonderful if your committee has communicated that you should not accept anything new for the year or until promotion because then you can reply automatically to such requests.

  There may be instances when you want to take on additional service, despite your committee advising you to not take on more responsibilities. In this case, you should give serious consideration to whether this service is essential for this stage of your career or if it should wait until after tenure. If you decide you want to accept, be upfront with your committee, articulate your appreciation for their support, provide your logic for why you went against their advice, and articulate how you plan to address their concerns. Consider this sample response to accepting a committee nomination for the American Psychological Association (APA) despite committee concerns:

  > Thank you for meeting with me to think about this service request. I thought long and hard about your concerns. In the end, I decided to accept this opportunity because it will contribute to my understanding of APA leadership, which aligns with my career goals and builds my national prominence, and it will increase my exposure to potential tenure letter writers in the field. Both national prominence and letter writers being familiar with my work are essential for my successful tenure application. Nevertheless, I heard your concerns about protecting my time before tenure. I spoke to the chair of the committee and negotiated sharing the position with a senior committee member to protect my time and increase the support I have

in the new role. I also told them that I would reevaluate the time commitment in 6 months to see if it conflicts with my tenure goals.

- **Establish your "no" committee.** While everyone can have a "no" committee, this is especially important for midcareer and senior faculty who do not have a review committee to consult. This committee could be convened as needed to discuss opportunities, review how they align with your values, discuss potential unstated tasks that may come with the work, and share their experiences with similar tasks that may inform your decision. It is helpful if your "no" committee is composed of peers at similar stages of their careers, with one or two more senior members that can discuss the longer term implications for your career.

- **Redefine (or shift) tasks.** Sometimes you will be "volun-told" to participate in service, perhaps by your department chair or university administrator, and it is strategic for you to say yes rather than no. And this may be especially the case for faculty at smaller institutions where the number of people available to do service is fewer. When this happens, look for ways to adjust the activity so that it aligns with your values, energy, and available time. You may also consider taking on this task, while also advocating to be relieved of another responsibility (e.g., "By taking on this additional role, I would like to request being relieved of my role as X").

- **Engage in collective action.** Because inequitable service loads among women and other minoritized faculty are a manifestation of how the academy is plagued by racism, sexism, and other -isms, it is imperative that feminist scholars also engage in collective action intended to shift and eradicate these oppressive structures. For instance, feminist scholars may create supportive networks, similar to consciousness-raising groups, during which feminist scholars convene to receive support and mentoring, and also collectively strategize ways to improve the conditions for feminist scholars. Through collective strategizing and action, you may deliver a strong no to institutions seeking to capitalize on the efforts of its most marginalized faculty.

Resources

Equity-Minded Faculty Workloads (ACE Network) Report: Equity-Minded-Faculty-Workloads.pdf

Harris, A. P. (2020). *Presumed incompetent II: Race, class, power, and resistance of women in academia*. University Press of Colorado.

National Center for Faculty Development, Diversity's Faculty Bootcamp, and other faculty-specific resources: https://www.facultydiversity.org/

Professor-ing podcast hosted by the National Center for Faculty Development & Diversity

Rockquemore, K., & Laszloffy, T. A. (2008). *The Black academic's guide to winning tenure—without losing your soul*. Lynne Rienner

References

Buchanan, N. T. (2020). Researching while Black (and female). *Women & Therapy*, 43(1/2), 91–111. https://doi.org/10.1080/02703149.2019.1684681

Buchanan, N. T., Perez, M., Prinstein, M., & Thurston, I. (2021). Upending racism in psychological science: Strategies to change how our science is conducted, reported, reviewed, and disseminated. *American Psychologist*, 76(7), 1097–1112. https://doi.org/10.1037/amp0000905

Buchanan, N. T., Settles, I. H., Wu, I. H. C., & Hayashino, D. S. (2018). Sexual harassment, racial harassment and well-being among Asian American women: An intersectional approach. *Women & Therapy*, 41(3–4), 261–280. https://doi.org/10.1080/02703149.2018.1425030

Carter-Sowell, A. R., Vaid, J., Stanley, C. A., Petitt, B., & Battle, J. S. (2019). ADVANCE Scholar Program: Enhancing minoritized scholars' professional visibility. *Equality, Diversity and Inclusion: An International Journal*, 38(3), 305–327. https://doi.org/10.1108/EDI-03-2018-0059

Case, K. (2013). *Deconstructing privilege*. Routledge.

Fox Tree, J. E., & Vaid, J. (2022). Why so few, still? Challenges to attracting, advancing, and keeping women faculty of color in academia. *Frontiers in Sociology*, 6, 792198. https://doi.org/10.3389/fsoc.2021.792198

Griffin, K. A. (2013). The calculus of yes and no: How one professor makes decisions about academic service. *Thought & Action*, 29, 35–43. https://eric.ed.gov/?id=EJ1017293

Griffin, K. A. (2019). Institutional barriers, strategies, and benefits to increasing the representation of women and men of color in the professoriate: Looking beyond the pipeline. In L. W. Perna (Ed.), *Higher education: Handbook of theory and research* (pp. 1–73). Springer. https://doi.org/10.1007/978-3-030-11743-6_4-1

Guarino, C. M., & Borden, V. M. (2017). Faculty service loads and gender: Are women taking care of the academic family? *Research in Higher Education*, 58(6), 672–694. https://doi.org/10.1007/s11162-017-9454-2

Hanasono, L. K., Broido, E. M., Yacobucci, M. M., Root, K. V., Peña, S., & O'Neil, D. A. (2019). Secret service: Revealing gender biases in the visibility and value of faculty service. *Journal of Diversity in Higher Education*, 12(1), 85–98. https://doi.org/10.1037/dhe0000081

Jones, M., & Day, S. X. (2018). An exploration of Black women's gendered racial identity using a multidimensional and intersectional approach. *Sex Roles*, 79(1), 1–15. https://doi.org/10.1007/s11199-017-0854-8

Jones, M., Hill-Jarrett, T., Latimer, K., Reynolds, A., Jones, A., Harris, I., Joseph, S., & Garrett, N. (2021). The relationship between the strong Black woman schema, depression, and coping among Black women. *Journal of Black Psychology*, 47(7), 578–592. https://doi.org/10.1177/00957984211021229

Jones, M., & Pritchett-Johnson, B. (2018). "Invincible Black Women": A culturally-informed group intervention with Black college women. *Journal for Specialists in Group Work*, 43(4), 349–375. https://doi.org/10.1080/01933922.2018.1484536

Kiyama, J. M., & Gonzales, L. (2019). "In academia, but not of it"—Redefining what it means to serve. In *The tenure-track process for Chicana and Latina faculty* (pp. 31–43). Routledge.

O'Meara, K., Kuvaeva, A., & Nyunt, G. (2017). Constrained choices: A view of campus service inequality from annual faculty reports. *The Journal of Higher Education*, 88(5), 672–700.

Pyke, K. (2015). Faculty gender inequity and the "just say no to service" fairy tale. In K. DeWelde & A. Stepnick (Eds.), *Disrupting the culture of silence: Confronting gender inequality and making change in higher education* (pp. 83–95). Stylus.

Settles, I. H., Buchanan, N. T., & Dotson, K. (2019). Scrutinized but not recognized: (In)visibility and hypervisibility experiences of faculty of color. *Journal of Vocational Behavior, 113*, 62–74. https://doi.org/10.1016/j.jvb.2018.06.003

Settles, I. H., Jones, M. K., Buchanan, N. T. & Brassel, S. (2021). Epistemic exclusion of women faculty and faculty of color: Understanding scholar(ly) devaluation as a predictor of turnover intentions. *Journal of Higher Education, 93*(1), 31–55. https://doi.org/10.1080/00221546.2021.1914494

Smith, E. M. (2019, May 21). Come and be Black for me. *Seattle Times*. https://www.thedaonline.com/culture/come-and-be-black-for-me-an-essay-by-ethel-morgan-smith/article_441f92f8-ee1c-11e6-9d7b-ab04c04993b5.html#comments

Social Sciences Feminist Network Research Interest Group. (2017). The burden of invisible work in academia: Social inequalities and time use in five university departments. *Humboldt Journal of Social Relations, 39*, 228–245. https://www.jstor.org/stable/10.2307/90007882

Thelin, J. R., Edwards J. R., & Moyen E. (2021). *Higher education in the United States: Historical development. Education Encyclopedia*. https://education.stateuniversity.com/pages/2044/Higher-Education-in-United-States.html

CHAPTER 14

Cultivating Communities

A Feminist Reframing of Networking Academia

- **Dionne Stephens**
  Florida International University

Not all women, in fact, very few, have had the good fortune to live and work among women and men actively involved in the feminist movement. Many of us live in circumstances and environments where we must engage in feminist struggle alone, with only occasional support and affirmation.

—bell hooks (1984, p. 112)

Although I embrace the need to carve out connections in the ivory tower, I hate networking. This statement often surprises people as I am not shy and love being around people. But the traditional concept of networking—as I was taught about it—is framed as a necessity in any field. The benefits of professional networks have been well documented: It will lead to more career opportunities, broaden your ability to gain access to the field's wells of knowledge, contribute to your capacity to be innovative, increase your pace of advancement, and enhance your status and authority (Davis & Warfield, 2011; Kiefer, 2011; Settles, 2020; Streeter, 2014). Studies have also noted that those who are successful at networking report higher levels in perceived quality of work and career satisfaction. This is because professional networks are a career-relevant resource that builds the social capital required for task and objective advancements (Kiefer, 2011; Streeter, 2014).

While these findings are supported by a large body of research, they provide evidence that networking privileges those who fit within the structures of academia. Specifically, those embracing the traditional goals and values of academic culture are most advantaged by framing networking as (a) primarily a potential for professional growth, advancement, and accomplishments or (b) an act of obligation that is part of the ivory tower culture of inclusion and requires creating a marketing narrative and sales strategy to promote ourselves as scholars (Fleming et al., 2015; Kiefer, 2011; Pollack et al., 2015; Streeter, 2014). In contrast, individuals with marginalized identities or research values, or social justice goals, have found that networking in academia is less beneficial. In fact, the reality of associated microaggressions and exclusionary slights associated with the traditional strategies can range from tiresome to traumatic (see Agosto et al., 2016; Anthym & Tuitt, 2019; Barber et al., 2021; Castillo-Montoya et al., 2022; Ricks, 2015). My identity as a first-generation, Black woman, non-American feminist informs my aversion to networking in academia. I am acutely aware that this is a space that validates certain voices of authority and legitimizes specific topic areas that do not reflect or include my own. These realities serve to continuously reinforce my marginalized positionality, and in turn make traditional networking approaches feel uncomfortable, phony, and inauthentic. This has played a significant role in my avoidance of putting myself out there at conferences or sitting right up front with questions for the conference speaker in hopes of leading to a coffee follow-up. I had viewed those who did it with ease suspiciously; I judged them as brown-nosing, exploitative, and disingenuous. Instead, I often choose to sit on the sidelines and jump in when it feels safe, which is not often.

For this reason, I was surprised when I put together a speaker list for a conference and came to the realization that I hadn't done too badly at developing relationships in academia. In fact, another organizing committee member reinforced this reality when she remarked, "Wow, you know a lot of the key people in the field." I did have a supportive network of colleagues, and these colleagues knew other colleagues they would willingly connect me with if I asked them to. But how had I built these relationships in light of my aversion to networking? These were people who I liked, wanted to be around, and respected for their skills and knowledge; what they could do for me, or I could bring to their table, was not central to our relationship. That was not what I was led to believe is effective networking, right?

The reality is that networking is not a one-size-fits-all endeavor, as it should encompass not just our professional identities and goals, but our personal identities as well. Recognizing this, I propose reimagining networking as a process of *cultivating a community*. By reimagining networking from feminist perspectives, we can nurture professional relationships that are characterized as supportive and aligned with individual values, skills, and practices that celebrate diverse academic identities. This centering of feminist values will further enhance the growth of supportive collaborations and equitable engagements across a variety of contexts and social issues. In this chapter I seek to help networking resisters reconceptualize the meaning of this important aspect of academia. By highlighting feminist values and norms we can align our social justice values and identities with the supportive and empowering professional relationships we cultivate. To build on this reconceptualization, I will also outline concrete steps for implementation through reframing, reflecting, and reorganizing strategies.

Reconceptualize Networking Meanings

For those of us who feel uncomfortable, excluded, or misaligned with traditional networking goals, I assert there is a need for us as feminists to think more holistically about the meanings of networking. Dismantling the margins and creating a space as *outsider within* or alongside academic norms requires cultivating relationships that center support, equity, and clear pathways of inclusion to ensure diverse ideas, individuals, and goals (Agosto et al., 2016; Davis, et al., 2020; hooks, 1984; Pruchniewska, 1984). Thus, instead of looking at networking as something you do to achieve a professional goal, we need to envision it as a process of expanding the spaces we and our allies can comfortably occupy. To do this, feminist scholars must reconceptualize meanings of networking to include community building, pursuits of passion, and meaning creation as central characteristics. In essence, it should be viewed as a process of building degrees of friendships in our professional spaces.

Community building. The first step toward engaging in feminist networking is viewing networking as a conscious approach to fostering a circle of support. It is only through establishing and investing in human connections that we can truly recognize and gain value from one another as scholars and collaborators (Davis et al., 2020; Deschner et al., 2020; Streeter, 2014). Having strong and healthy working relationships makes engaging in our work enjoyable because being part of a close-knit group increases productivity and innovation (Agosto et al., 2016; Streeter, 2014). This results in more opportunities to focus on our personal development in the context of our career responsibilities.

So how do we start planting these seeds for cultivation? Often the initial conversations we initiate to foster relationships are framed as trivial and trite. This is because many of us think about it in terms of the entry to a set professional goal attainment process. As feminists, we can shift the ways we use these forms of small talk to establish a foundation toward building allies, peers, or even friends, rather than only work colleagues, manuscript coauthors, or research collaborators. Just this shift in naming the potential relationships opens the doors for feelings of "natural" connection and a focus on collaborative growth. Valuing nonwork-related discussions in these early small-talk interactions can forge a closeness around sharing identities, points of similarity or difference, and daily life realities. When we frame conversations as community building, rather than career enhancing, these professional relationships become grounded in mutual respect and commitment to each other's goals (Castillo-Montoya et al., 2022; Deschner et al., 2020; Knight et al., 2013). This becomes the foundation of the "We is always stronger than me" networking mantra. In turn, our professional community of colleagues will have also a greater commitment to collaboration, productivity, and accountability with one another.

Pursuit of passions. As building a community is a form of investing in ourselves and our identities, it would be useful to think of networking as a way to gain more knowledge, feedback, and support for doing what we love. This shift makes the process less overwhelming. When we move away from focusing on what drives us to what seems practical, we are more apt to feel detached and are less likely to be successful in our dedication to our work. Having those around us who embrace the value of our work is critical for nurturing our professional growth and personal commitment (Agosto et al., 2016; Streeter, 2014). When networking is framed as a way of supporting our passions, we are more likely to invest productive time and energy into relationship building, increasing our chances for work goal success. In turn, we get more personal and professional fulfillment when we achieve these goals.

Creating meaning and value. Related to the pursuit of passions are the meanings and values that we give to our work. In so many ways, feminists and those with marginalized identities are not given the platform to be validated as voices of authority or their work is not viewed as valuable. In fact, a longitudinal study found that a primary reason that Black researchers disproportionately did not receive National Institutes of Health (NIH) funding was that their topics of interest, which were overwhelmingly community focused, were viewed as less important (Hoppe et al., 2019). A follow-up of this study further found that the agencies that supported the type of work Black scientists proposed were less well resourced (Lauer & Roychowdhury, 2021). Similarly, both topics studied by women and people of color (POC) are cited less; even among popular areas of research, women and POC receive less recognition via citations (Kozlowski et al., 2022). While these are concrete examples of the impact of evaluations of work within the current system, it is often the day-to-day comments and indignities we may face in our isolated programs that highlight the need for having people in our corners who understand the meaning of what we do. Developing a community that understands and promotes the value of our work across the field and outside of academic settings is essential for making change at all levels.

Restructuring Networking Strategies

Once you have shifted your networking lenses, the next step is to restructure how you approach this process. Traditionally, the focus has been on transactional goals: what you need and what others can gain from you (Fleming et al., 2015; Kiefer, 2011). I assert that we move away from this exchange relationship approach to one of equitable mutual benefit and support. This means not only considering your career objectives, but also embracing three strategic goals that center your core values: Reframe your networking capital, reflect who is already in your network, and reassess your target spaces.

Reframe your networking capital. Carefully naming both your instrumental and social strengths is an important practice. We are often taught to develop elevator speeches that focus on our research topics and skills. Being able to share our professional expertise, specific skills, and foundational training is a key component of networking. Often people just focus on this when they prioritize the exchange on networking per se. But if you are focusing on cultivating a community, you also need to be able to articulate your professional identity and your value beyond the quantifiable "what is on the CV." While "hard skills" (e.g. software competencies, methodological expertise, administration skills, language proficiencies) without question are critical for professional development, consider the interpersonal and social traits known as "soft skills" you bring to the table. Being skilled at organizing teams, knowing how to critically think outside the box, excellence in negotiation or deal making, facilitating difficult conversations, and being a task master—these are all soft skills that are critical for a successful collaboration. For these reasons, carefully consider these relationally focused aspects of yourself as they will directly shape the depth and quality of your connections. Our ability to attract a community, sustain engagement in community, and have a positive long-term reputation with colleagues, collaborators, and future mentees/students is grounded in who we are and our values, often more than our hard skills (Agosto et al., 2016; Deschner et al., 2020).

In addition to focusing on your strengths, acknowledge those areas where your skills may be more limited, and communicate clearly with potential collaborators. It is as important to know why someone may not mesh with your work style as it is to know why they would want to work with you. Do they have difficulty meeting deadlines? Are the tiny details unimportant to them? Does it matter whether we meet regularly to talk about our progress? For me the answer is yes, yes, and yes. Knowing this about me is important to determine the path you would take for certain activities. Being clear up front about where you can and cannot work together will ensure you can maintain relationships and productive professional collaborations.

Reflect on who is already in your network. When we think of networking, we often think outside instead of looking around us. Take stock and look at what cards you already hold in your hand. Begin this by brainstorming about who your connections are and who they might know. Be sure to move beyond this to start thinking about who these people can connect you with. These not-yet-met but tangentially connected people are part of your network. It just requires figuring out where they sit in your community, the invisible college or scholar squad.

The invisible college. The concept of the invisible college has existed for decades and serves as a central piece of academic culture (see Chapter 4, this volume). Essentially, the belief is we are associated by our areas of focus, methodological practices, and training norms in ways that are fairly structured and clear across the ivory tower. Those you should count as being in your invisible college are those in your field of work that "get" what you do or are willing to contribute to your success. They may not be our work "best friends" or people who we talk with regularly. However, you are connected enough to reach out if you need information or support relevant to your work. They will be there to give you instrumental help and some degree of emotional labor when you ask. An example is the Institute for Academic Feminist Psychologists, which brings together scholars with diverse feminist-focused interests (see Introduction). My participation in the gathering has increased my network of potential collaborators tremendously. Similarly, think beyond fellow academics, including librarians and support staff. I consider my department's grants manager part of my invisible college; she keeps me abreast of opportunities and new ways to work on projects, while also reaching out when she needs a faculty member to advocate on her behalf.

The scholar squad. Next, you should be clear about who is in your scholar squad. These are your "ride-or-die" folks beside you in the trenches with whom you can feel free to be open and vulnerable about professional stressors or achievements. They are different from friends as these relationships incorporate a career focus. Their cultural understanding of your work/life balance needs is also something those outside of academia often can't help you with. Not simply your cheerleaders, your scholar squad should be able to tell it to you like it is. Their consistent honesty in calling out your strengths and weaknesses are what make them valuable. Over time, this circle will shrink and expand as needs, life experiences, and career paths unfold. Thus, expect that these relationships can blossom into more of a personal friendship, or need to be pruned back to just a professional association at various points of your career journey.

Reassess Your Target Spaces

Without question, conferences remain one of the most important sites for professional networking. These are often the main gathering events for professional organizations across all fields. It brings together our invisible colleges and scholar squads. The value given to these spaces in the field cannot be denied. However, the COVID pandemic highlighted that while these gatherings could practically be held virtually, the interpersonal value that comes with in-person meetings was missing. In-person interaction is central in cultivating networks that intentionally empower, support, and prioritize social justice change that are the foundations of feminist community building (Cole, 2009; Emejulu, 2011; Wilson et al., 2010).

It is important to recognize just attending is not enough. You need to find ways to make inroads into what can be an overwhelming setting. One way to navigate this is by attending regional or topic-specific conferences to increase the likelihood of making connections. These smaller gatherings provide more intimacy and more face time with both presenters and other attendees. Similarly, focus on subgroup or division-specific events within larger conference settings; these more personalized spaces provide opportunities to develop relationships within the larger event. The American Psychology Association's (APA) Division 35: The Society for the Psychology of Women, for example, typically hosts pre-conference workshops, affinity group meetings, and specialized topic programming during APA-sponsored events. You can plan ahead by perusing the meeting websites or the division's Facebook pages in the weeks leading up to the gathering. Identifying these smaller meeting sessions provide additional time for interaction because they are allotted time slots outside the regular conference schedule. Further, they provide a collaborative, friendly environment to have deeper discussions than are typical during formal presentation hours.

Another way to strategically network at conferences is to create your own opportunities for cultivating connections. A member of my scholar squad wanted to connect her graduate student with a leader in a specific area of research who neither knew well. When the APA put out a call for symposia proposals to be presented at their annual conference, my scholar squad member organized a panel to ensure the student not only met the field leader but had an opportunity to have multiple occasions to engage both professionally and personally. Similarly, volunteering at a conference or being part of a planning committee gives you direct access to knowing who is attending, when they will be there, and where they will be. Again, think about where you are in the academic pipeline when taking these things on. Those who are pre-tenure, for example, should determine their level of contribution based on the time and realistic value that your evaluative unit will give to it when reviewing your tenure dossier.

Linked to engagement at conferences is your role in professional organizations; they offer several opportunities to join committees. Although we are often warned not to engage in too much service, for feminists and others who are marginalized, being strategic in selecting service work is an effective networking tactic (see Chapter 13, this volume). Select committees that align with your goals and prioritize cultivating relationships with potential allies and coconspirators. Be sure to take advantage of these early in your career. Often there are stage-appropriate roles that will make engagement easy. For example, I was on the graduate student editorial board for *Psychology of Women Quarterly*, and the assignments and guidance they gave was appropriate for my knowledge level and time priorities. The connections I made through this work got the attention of editors who were also contributing to other journals. This easily opened editorial opportunities during the early stages of my tenure road. However, over time, you should reevaluate whether the returns are worth the effort at that point in your personal and professional life. In other words, do not continue service positions when the perceived benefits are no longer needed or valuable to your trajectory plans. Also, part of community cultivation is stepping aside to allow someone else an opportunity that you have already experienced.

Finally, the nature of our work as feminists and social justice advocates is often isolating within traditional psychology spaces. We often face unique barriers due to research foci, which can prohibit our full engagement within our departments or programs. Thus, it is critical that we go outside our field and engage in truly interdisciplinary community cultivation. For example, I have joint faculty status in Women's Studies and Latin American and Caribbean Studies. These connections not only serve to expand my professional networking opportunities, but also have led to several interdisciplinary publications. Similarly, I have worked with peers in Public Health and Nursing to explore grant and training opportunities. This resulted in the development of an interdisciplinary global health research abroad program; we have gone on vacation immediately following the program's end to relax and bond together.

Increasingly universities are moving toward cluster hires, and you should reflect this in your own networking strategies. There are clear practical reasons for doing this. Aligning with a community that has diverse perspectives on your work will increase your publications and grant opportunities related to, as well as outside, your specific area of research. By recruiting from outside your field, you also create a broader network of potential letter writers and collaborators for projects. More important, crossing disciplines increases our ability to engage in critical and intersectional approaches to disseminating our work. By expanding our communities beyond discipline silos, we expand the ways in which research values, goals and training are conceptualized (Cole, 2009; Matsick et al., 2021; Wilson et al., 2010).

You don't have to go far to get started; look at other departments in your current institution for connections. Having someone within your organization to meet for coffee or attend campus and local events with is important; at some point, you could even become close enough that you can connect in personal spaces and activities (e.g., visiting each other's home or taking short trips together). Deepening your connections across campus can also provide you practical insights about your institutional experiences, which you can examine alongside emotional realities. Also, consider applying for trainings and fellowships that allow time and space to interact with others outside your field to expand your network reach. You never know what new insights about your own work you will gain, and the doors it can open for you. A former doctoral student attended an international meeting on complex systems methodologies where she met her future postdoctorate mentor on the bus from the airport. They talked about how she wanted to learn a method not yet normed in our field, and he continued to follow her doctoral journey, inviting her to join his team upon graduation.

Using social media platforms. Although social networking technology has been around for some time, it is only in the last decade that academics have begun to actively use this tool for their own networking efforts. At this point, the use of social media platforms are normative modes of social interactions in academia; at the most basic level, conferences are no longer our primary mode of connection. Now we use Zoom and other platforms to not only communicate, but host professional gatherings such as lectures, webinars, and symposia. Although the risk-benefit ratio of networking on social media sites is still up for debate (Jordan & Weller, 2018; Meishar-Tal & Pieterse, 2017; Van Noorden, 2014), as feminists we cannot ignore the ways in which it can expand our often-isolated career networks. These spaces have played a central role in building and sustaining relevant connections across scholars. We can now more easily connect with peers and colleagues or seek out new information and disseminate new ideas from our offices or homes. For those of us who may feel isolated as one of just a couple (or only one) of the feminists, racial/ethnic, gender, and/or sexual minority scholars in our department, social media spaces like these can be a lifeline for support and engagement. It can also become a space for rallying. For example, the absence of structured support and informal community led Black women in medical fields to use social media as a forum to heal from shared experiences related to the intersections of race and gender identity and to speak out against injustice (West-Livingston et al., 2021).

Start off by picking the low-hanging fruit and join existing social media spaces. For example, Facebook groups, Instagram, and Twitter are current spaces for sharing news information and opportunities. Even if you are not big on having a regularly updated profile, you should join the spaces that align with your career goals and values for these purposes. There are many options available that not only align with our professional identities but break down into the most salient aspects of our identities. For example, Binders Full of Women of Color (WOC) is a very active *closed group* for women academics identifying as BIPOC (Black, Indigenous, people of color), where opportunities, personal stories of struggle, questions, or advice-seeking posts are shared. In the Black/African American Scholars Facebook group,

I connected with a Dutch student seeking a psychology researcher with expertise in hip hop for her dissertation committee, and I was connected to another Facebook group for Black women runners by a member sharing one of her safe spaces for unwinding after leaving campus (Black Girls RUN!). Just identifying these spaces will be a great first community-cultivation step you can take. While I occasionally engage in these spaces, more often I find comfort in reading the words of the communities' posts and knowing that I can reach out in these spaces for professional feedback when needed.

While these kinds of spaces will provide an established community, is not enough for us to go to or remain as observers in established groups. We as feminist scholars need to put ourselves out for a couple of reasons. First, social media is now the most common way students, media agencies, and nonacademics find us. Second, beyond just a presence, these tools offer elements such as the construction of a personal profile and interactivity with peers along with specific tools for academic requisites, such as uploading and tagging articles and tracking citations (Jordan & Weller, 2015; Melvin & Chan, 2018). Several studies have noted that academics use social media searches in evaluations of colleagues and mentoring activities and to find research partners (Gruzd et al., 2011; Luc et al., 2018; Meishar-Tal & Pieterse, 2017; Thelwall & Kousha, 2014; Van Noorden, 2014). One way you can initiate connections is through writing policy briefs, op-eds, or blogs. These types of public scholarship and dissemination get your work out to a wider audience and will put you on the radar of those who have shared interests. It can also open the doors to more opportunities as this kind of scholarship often gets the attention of media agencies and other key power brokers. Further, the emergence of marginalized voices in these ways allows for the construction of alternative narratives and creation of safe spaces for hidden allies (Clark-Parsons, 2017; Pruchniewska, 2019). Thus, networking via social media builds connections and is increasingly the primary mode for communicating our individual research identities when engaging in networking.

Without question, there are several risks related to having an online presence if you are identified as a member of a marginalized group and engaged in or present support for social justice–informed research (e.g., Burns, 2017; Emejulu, 2011; Kamola, 2019; West-Livingston et al., 2021). However, it is critical that feminist scholars carve out and take active ownership of spaces across social media platforms. At the most basic level, you should have a website that is representational of yourself. My institution has so far allowed me to the freedom to design and maintain my faculty site; it clearly reflects who I am as a scholar. The software I use to maintain my site is included in my grants as I use the same program to develop research project websites. Similarly, start-up funds and internal awards will also readily cover this expense. Otherwise, figure out the free options on campus or off campus.

I also created a personal site that serves to connect with nonacademic individuals; the content in that space is structured to prioritize the information that my community collaborators and media inquirers would prioritize. Other members of my scholar squad have active Twitter and Instagram accounts that provide them opportunities to send short updates about their personal achievements and/or professional productivity on a regular basis. During this period of increased social injustices, including attacks on academic freedom, disinformation about critical race theory and backlashes against movements like Black Lives Matter, having regular and easy access to colleagues' voices in these technologically mediated spaces is empowering and comforting (Luc et al., 2018; West-Livingston et al., 2021). We must hold firm in maintaining our presence and support across these platforms. This may require 1 hour a week of work—but remember it is about yourself and your career identity. So, this should be a time of self-celebration and not framed as a burden. If it becomes one, step back and restart when you are ready to put yourself out there again.

Maintain the Momentum

We often get excited when we connect with others who share our interests and research values as feminists; it is like connecting with a long-lost friend after wandering around a cold, unwelcoming city. Often, we'll sit over coffee at a conference for hours, or chat on Zoom about great ideas. But life happens, and it is not uncommon that a strong connection becomes weaker as we move back into our regular work grinds. Therefore, we must be very deliberate in not only cultivating relationships but maintaining them (Deschner et al., 2020; Emejulu, 2011; Wilson et al., 2010). Here are three basic steps that will help you keep building your bonds.

After you have made that initial contact, be clear on your commitment to stay connected—document it! This is not simply to record what you've started to cultivate; be concrete on your next follow-up steps. Write down what you talked about, what was promised, and any technical tips that were shared. Also, be sure to note what you owe to that person and what they owe you, be it an article, connection to another scholar, or even a recipe. Keeping track of these items will make the next steps easy and show your desire to invest in this new relationship.

Next, do the short-term follow-up. Look back at that initial contact list and follow through. Continuing to stay in contact will take some initial effort but will come naturally once you embed them into your daily workspaces. For example, add all their information to your contact sites, bookmark their websites, and visit their research papers. Keep track of their work by following their ResearchGate or Academia.edu pages. Request Google notifications of their newest publications. Friend them on Facebook and Twitter. You'll be more inclined to reach out when things pop up from or about them (Clark-Parsons, 2017; Huang & Liu, 2017; Pruchniewska, 2019). These informal opportunities to communicate with one another will, in turn, contribute to the growth of this community connection. If you are looking for longer term in-depth interactions (e.g., writing a paper or developing a grant), you may want to schedule monthly meetings. These can be simple 30-minute check-ins that are follow-ups of email conversations. Using active engagement approaches (talking) alongside efficiency efforts (Google Docs, email messaging) will serve to increase productivity and human connections.

Finally, don't sit back and relax once you get your networking rhythm. Remember, networking is an ongoing process. Just as your friendships change when you move through your various life stages, so should your relationships at work. Embrace that this process will involve expanding and shedding network members as your life, values, and goals change. This is particularly important as you move up the academic ladder because your knowledge base and power will shift. Think back to an initial goal of reimagining networking as a process of cultivating a community. A feminist position would further assert that our shared goal is the expansion and maintenance of supportive spaces within and around our work environment (Agosto et al., 2016; Deschner et al., 2020; Tsouroufli, 2012; Wilson et al., 2010). Thus, once you are connected, be deliberate in your efforts to connect those who need to be introduced to other individuals or a community like yours. Reach out to those who are sitting on the sidelines or hiding behind the margins. Help them learn the language and strategies for successful feminist networking. This will ensure that our invisible colleges and scholar squad members continue to take up space for change in academia.

Concluding Thoughts

It is critical that networking is viewed as an ongoing professional and personal activity. Although there is greater emphasis on deliberate networking in the early stages of our careers, it is essential that we continue cultivating our networks and relationships over the long-term. Networking needs and goals will change according to the stage of your career, organizational location, and availability of institutional resources (Agosto et al., 2016; Deschner et al., 2020; Ricks, 2015). This means it is critical that you revisit these strategies throughout your career journey. Just as your career trajectory changes, so should your work on expanding your communities. Additionally, embrace yourself throughout this community cultivation process. Be clear on what you have, what you need, and your goals for the collaboration. As you move through your career, prioritize all aspects of your life such as longer term career goals, time, work–life mix, and measures of productivity. How you do this will be greatly influenced by those around you, so you need to make sure that you have healthy and honest sounding boards that value you as a whole person, not just a career colleague.

Feminist networking is not about reinventing the wheel, but redefining what it means to cultivate a supportive community. Thus, taking this journey is not only about improving things for ourselves, but creating a movement centering equity across academic spaces. By disrupting traditional frameworks of networking, we can increase the number of individuals that embrace these same values while shifting cultural norms around engagement and interpersonal relationships across our professional contexts.

References

Agosto, V., Karanxha, Z., Unterreiner, A., Cobb-Roberts, D., Esnard, T., Wu, K., & Beck, M. (2016). Running bamboo: A mentoring network of women intending to thrive in academia. *NASPA Journal About Women in Higher Education, 9*(1), 74–89.

Anthym, M., & Tuitt, F. (2019). When the levees break: The cost of vicarious trauma, microaggressions and emotional labor for Black administrators and faculty engaging in race work at traditionally White institutions. *International Journal of Qualitative Studies in Education, 32*(9), 1072–1093. http://dx.doi.org/10.1080/09518398.2019.1645907

Barber, P. H., Hayes, T. B., Johnson, T. L., & Márquez-Magaña, L. (2020). Systemic racism in higher education. *Science, 369*(6510), 1440–1441.

Burns, J. (2019, March 19). Black women are besieged on social media, and White apathy damns us all. *Forbes*. https://www.forbes.com/sites/janetwburns/2017/12/27/black-women-are-besieged-on-social-media-and-white-apathy-damns-us-all/?sh=35bf32b4423e

Castillo-Montoya, M., Hunter, T., Moore, W. C., & Sulé, T. (2022). Why the caged bird sings in the academy: A decolonial collaborative autoethnography of African American and Puerto Rican faculty and staff in higher education. *Journal of Diversity in Higher Education*. Advance online publication. https://doi.org/10.1037/dhe0000395

Clark-Parsons, R. (2017). Building a digital girl army: The cultivation of feminist safe spaces online. *New Media & Society, 20*(6), 2125–2144. https://doi.org/10.1177/1461444817731919

Cole, E. R. (2009). Intersectionality and research in psychology. *American Psychologist, 64*(3), 170–180. https://doi.org/10.1037/a0014564.

Davis, D. J., & Warfield, M. (2011). The importance of networking in the academic and professional experiences of racial minority students in the USA. *Educational Research and Evaluation, 17*(2), 97–113. https://doi.org/10.1080/13803611.2011.597113

Davis, T., Greer, T., Sisco, S., & Collins, J. (2020). "Reclaiming my time" amid organizational change: A dialectical approach to support the thriving and career development for faculty at the margins. *Advances in Developing Human Resources, 22*(1), 23–40.

Deschner, C. J., Dorion, L., & Salvatori, L. (2020). Prefiguring a feminist academia: A multi-vocal autoethnography on the creation of a feminist space in a neoliberal university. *Society and Business Review, 15*(4), 325–347. https://doi.org/10.1108/sbr-06-2019-0084

Emejulu, A. (2011). Re-theorizing feminist community development: Towards a radical democratic citizenship. *Community Development Journal, 46*(3), 378–390.

Fleming, G. M., Simmons, J. H., Xu, M., Gesell, S. B., Brown, R. F., Cutrer, W. B., Gigante, J., & Cooper, W. O. (2015). A facilitated peer mentoring program for junior faculty to promote professional development and peer networking. *Academic Medicine: Journal of the Association of American Medical Colleges, 90*(6), 819–826.

hooks, b. (1984). *Feminist theory: From margin to center.* South End Press.

hooks, b. (2000). *Feminist theory: From margin to center* (2nd ed.). South End Press.

Hoppe, T. A., Litovitz, A., Willis, K. A., Meseroll, R. A., Perkins, M. J., Hutchins, B. I., Davis, A. F., Lauer, M. S., Valantine, H. A., Anderson, J. M., & Santangelo, G. M. (2019). Topic choice contributes to the lower rate of NIH Awards to African American/Black scientists. *Science Advances, 5*(10). https://doi.org/10.1126/sciadv.aaw7238

Huang, L. V., & Liu, P. L. (2017). Ties that work: Investigating the relationships among coworker connections, work-related Facebook utility, online social capital, and employee outcomes. *Computers in Human Behavior, 72*, 512–524.

Jordan, K., & Weller, M. (2018). Communication, collaboration, and identity: Factor analysis of academics' perceptions of online networking. *Research in Learning Technology, 26*. https://doi.org/10.25304/rlt.v26.2013

Kamola, I. (2019). Dear administrators: To protect your faculty from right-wing attacks, follow the money. *Journal of Academic Freedom, 10*. Retrieved from https://www.aaup.org/reports-publications/journal-academic-freedom/volume-10

Kiefer, J. C. (2011). Tips for success: Networking is not a bad word. *Developmental Dynamics, 240*(11), 2597–2599. https://doi.org/10.1002/dvdy.22740

Knight, D., Duncan, L., Morris, J., & Davidson, D. (2013). *Research mentoring experiences of racial/ethnic minority professional psychology doctoral students* [Data set]. PsycEXTRA. https://doi.org/10.1037/e598102013-001

Kozlowski, D., Larivière, V., Sugimoto, C. R., & Monroe-White, T. (2022). Intersectional inequalities in science. *Proceedings of the National Academy of Sciences, 119*(2). https://doi.org/10.1073/pnas.2113067119

Lauer, M. S., & Roychowdhury, D. (2021). Inequalities in the distribution of National Institutes of Health Research Project Grant funding. *ELife.* https://doi.org/10.7554/elife.71712.sa2

Luc, J., Stamp, N. L., & Antonoff, M. B. (2018). Social media in the mentorship and networking of physicians: Important role for women in surgical specialties. *American Journal of Surgery, 215*(4), 752–760. https://doi.org/10.1016/j.amjsurg.2018.02.011

Matsick, J., Kruk, M., Oswald, F., & Palmer, L. (2021). Bridging feminist psychology and open science: Feminist tools and shared values inform best practices for science reform. *Psychology of Women Quarterly, 45*(4), 412–429.

Meishar-Tal, H., & Pieterse, E. (2017). Why do academics use academic social networking sites? *The International Review of Research in Open and Distributed Learning, 18*(1). https://doi.org/10.19173/irrodl.v18i1.2643

Melvin, L., & Chan, T. (2014). Using Twitter in clinical education and practice. *Journal of Graduate Medical Education, 6*(3), 581–582. https://doi.org/10.4300/jgme-d-14-00342.1

Pollack, J., Forster, W., Johnson, P., Coy, A., & Molden, D. (2015). Promotion- and prevention-focused networking and its consequences for entrepreneurial success. *Social Psychological and Personality Science, 6*(1), 3–12. http://dx.doi.org/10.1177/1948550614543030

Pruchniewska, U. (2019). "A group that's just women for women": Feminist affordances of private Facebook groups for professionals. *New Media & Society, 21*(6), 1362–1379.

Ricks, S. A. (2015). *Psychological tight spaces: One Black feminist scholar's journey into academia.* Library Partners Press.

Settles, I. H. (2020). Meaningful moments: How mentors and collaborators helped transform career challenges into opportunities. *Women & Therapy, 43*(1–2), 58–73.

Settles, I. H., Jones, M. K., Buchanan, N. T., & Dotson, K. (2021). Epistemic exclusion: Scholar(ly) devaluation that marginalizes faculty of color. *Journal of Diversity in Higher Education, 14*(4), 493–507. http://dx.doi.org/10.1037/dhe0000174

Streeter J. (2014). Networking in academia. *EMBO Reports, 15*(11), 1109–1112.

Thelwall, M., & Kousha, K. (2014). Academia.edu: Social network or academic network? *Journal of the Association for Information Science and Technology, 65*(4), 721–731.

Tsouroufli, M. (2012). Breaking in and breaking out a medical school: Feminist academic interrupted? *Equality, Diversity and Inclusion: An International Journal, 31*(5/6), 467–483. https://doi.org/10.1108/02610151211235479

Van Noorden, R. (2014). Online collaboration: Scientists and the social network. *Nature, 512*(7513), 126–129.

West-Livingston, L. N., South, E. C., Mabins, S., & Landry, A. (2021). When screens become mirrors: Black Women in medicine find belonging through social media. *AEM Education and Training, 5*(S1), S98–101. https://doi.org/10.1002/aet2.10669

Wilson, R. J., Abram, F. Y., & Anderson, J. (2010). Exploring a feminist-based empowerment model of community building. *Qualitative Social Work, 9*(4), 519–535.

CHAPTER 15

Another Country
Thriving Through the Travels and Travails of Interdisciplinary Scholarship

- **Patrick R. Grzanka**
  University of Tennessee, Knoxville

- **Elizabeth R. Cole**
  University of Michigan

Interdisciplinarity is one of the most exciting, complex, and intellectually stimulating advances within the contemporary academy (Jacobs & Frickel, 2009). Being an interdisciplinary feminist scholar and managing a joint appoint between two disciplines (e.g., psychology and sociology), or even an interdiscipline (e.g., women's and gender studies), means linking important ideas and questions in a given discipline to broader conversations in ways that can tear down arbitrary academic boundaries and produce genuinely transformative knowledge. Doing interdisciplinary work, and having a joint appointment, can also mean learning and navigating two (or more) bodies of knowledge, two curricula, two sets of colleagues, two cultures and practices, and sometimes two different sets of criteria—both explicit and implicit—for excellence and success. Thus, choosing to take a joint appointment presents a challenge of how to use these positions to enrich our life and scholarship, and eventually to change the academy, without sacrificing our own productivity and well-being. Unfortunately, some early career scholars anticipate that the burden of these dual demands outweighs any possible benefit to be gained in terms of intellectual value and career rewards, leading them to avoid interdisciplinary work and joint appointments. In this chapter we offer some insight into what makes interdisciplinary work worthwhile and how to make joint appointments support you and your work, not deplete you.

We (Liz and Patrick) are both scholars who have spent our entire careers working in joint appointments and publishing across disciplinary boundaries, though we occupy different and overlapping social positions (Liz is a Black, biracial, straight woman and Patrick is a white queer man, both cisgender, able-bodied [for now], and tenured full professors, although we are of two different generations). We have come to think of our careers as protracted journeys across disciplinary spaces, almost like studying abroad or traveling to distant places in which we have had to learn new customs and languages through a process of immersion and translation. Just as traveling in another country makes you see new things when you return home, interdisciplinary travel can help us imagine ways that disciplines can be different. Making interdisciplinary careers is still a bit of a revolutionary act in our own "home" discipline of psychology and in the academy more broadly. Though these travels have undoubtedly introduced complexity and challenges in our careers that may not have been there if we had taken more established journeys to tenure, we also feel compelled to underscore the unquantifiable dividends of interdisciplinarity that we have both been so privileged to experience. Learning a new language in a country where you don't read or speak the dominant language can be alienating and isolating. It can be difficult and even traumatic at times. But we are hard pressed to think of a single person who would give up having learned how to communicate effectively, fluently in another country.[1] What follows in this chapter is our attempt to transform the dividends of those travels into practical advice for scholars embarking on similar journeys.

Liz

Although my PhD was in psychology, as a graduate student I began a major collaboration with a sociologist in communications studies. This project resulted in a coauthored monograph, not the type of publication that anyone would encourage a doctoral student in psychology to undertake. As a graduate student I took courses in social work and public policy and taught in Afro-American Studies and Women's Studies. Looking back, I think that everything that is novel or, frankly, important about my scholarship is directly related to what I learned from my colleagues and in my teaching beyond psychology, including my understanding of politics, history, social structure, and culture. Other disciplines provide deep, rich literatures to theorize and understand these contexts in sophisticated ways. My joint appointments facilitated these experiences and conversations. They also have provided three communities and cultures that offered different kinds of support, both intellectual and social. Throughout my career I have sometimes felt like I didn't belong in the social spaces of academia, and having a second department has been an important refuge.

---

1. Our title gestures toward James Baldwin's 1962 novel *Another Country*, which was notably composed during his travels from New York City to Paris and back; he ultimately completed it while writing in Istanbul.

Often, we speak of joint appointments as if they are one kind of position, but in fact they take different forms. At my first university joint appointments were rare. My joint status did not designate specific fractions of effort and was administered informally. Three key features facilitated my success in this arrangement: (a) my department chairs were excellent mentors devoted to my success, who had already established a friendly relationship prior to my arrival; (b) by chance my departments were located across the hall from each other, and this physical proximity further facilitated the chairs' communication and my movement between the two units; and (c) although the terms of the arrangement were only lightly defined, it was implicitly clear to me that my evaluations would be primarily in psychology, and this understanding provided important guidance about expectations.

I arrived at my second (and current) job with tenure, at a university where joint appointments were common, and procedures governing them were relatively well defined. My position was explicitly split evenly between two interdisciplinary units (Women's Studies and Afro-American and African Studies), which meant that both units were used to evaluating interdisciplinary work by scholars with joint appointments. I've been here for more than 20 years, although the configuration of my appointment has changed according to my interests and other responsibilities, including time spent in significant administrative roles. From this vantage point I know a lot about how to administer joint appointments well.

Patrick

Throughout my entire career my work has been interdisciplinary. I am trained in an interdisciplinary field (American studies); my first job was in an interdisciplinary unit with a primary teaching focus; and my current job is as a professor of psychology and chair of an interdisciplinary women, gender, and sexuality (WGS) studies program. I've had a complicated relationship to my own training and career path over the years, including quite a bit of internalized shame over not having a more traditional pedigree. Indeed, being terminally "undisciplined" has at times been a source of profound anxiety for me: I've been called too psychological for the sociologists, too empirical for the cultural studies folks, and—because I don't hold the PhD in it—flat out *not* a psychologist. I used to take all of these criticisms as mortal wounds and symbols of my perpetual inadequacy. Now, from a position of tenured full-professor privilege, I treat my wily academic upbringing as a badge of honor.

Part of the journey from shame to self-actualization has involved a nonlinear process of coming to understand how disciplinary insider status functions in disciplinary spaces, divesting from the anger and hurt I felt from being targeted by disciplinary boundary policing, finding support and mentorship from people both within and outside the academy, and developing a sense of self and purpose in my scholarship and work that is less dependent on validation from disciplinary-trained academics. I now know that when I'm experiencing boundary policing in action, it's not just in my head: There's an entire sociological concept—boundary work (Gieryn 1983)—designed to capture the heterogeneous ways scholars produce and reify disciplines, often in the interest of maintaining power in the name of "quality" (e.g., Liz and I discuss this in-depth in our paper about "bad psychology"; Grzanka & Cole, 2021; see also Lewis, 2021).

As we discuss throughout this chapter, not all interdisciplinary appointments are the same, and there is no one-size-fits-all approach to doing interdisciplinary work in contemporary academic institutions, many of which purport to support and value interdisciplinary work while actively and passively making interdisciplinary careers painful or impossible (Jacobs & Frickel, 2009). But one key thing I have learned about interdisciplinary careers is that it is generally far easier to have a disciplinary degree and then succeed in an interdisciplinary appointment rather than pursue a disciplinary appointment with an interdisciplinary degree. This is a harsh reality, but it is the truth.

A Strengths-Based Approach to Interdisciplinary Careers

Interdisciplinarily trained, inclined, and informed scholars come to their work with tremendous gifts and strengths, and joint appointments increase the probability that the contributions their scholarship makes can be understood and appreciated. This work of interdisciplinary scholars is critical because their presence—as teachers, scholars, and interlocutors engaging with colleagues' work—is also a contribution to the development of the fields in *both* departments. Most disciplines were created many years ago when universities operated differently, served different student bodies and engaged different communities and audiences and populations, and addressed different problems that were understood in different ways. In some ways these divisions don't serve our students or our scholarship today. The presence of interdisciplinary scholars helps the disciplines stretch and change.

However, the nature of interdisciplinary travels is that it can be difficult to master the nuances of theory, culture, methods, and norms in more than one discipline. The process of becoming fully acculturated into a disciplinary framework/epistemology/lexicon does not happen overnight, particularly when you are trying to do this across multiple fields—all the while just keeping your head above water in graduate school (Calarco, 2020)! It's next to impossible to speak the language of multiple disciplines (i.e., code-switch); understand the arbitrary and nuanced idiosyncrasies of disciplinary organizations, which are key to succeeding on the job market; and to publish manuscripts in a sufficient number of prominent disciplinary venues to maintain perceived legitimacy in more than one discipline at the same time. One of the unfair privileges of disciplinary work is typically having to know only one discipline's body of literature, which is an enormous feat in and of itself. The obstacles we've described thus far are also certainly germane to more traditionally trained scholars who may find themselves in interdisciplinary spaces for the first time while on the tenure track.

We understand a meaningful and rewarding career as an interdisciplinary scholar in a dual or interdisciplinary appointment is both a deeply personal and structural journey. In other words, it represents a personal and individual path that others cannot dictate, and which should ultimately be driven by one's scholarly goals and teaching interests: What audiences do you wish to speak to? What impacts—in the academy and beyond—do you aspire to make? The choice may also be influenced by your own values and your needs with regard to home, health, and happiness. For example, we find our work with students in WGS particularly rewarding and important because of their commitment to work for social justice. At the same time, it involves moving through and beyond institutional forces that should not be any one individual's responsibility to change. In our own travels down this sometimes complicated, but almost always rewarding, vocational road we have made some observations about how to progress while enjoying the trip. Though our recommendations are based on our experiences in psychology as one of our core disciplines, we expect these strategies and recommendations can apply to feminist scholars in a variety of fields as well.

Preparing for an Interdisciplinary Job

Our advice for junior faculty begins in the late graduate school phase, particularly when folks are first on the job market. Articulate your skills and interests in terms that are legible to those who are doing the hiring. An important value of interdisciplinary work is the way it tends to break down traditional disciplinary concepts, but this can be extremely confusing to scholars who are more firmly entrenched in the culture and worldview of particular disciplines. Make sure you can be *heard* by clarifying your teaching and research skills in terms of courses that are traditionally taught in the discipline to which you are applying. For example, if you are a feminist scholar of emotions applying to a joint appointment with psychology and women's and gender studies, you might explain that you are prepared to teach both a basic course in emotions as well as psychology of gender (i.e., service courses), and could also offer upper level electives in gender and emotion. Be prepared to explain what feminists have contributed to understanding key constructs in psychology; likewise, you should be prepared to explain the value of psychological methods to feminist, queer, and trans scholars in the humanities who may be skeptical of quantification broadly (Grzanka, 2019), not to mention psychology's epistemic assumptions and legacy of positivism. (We'll share a little secret: Most critical humanities scholars are deeply skeptical of the quantitative empirical social sciences.)

Your job talk should aim to engage multiple audiences by inviting people into the conversation. Define your key terms, even ones that you assume some in the audience take for granted. Your ability to explain these concepts well can show that you are a good teacher! For example, how we present tables and graphs often presumes fluency with statistical analyses. Be prepared to narrate your findings for people who are most familiar with looking at the graphical representation of data in newspapers like *The New York Times*. A central part of being clear is speaking across disciplinary boundaries, particularly when communicating with those who are trained in vastly different methods and languages. The prescriptions of psychological job talks, for example, can be extremely alienating to nonpsychologists, and they can confuse or even irritate the uninitiated, including those who may be suspicious of psychology's relevance or contributions to feminism, social justice, and so forth. All of this advice also applies to presentations you make at interdisciplinary conferences.

Because you ideally need to understand who holds the keys to your future in any institution, try to get to know your audience before you come to campus. For example, it's essential to know which unit is going to have the most influence in the hiring and tenure/promotion process. If you will be joining the ranks of others who have held joint positions or interdisciplinary appointments at your institution, understanding the experiences of these more senior scholars, particularly those who have successfully been promoted and tenured, is invaluable. Before accepting an offer, ask them to chat with you. Most will be excited to share their experiences with junior scholars and may be forthright about obstacles you should expect on the road to tenure and promotion. This is information you won't glean from a university website. The same idea applies once you start your position. You should have as robust an understanding as possible of which unit(s) will play the largest role in decision-making around your job, including what classes you teach, when you will be eligible for any pre- or post-tenure research leaves, and what kinds of service obligations you will expected to perform prior to your first promotion.

Making the Interdisciplinary Job Work

Once you start a position, the most important issue, particularly in joint appointments, is understanding the metrics and expectations for success (for types of scholarship, outlets for publication, teaching expectations, service, and processes for evaluation). This demands communication between department chairs. Navigating joint appointments will often mean that junior scholars need to "manage up," asking for clarification and making sure each chair has information from the other department. Ask for transparency if it is not provided to you: "Dear _____: As I prepare for my annual review in both units, I am hoping you can provide me with specific information about how my dual obligations will be treated by both units in terms of teaching and service, in particular. I want to make sure I am representing my work accurately to both units and am setting myself up for a transparent and fair evaluation. I appreciate your help and support in this process." You have a right to this information, and there's no shame in not knowing (you can be sure that some of your peers don't know either). To avoid burdening jointly appointed faculty with disproportionate service, one model is for junior faculty to do service to only one department at a time, alternating years. If this sounds attractive to you, ask your chairs whether it is possible. Don't assume that usual practices can't be changed. This kind of self-advocacy can take some effort and skill, but it's worth it to cultivate it.

Early on, think about assembling your team. Don't wait to identify potential mentors in your institution who have successfully negotiated similar appointments; there are advantages to having mentors both within your unit(s) and outside your unit(s). Ideally, you will have both. Mentors within your unit(s) will be able to offer insider knowledge that others will not have. They have been through many of the same processes you are currently navigating and will help you avoid mistakes that waste time and can be demoralizing, such as submitting a paper to a journal with a notoriously bad or slow editorial process or agreeing to serve on a committee that is poorly managed. On the other hand, mentors outside your unit(s) will have institutional knowledge that may be limited within your unit(s), and they may help you see the structure of the university in ways that your direct colleagues cannot. Join multidisciplinary mentoring groups at your university if they exist; attend campus-wide social events when you have the emotional bandwidth; and reach out to faculty whose work you admire for lunch and coffees, or ask them to attend lectures with you. As a junior faculty member on campus, your college/university colleagues are generally quite invested in retaining talented junior faculty (you!) and are excited to make connections and share advice. Granted, this will come easier for extroverts like Patrick than it will for introverts like Liz. If you're more the latter, try setting yourself a modest goal like making one contact each month. Further, it's helpful to have confidants outside of your unit(s) whom you can bounce ideas off, especially when you're trying to solve a complex problem, whether it is intellectual, bureaucratic, or political.

Finally, identify mentors outside your university whose career trajectory is one that you aspire to; this is good advice for anyone but is especially important for interdisciplinary scholars who may be mold breaking (i.e., a "unicorn") or dissimilar from virtually all/most of your peers. For example, when Patrick was on the job market, he noticed that Liz was attending the same interdisciplinary conference and he was giving a talk about intersectionality that spoke directly to her work. He reached out to her while en route to the conference, and Liz enthusiastically responded to the idea of meeting up, which Patrick initiated over email: "I am so thrilled that you'll be at this meeting. I know your schedule is likely already full, but I was wondering if you'd have any time for coffee while we're both at the conference, because I would so appreciate your feedback on this new paper …" Though all emails won't result in decade-plus friendships (and collaborations), this type of outreach can produce career-changing interactions—but they won't happen if you don't initiate the contact. (Liz always asks junior scholars at conferences to send her their papers, and they rarely do.)

Patrick found Liz because of her papers, but another fruitful strategy for identifying potential outside mentors is to find five to 10 people whose careers you aspire to and study their CVs. CV scanning can sometimes result in a shame spiral, but that's not what we're talking about. Studying the CVs of your aspirational colleagues is a great way to figure out things that you may not have been taught in graduate school (we certainly weren't!), such as which conferences to attend; journals that are friendly to the kind of questions you ask and methods you use; awards to apply for; and funding agencies from which to consider pursuing grants. This is all the more important for interdisciplinary scholars because there is no direct path toward an interdisciplinary career. If you develop relationships with outside mentors, they may become strategic allies in job applications, as well as the tenure and promotion process. But Liz notes that sometimes the best allies do not make the best letter writers, so it can be useful to consult other senior mentors for any relevant feedback about the kind of recommendation/review someone generally offers (e.g., "I was just wondering what you thought of Patrick as a potential letter writer?"). (Liz and Patrick both routinely invoke the same person they would *never* ask for a letter!) On the other hand, be on the lookout for unlikely allies. We have seen many scholars make the unfortunate mistake of assuming people in your discipline will not be your ally or even champion based largely on subfield rivalries or prejudices developed in graduate school. For example, as assistant professors, Liz got great support from the clinically oriented faculty member in her unit, and Patrick's biggest champions were traditionally trained experimental social psychologists.

Feedback—about scholarship, teaching, and service—is central to academic life, both to improve the quality of our work and to share ideas, resources, and strategies. The ability to give and receive feedback is one of the most fundamental processes in the development of a scholarly identity. Acclimating to consistent feedback on your scholarship begins in graduate school, and interdisciplinary scholars may get even more critical feedback than traditionally trained disciplinary scholars for all the reasons we named, including the time it takes to learn multiple disciplinary cultures, languages, styles, idiosyncrasies, methods, and so on. You will receive lots of feedback during your career, both as a junior scholar and beyond, and sometimes it will be disappointing and sometimes it will sting (hard). Although it can be truly difficult, it's important to use feedback as an opportunity to improve your work, not as a referendum on the quality of your contributions. (We both confess to consigning important projects to the back of a file drawer—when those existed—for several years after a harsh review.)

But you should consider even challenging responses to your work deeply and understand that guidance aimed at achieving success within an unfair system need not be a sign of collusion with that system. At times, senior feminist scholars who have successfully navigated academia *and* who are extremely invested in you and your success will give you feedback that you may think is wrong. In some cases, it may ultimately not be the right feedback for you. Certainly, we have both decided against taking the advice of trusted advisors on occasion. But when dealing with supportive colleagues and good-faith actors, such as editors who want to help you improve your work, you should always work to find the value in the feedback you receive.

One easy way to deflect constructive criticism or dismiss feedback as unhelpful or even unsupportive is to decide that senior scholars are merely giving you this feedback because they have mastered the use of the proverbial master's tools (Lorde, 1984). In other words, it's easy to dismiss some forms of feedback—particularly when it's about meeting standards of a discipline or changing an approach or direction in the interest of getting tenure—as giving in to harmful forces you are committed to resisting. But to automatically reject feedback as rooted in complicity in systems of domination—for example, white supremacy, patriarchy, or the interests of the neoliberal university—may actually undermine your capacity to change the systems you want to resist (e.g., Zambrana, 2018). Learning the tools does not necessarily mean internalizing the most inegalitarian or oppressive elements of academia. A broad and deep network of feminist scholars in your corner whom you trust to give you supportive, smart, and critical feedback is one way to get good at navigating harmful systems so that you can ultimately help transform them.

Relatedly, chasing brilliant ideas that will transform disciplines takes time (Dill et al., 2009). As we have stressed, all junior scholars need to know what's expected of them to earn tenure. As an interdisciplinary and/or dual-appointment scholar, you especially should have a sense of what your departments' expectations are for your annual publications and scholarly output. For example, your personal intellectual priority may be to write a groundbreaking book that expands on your dissertation project. But if your tenure home is not a "book department" (i.e., a department that does not require or value books for tenure), then focusing exclusively on a book during your time as an assistant professor will undermine your tenure case. Instead, you may need to put the book into what we call the "B line" of your research program and prioritize articles in the "A line." The A line of any research program represents your primary contributions and primary effort; the B line is secondary and gets your attention when there are pauses in the A line, such as when A-line manuscripts are under review or you need to step away from that line of work to refresh your mind (or nourish your soul).

On the other hand, if you are in a department that expects two to three or more publications annually, the book project may need to be relegated to the C or D line. That doesn't mean abandoning a book project (Liz: Seriously, step away from the file drawer!). It just means making sure that you attend to the (typically faster) process of publishing articles while you are serving your probationary period (i.e., the period prior to tenure review). Conversely, if your tenure home is a book department—as so many WGS units are—articles should be your B line while your book occupies the privileged real estate of the A line. Remember, too, that a career is a long game, and those dazzling contributions will eventually materialize, but you have to get tenure in the meantime. For example, Liz published her (Patrick: "groundbreaking, revolutionary, capital-I Important!") *American Psychologist* paper on intersectionality 10 years after getting tenure. And though Patrick published two edited books before getting tenure, he deferred finishing the extremely time-consuming monograph book project until after tenure *and* promotion to full professor.

It's never too early to think about scholars whom you might choose to write tenure letters for you. Even the 1st year on the tenure track is not too early to begin being strategic about who will be evaluating your tenure portfolio. Letters evaluating your scholarship written by faculty outside your university are often the most heavily weighted elements of your tenure portfolio, particularly at research universities. Some colleges and universities allow faculty to recommend external reviewers who are qualified to write on their behalf. Nevertheless, it is essential that you understand your department and school's bylaws and regulations governing this process. Typically, letter writers should be people with whom you have never collaborated (i.e., published), though you may know them as professional acquaintances or have served on panels together. (Although Liz and Patrick met 12 years ago, we didn't write together until recently for exactly this reason!) Talk to department leadership about the expectations not only for the kinds of institutions (i.e., perceived prestige, Carnegie designation [e.g., R1]) from which your letters can come, but also the representation of disciplines among your letter writers. Cultivating professional relationships with possible letter writers can happen at conferences and other professional meetings, but another useful way to get to know potential evaluators is by inviting them to your campus to speak in departmental colloquia, for example, and by accepting invitations to do the same. Campus visits like these are great opportunities to talk with respected senior colleagues (i.e., potential external letter writers) about exactly the kinds of things about which we have suggested you be strategic: where to publish, how to navigate obstacles in the peer review process, balancing interdisciplinary demands on your time, and so forth.

In Patrick's appointment, which is fully in psychology despite service obligations to WGS, only other psychology faculty would vote on his tenure and promotion. In this case, one might assume that only psychologists would be preferred for external reviews. But Patrick's department head wanted interdisciplinary representation in the letter writers to better speak to the impact of his work in other fields. This is not always the case, however, and you do not want to be surprised. The expectations of those who will vote on your tenure case (i.e., your colleagues) should inform the questions of audience we referenced, such as where you are publishing your work. For example, it may be difficult for an external reviewer to speak favorably of your scholarly impact if you have not published in journals that are considered essential or well regarded in your field. On the other hand, often the flagship disciplinary journals are reluctant to publish interdisciplinary work; the right external reviewers can help explain how other journals are regarded and why they are the appropriate venues for your scholarship.

The question of where to publish sometimes raises uncomfortable questions about pressures to meet norms or standards with which you do not agree and/or do not feel consistent with who you are as a scholar and a person. We are not encouraging you to "sell out" or be disingenuous; it's also not advisable to contort yourself into a scholar you are not. Such a strategy is deeply unsustainable and painful. We are suggesting that in order to create the spaces you want to do creative and even transgressive work, you must clearly identify the hurdles to overcome and make sure you have a path to do so. Collaborations are fantastic ways to do this. By partnering with people who have had success placing articles in journals you might aspire to, you increase your chances by learning from their successes and mistakes. In fields where coauthorship is less common (e.g., history, literature), reaching out to scholars who have published similar or relevant scholarship in your aspirational venues is another way to assess critical factors that may help you balance your multidisciplinary obligations and chart a path to tenure: What was the peer review process like at that journal? How long did it take from submission to publication? Were the reviews constructive?

Disciplines have idiosyncrasies that are not always immediately apparent, even to sophisticated scholars (like you!) who already have spent years in academia. Different disciplinary cultures require different strategies, and these cultures might vary widely even between departments/programs in the same discipline. In a huge psychology department (like the ones we work in), attendance at brown-bag or colloquium lectures is not necessarily going to even be noticed and so might not be the best use of your time, particularly when the speaker or topic is not remotely relevant. But in a smaller WGS unit with only a handful of faculty, attending program lectures may be an essential way for colleagues to see your commitment to the unit. Similar dynamics almost certainly apply to conferences. If your colleagues (and potential external letter writers) have an unwritten but nonetheless consequential expectation that your attendance is expected at specific meetings, you should know this early and start planning and budgeting accordingly. Assuming you do not have infinite funds or energy, it makes sense to think about where and when you need to be directing your limited sources to professional development.

Teaching is also an important part of the journey. Teaching expectations can vary widely between units. For example, one of your units may care deeply about teaching and expect stellar evaluations from peers and students prior to tenure; another may not care much about teaching at all until the post-tenure stage. In some departments, it's common for faculty to teach one course routinely or exclusively before applying for promotion, whereas others prefer to see a diversity of courses and modalities (i.e., lecture, seminar, online). Understanding these expectations and the values of your school or college will help you set realistic and attainable teaching goals while balancing research and service demands, which may similarly vary widely. Patrick observed no fewer than seven colleagues' courses in his 1st year on the job; visiting others' courses, particularly those of recently tenured faculty members', is a great way to get a sense of teaching expectations.

At times, navigating these diverse demands can be stressful, unsettling, and ultimately alienating from the joys of teaching. Struggles in the classroom can completely derail an otherwise productive and joyful semester. Accordingly, within-unit mentors are essential for anticipating and handling pedagogical issues that are inevitable when teaching in multiple campus units.

Mentors (including peer mentors) can help you avoid mistakes that might otherwise feel inevitable and to increase your confidence when commanding authority with students, particularly those students who might be inclined to challenge your authority or expertise. Fortunately, there are outstanding resources for developing critical feminist pedagogy from interdisciplinary luminaries in our field, such as Kim Case (2013, 2017), Mary Kite (Kite et al., 2021), and Wendy Williams. And if there is a teaching center on your campus, don't hesitate to seek their support. You will eventually write a teaching statement for your tenure portfolio, and your investment of effort to improve your teaching will be a key part of the narrative.

On the Dividends of Interdisciplinary Travel

The focus of this chapter was on the very tangible barriers that institutions of higher education present to interdisciplinary and dual-appointment faculty members. We have provided advice to early career scholars that we have learned on our journeys from graduate students to full professors. We have stressed the ways these institutions impede the very kinds of transformative scholars and visionary concepts they claim to (want to) cultivate. But this is not the only part of an interdisciplinary scholar's journey, and the challenges we faced were not the only part of our respective stories. We have been successful by traditional academic metrics, made wonderful friends, and done work that brings us joy and fulfillment. We would be remiss to conclude without emphasizing the very tangible benefits of our interdisciplinary careers. For us, interdisciplinary travel has meant having not one but many homes, which comes with the kind of support from diverse networks of scholars and collaborators that have increased our resilience to the challenges of academic life and have enriched both our scholarship and our fulfillment in our careers. Just as home can be complicated, we have not romanticized the difficulties that accompany interdisciplinarity. Nonetheless, to return to our opening metaphor, having traversed so many discourses has brought us both stamps in our intellectual passports without which we cannot imagine doing the work we do today.

References

Baldwin, J. (1962/1992). *Another country* (5th ed.). Vintage. (Original work published 1962)

Calarco, J. M. (2020). *A field guide to graduate school: Uncovering the hidden curriculum*. Princeton University Press.

Case, K. A. (Ed.) (2013). *Deconstructing privilege: Teaching and learning as allies in the classroom*. Routledge.

Case, K. A. (2017). *Intersectional pedagogy: Complicating identity and social justice*. Routledge.

Cole, E. R. (2009). Intersectionality and research in psychology. *American Psychologist*, *64*(3), 170–180. https://doi-org.proxy.lib.umich.edu/10.1037/a0014564

Dill, B. T., & Zambrana, R. E., & McLaughlin, A. E. (2009). Transforming the campus through institutions, collaboration, and mentoring. In B. T. Dill & R. E. Zambrana (Eds.), *Emerging intersections: Race, class, and gender in theory, policy, and practice* (pp. 253–273). Rutgers University Press. https://doi.org/10.36019/9780813546513-013

Gieryn, T. (1983). Boundary-work and the demarcation of science from non-science: Strains and interests in professional ideologies of scientists. *American Sociological Review*, *48*(6), 781–795. https://doi.org/10.2307/2095325

Grzanka, P. R. (2019). Queer survey research and the ontological dimensions of heterosexism. In A. Ghaziani & M. Brim (Eds.), *Imagining queer methods* (pp. 84–102). NYU Press.

Grzanka, P. R., & Cole, E. R. (2021). An argument for bad psychology: Disciplinary disruption, public engagement, and social transformation. *American Psychologist*, *76*(8), 1334–1345. https://doi.org/10.1037/amp0000853

Jacobs, J. A., & Frickel, S. (2009). Interdisciplinarity: A critical assessment. *Annual Review of Sociology*, *35*, 43–65. https://doi.org/10.1146/annurev-soc-070308-115954

Kite, M. E., Case, K. A., & Williams, W. R. (Eds.) (2021). *Navigating difficult moments in teaching diversity and social justice*. APA.

Lewis, N. A., Jr. (2021). What counts as good science? How the battle for methodological legitimacy affects public psychology. *American Psychologist*, *76*(8), 1323–1333. https://doi.org/10.1037/amp0000870

Lorde, A. (1984/2007). *Sister outsider*: *Essays and speeches*. Crossing Press. (Original work published 1984)

Zambrana, R. E. (2018). *Toxic ivory towers: The consequences of work stress on underrepresented minority faculty*. Rutgers University Press.

CHAPTER 16

That Tenured Feeling of "What Now?"
Recalibration, Power, and Focus

- **Asia Eaton**
  Florida International University

- **Kim A. Case**
  Virginia Commonwealth University

You did it. You persevered—and more. You defied the odds by earning the highest degree available in your discipline, again when you secured a tenure-track job, and again by performing so well in that position that you earned a higher level of job security than can be found in most fields of work. You have inspired and supported students, some of whom consider their lives better for having known you. You have contributed to the scientific literature, advancing what we know about and can do to create social justice. You developed and grew professional connections that will continue to bear fruit. You contributed your expertise, insight, and leadership to service commitments that built and strengthened structures and processes you care about. You devoted years of your life on earth to this pursuit and sacrificed in ways beyond number. If you are a member of any marginalized or underrepresented communities in academia (e.g., a woman of color, a queer person), you survived additional challenges and systemic barriers to blaze a trail your ancestors are surely proud of and that more junior scholars will benefit from.

The way you construct your personal and professional life from here on out will be mostly measured against your own standards, not external ones. The character of your work can now take shape to fit your goals. In light of this, the suggestions and thoughts we offer on immediate post-tenure life are free for you to use as fits your career plan. In the following sections, we suggest you first and foremost take time to celebrate and relax, then use your power to speak up for more vulnerable individuals within and outside the academic system. Once you have gained stability, energy, and voice, you can recalibrate and refocus your efforts on what you are most passionate about. Finally, we suggest you return your focus to your career goals, including promotion to professor (for details on this goal, see Chapter 17, this volume).

Our Intersectional Social Locations

We would like to describe our social locations and scholarly backgrounds to frame our experience with and approach to post-tenure issues. I (Asia) am a white, heterosexual, cisgender, single mother with class privilege. I am a feminist social psychologist at an R1 Hispanic-serving public institution in Miami, Florida, where I have been since my post-doc. My lab studies how gender intersects with identities such as race, class, and sexual orientation to affect individuals' access to and experience with power. Most of my scholarly efforts these days are dedicated to the mentorship of graduate students in community-partnered social justice research.

I (Kim) am privileged as a white, heterosexual, able-bodied, cisgender, upper middle-class citizen of the United States from birth, and English is my first language. As a working-class (culturally and psychologically) woman from East Tennessee (Case, 2017; Rios & Case, 2020), I also face classism, sexism, and marginalization as a religious minority. Most of my career thus far was spent serving first-generation students of color at a Hispanic-serving state teaching university in Texas. In my current position as an academic administrator at an R1 state university in Virginia, I now provide faculty development full-time. My current scholarship explores effective social justice and antiracist pedagogies, ally development and the psychology of whiteness, and faculty development programs to promote equity.

Celebrate and Relax

In our experience, academics rarely celebrate their accomplishments. There are myriad reasons for this, which may be compounded for feminist scholars. First, many academic pursuits are long-term, requiring multiple years of dedication, revision, and resiliency. When we finally complete the task at hand, it can feel a bit anticlimactic. Achieving tenure may be the archetypal example of this, given that it represents a lifetime of work and a year-long vetting process. Academic culture has also become increasingly fast-paced, short-sighted, and demanding (Mountz et al., 2015; Stengers, 2018). Each accomplishment demands another, with no end in sight.

In addition, for feminist scholars, drawing attention to your accomplishments may seem to clash with social prescriptions, specifically that women, and others from marginalized backgrounds, shouldn't self-promote (e.g., Moss-Racusin & Rudman, 2010; Smith & Huntoon, 2013). We, as feminists, should devise creative ways to promote feminist work, including amplification of each other's work (Chapter 14, this volume). Feminist scholars may also engage in collaborative, community-partnered, and service-oriented work that we feel less personal ownership over (e.g., Hill et al., 2000).

We suggest that in spite of these hesitations you make the time to officially celebrate this milestone. What this means is, of course, unique to each individual. Perhaps you have been wanting to travel, spend time with loved ones, or enjoy some time alone. Or maybe you would like to purchase a treasured item, throw a party, or complete a bucket list experience. Take some time to thoroughly consider what would give you joy and a feeling of accomplishment. Remember, too, that celebrating tenure does not have to be a one-time event. It can be a commitment to an old or new hobby you didn't previously have time for. It can be changing how you interact with family members, students, or friends. It can take the form of a year-long decision to try something new. For me (Kim), this meant finding and joining an Appalachian clogging dance team after 6 years of working far too many hours. I had been a clogger in middle school, and returning to this love of dance became my strongest stress relief, coping mechanism, and pure joy for the next 10 years.

Whatever method(s) of celebration you adopt, we also suggest that you intentionally take time to relax and fall back from the front lines of work. You're safe now. Take a chunk of time off from the hopefully not-too-frantic pace at which you were working. When your high-achieving mind wanders toward anxiety about becoming professor, remind yourself that you are relaxing, and it is your right and your job to table that concern for the time being. You can even put a note in your calendar reading "now turn to the next stage of promotion." We suggest that you aim to submit for promotion to full no more than 6–10 years post-tenure.

Lean Into Your Power

You may not feel like you have much power in your university or college. After all, you likely experienced isolation and marginalization in connection to your teaching and scholarship as a feminist. For many readers, your very presence in the academy, just being who you are in your particular social locations, caused a disruption to the white middle-/upper-class patriarchal culture. At the same time, you succeeded in meeting the criteria for tenure and promotion at your institution, no matter how challenging the journey or faulty the criteria. Your university has officially accorded you a substantial level of power and status. With that new title comes job stability, financial benefit, and power you can use to advance your feminist social justice goals (e.g., establishing new departmental criteria for tenure). Your voice counts in a new way. Using your feminist intersectional perspective, we call on you to intentionally use your power and privilege to further advance social justice.

Your Justice Work as a Tenured Feminist Scholar

In my (Kim's) group coaching for midcareer academics, I urge social justice faculty to "embrace your inner Lizzo!" The Lizzo-focused module is all about how much we critique and diminish ourselves—just as the systems have taught us to do. What if you embraced all the unapologetic confidence and vulnerability of Lizzo as a feminist scholar? What if you embodied your social justice values out loud? I (Kim) am here to tell you, if you do this, the right people in academia will arrive, support you, and carry you through when you need them. After years of having my confidence eroded by supposedly feminist but patriarchy-identified bullies in women's studies, I finally reclaimed my strength, expertise, and voice. Once I accepted that I could manage whatever the bullies threw at me, the academics who recognized my worth began showing up all around me. Yes, this requires vulnerability and feels scary. By sharing this, I hope you will remember that you are valued and reach out to your support systems.

Which Justice? Whose Justice?

To be clear, we assume and expect that all feminist scholars do and will pursue justice for women and girls, but also work well beyond the single-axis category of systemic sexism (Grzanka, 2018). As a label, "feminist" has been associated with "white feminist" (Signorella, 2020), a legitimate critique of the lack of racial justice within mainstream feminism and academic feminism (Aziz, 1992). Allow us to take a moment to clarify that feminist scholars must engage racial justice, intersectionality, and the full intricate web of oppressive systems. Your justice work as a feminist scholar must include actively disrupting systemic oppression based on sexuality, ability, gender identity, social class and income, race, ethnicity, nation of origin, language, documentation status, and religion (see Academics for Black Wellness and Survival; www.drkimcase.com). This is not an exhaustive list of coconstructed, intertwining, and intersectionally influential systems within the matrix of domination (Collins, 1990).

Advocate and Amplify

What does a tenured feminist scholar do to speak up for justice? There are some concrete behaviors we suggest for harnessing your power and privilege within the academy:

- Speak up. If you felt unsafe on the road to tenure and chose to remain silent on some issues close to your heart, you can begin to reclaim your voice. You can help speak up about social justice issues affecting undergraduate and graduate students, staff, and nontenure-track and untenured faculty. For example, the lack of diverse representation within most academic decision-making bodies remains unacceptable. How can you use your voice to bring attention to and authentically include those who typically remain invisible as well as those directly impacted by the decisions?

- Advocate. Be that person on the committee who brings up equity issues and shares ideas for how to address them. Push for inclusion, whether it be curricular transformation, policy overhauls, or urgent task forces where major institutional change can happen.

- Amplify. Are you witnessing white people repeating the ideas of faculty or students of color without getting recognition? As soon as you can get in the queue to contribute to the meeting, amplify by crediting back to the original source to make it clear who the original idea generator was. If you err, be receptive when realizing that you failed to correctly attribute an idea to its creator.

- Sponsor. Use your privilege and influence to tell people about the great work being done by less powerful or visible scholars. Sponsors elevate the work of students and more junior scholars by centering and celebrating their voices and contributions. Invite nontenure-track or otherwise marginalized faculty onto your projects. Invite undergraduates and graduate students to present with you in spaces that can bring them positive visibility and connections.

- Organize. Noticed that your promotion and tenure policy does not value equity and inclusion pedagogy or scholarship? Notice that women in the department are carrying 70% of the service work? Do something about it. Organize for justice and align with more powerful people across the institution. Get organizing advice from feminist scholars outside your own university.

- Center the voices and perspectives of early career faculty, non-tenure-track faculty, invisible staff members, undergraduate and graduate students, and perhaps even community members. Be careful not to take over and speak for others without being educated and aware of your own role. Work to support these less powerful groups to be "in the room" and speak for themselves.

- Keep learning. Every reader occupies an intersectional social location that includes one or more forms of privilege in the matrix of domination (Case, 2013; Collins, 1990). In your privileged social identity roles as an ally (accomplice, coconspirator), stay in tune to continuous learning. Reflection and awareness are essential to minimize the chances of harming the efforts and well-being of the marginalized group members. Your ally actions should not burden marginalized group members with more work or the emotional labor of helping you manage your ally journey.

- Find ways to sustain your justice work by curating your own social support network to avoid burnout.

Curate Your Service

More than ever, you have the power to intentionally select your service efforts. Specifically, we recommend that your service work moving forward be values driven (Chapter 13, this volume) instead of obligatory. We suggest you opt out of voluntary service that doesn't have personal meaning, doesn't benefit your career, or doesn't benefit the field of feminist psychology. You now have the privilege of mentoring more junior feminist scholars, of working to diversify your department, or of creating feminist service that hadn't before existed.

For me (Asia), one of my priorities after getting tenure was to challenge predominant academic priorities and reward structures. Specifically, my goal was to raise awareness and support for public psychology—a model of psychology that requires research, teaching, and service activities engage with social problems, that academics involve the public in their work, that scholars be public facing, and that we rethink how we define psychology and psychological expertise (Eaton et al., 2021; Ozer et al., 2021). Part of this required that I do more national and public service, including writing op-eds, blog posts, doing expert witness work, and more. This passion project has begun to change local and national dialogue on what constitutes rigorous and legitimate psychological practice and research, and it gave me the local and national recognition that my university appreciates in the promotion process.

Of course, intentionally curating your service assignments creates the question of who will perform the tasks we don't assign as much value to—the ones that don't align with our careers and professional ideology. As feminists, it is common to consider the extent to which our behavior might negatively impact more vulnerable people. To this, we offer two thoughts. First, are these essential tasks? Perhaps some of these service efforts can be abandoned without major consequence to vulnerable others. Second, for those tasks that are essential but not values driven, we nonetheless suggest that, at least for the time being, the person responsible for them be someone other than you.

Finally, the wise NiCole Buchanan made an additional argument in favor of declining low-value and/or high-cost professional responsibilities as a woman of color (Chapter 13, this volume). At the Association for Women in Psychology conference in 2016, she noted that if she continued to perform excessive service work for her unit, including service related to equity and inclusion, then they would never hire anyone else like her. In essence, overworking ourselves perpetuates the system of inequities. Give the units you serve the opportunity to experience their profound need for your perspective, expertise, and labor.

As you think about leaning into your new power as an associate professor, these questions might foster useful reflection:

- How does your own social identity, background, family culture, and ties to community impact how you might think about life after tenure?

- What does it mean for you to be a feminist leader with tenure and power?

- Where do you want to focus your power for justice and change: university, public policy, the broader discipline, community work, social justice teaching, and/or scholarship?

- Are you interested in public, translational, community-engaged scholarship and/or service?

- What if you chose to be your most radically authentic self, not just outside academia, but also within academia?

Recalibrate and Refocus

In the process of determining which responsibilities to let go of or decline, and finding your voice in speaking up for others, you will likely come up against a larger question: What exactly *do* you want to do, contribute, and move forward? You know your CV by now. Is this who you want to continue being, professionally speaking? Where does your passion lie? Where are you making the most traction? What are your long-term hopes and dreams? For many of us, the post-tenure process is a period of deep reflection on whether the efforts we undertook to get to this privileged place were (a) properly directed and (b) worth it. Beauboeuf-Lafontant et al. (2019) provide a fresh perspective on the post-tenure period as a unique intersection of your own agency and your institution's reward systems and opportunities.

Review how you spent your time and effort on the path to tenure, considering both the number and nature of your commitments. What topics have you been researching? What classes have you been teaching? How much time have you spent at conferences versus grading versus exploring new literature versus mentoring? Get in touch with what you want rather than what you have been told to want. Do you want to continue working at the same pace, with the same organizations, on the same topics, with the same collaborators? What about your work gets you excited to get out of bed in the morning, and how can you nurture that?

For me (Asia), my professional purpose and joy is found in mentoring graduate students in the scientific process, centering their passions and strengths in service of social justice research. Pre-tenure, I was heavily involved in mentoring PhD students in my lab. I continued this work post-tenure, at one point having 10 PhD students across two programs (an overcommitment). As a feminist social psychologist in a department without a social psychology program, I had survived tenure by becoming a core member of our Industrial-Organizational program and our Developmental Science program. While I was able to conduct meaningful research in these areas that aligned with my training, I never felt fully at home and was constantly having to learn literatures outside my areas of expertise and interest.

After earning tenure, with the help of Dionne Stephens (a colleague at FIU), I sought to create a new PhD program at my university in Applied Social and Cultural Psychology. Creating, and ultimately directing, a new graduate program was a dream project for me, where I could both live my values and fully use my skills and knowledge. To make more room in my life for this endeavor, I left a number of editorial positions, as well as some university and national committees. Tenure also provided me the time, perspective, and energy I needed to reevaluate my marriage, and the confidence and financial stability to move on.

For me (Kim), my recalibration meant asking powerful questions about my justice-oriented career goals. The professional goals that get me excited about my work are tied to advancing inclusive, equity-minded, antiracist, social justice teaching practices across the curriculum, across the disciplines, across the full landscape of higher education. I love my students and the joy of serving their learning journeys, expanding empowerment, and growing confidence. And yet, I wanted more. My drive to make the broadest impact possible drew me to faculty development and institutional change as my life's purpose. I took an extremely scary leap and edited my first book on privilege pedagogy and how privilege shows up in our teaching and learning (Case, 2013). I did not embark on the torture of book editing as a strategic career move. I did this because *Deconstructing Privilege* is the book I wish someone had given to me when I started teaching. In fact, this book you are reading is another book I wish someone had given me when I earned my PhD.

Although my goal was clearly to earn professor as soon as possible, I did not make my career plan based on that goal. The desire for that next promotion was mostly fueled by my low academic salary and need for a substantial increase that would accompany promotion. Honestly, I focused on what gave me the most meaning and purpose. Professor was icing on the fulfillment cake. More on that later. At the same time, I was not naive enough to ignore my university's standards for promotion to professor. As freshly minted associate professors, Jeannetta Williams and I built a midcareer peer mentoring process to make our individual action plans for promotion (Williams & Case, 2019). One of our top priority actions was to gather as much information, data, and feedback about our institution's previous patterns of approval and rejection of promotion so that we could build a solid case for how we met those standards.

In the process of realigning your professional efforts to better reflect who you want to be and what you want to accomplish, be mindful of the direction these efforts will take your career. If continuing your career in academia, you will need to integrate your efforts with university standards and expectations for achieving professor status. If you plan to leave academia, this may be the time to turn away from the academic track and develop a side hustle or exit strategy. Post-tenure, I (Kim) also developed my soul's work focused on coaching and consultation with social justice academics. Working with faculty and universities on antiracist and intersectional pedagogies and supporting midcareer feminist scholars has my "passion project cup" overflowing with joy! How will your efforts moving forward get you closer to these goals?

As you aim to recalibrate and refocus in your new status as an associate professor, these questions might help you with that process:

- What supports do you have that will enable you to refocus and recalibrate successfully?

- What learned and/or false beliefs are you carrying with you that you may need to reframe or shed to live your best post-tenure life?

- What updates and changes do you need to make to your career support systems (e.g., mentors, sponsors, social support)? You are at a new stage and need to reconsider who will be part of your team. Now is the time to identify and develop relationships with feminist scholars who have what you want or can help you navigate the path.

- What about your hobbies and passions outside work? Are there things you lost that you want to reclaim?

- What does work–life integration or balance look like for you after tenure?

Our Wishes for You

We hope this chapter has given you permission to celebrate and relax, and encouragement to use your power to speak up and carefully curate your scholarly endeavors moving forward. There are countless ways to live with joy, meaning, and safety post-tenure, and our thoughts and experiences represent a tiny window into what is possible or ideal. Further, there is no "wrong" way to approach your post-tenure experience. Perhaps you are reading this because you don't feel you've made the most of your time post-tenure. Maybe you lingered a little "too long" in celebration or relaxation. Or maybe you refocused your efforts on projects that did not bear the intended fruit (or not yet!). Do not despair. You can restart, reinvent, and even rewind as you move to the next stage of promotion (Chapter 17, this volume). We thank you in advance for lifting other feminist scholars as you climb and providing them a successful model of what it is to be an authentic, values-driven, power-sharing academic.

Resources

Baker, V., Lunsford, L., Neisler, G., & Pifer, M. (2019). (Ed.). *Success after tenure: Supporting mid-career faculty*. Stylus.

Case, K. (2017). Insider without: Journey across the working-class academic arc. *Journal of Working-Class Studies*, *2*, 16–35. https://doi.org/10.13001/jwcs.v2i2.6081

Castaneda, D., Flores, Y. G., & Flores Niemann, Y. (2020). Senior Chicana feminist scholars: Some notes on survival on hostile contexts. In Y. Flores Niemann, G. Gutierrez y Muhs, & C. G. Gonzalez (Eds.), *Presumed incompetent II: Race, class, power, and resistance of women in academia* (pp. 83–94). Utah State University Press.

Croom, N. N. (2017). Promotion beyond tenure: Unpacking racism and sexism in the experiences of Black womyn professors. *Review of Higher Education: Journal of the Association for the Study of Higher Education*, *40*(4), 557–583. https://doi.org/10.1353/rhe.2017.0022

Sulé, V. T. (2014). Enact, discard, and transform: a critical race feminist perspective on professional socialization among tenured Black female faculty. *International Journal of Qualitative Studies in Education*, *27*(4), 432–453. https://doi.org/10.1080/09518398.2013.780315

References

Aziz, R. (1992). Feminism and the challenge of racism: Deviance or difference? In H. Crowley & S. Himmelweit (Eds.), *Knowing women: Feminism and knowledge* (pp. 291–305). Polity Press.

Beauboeuf-Lafontant, T., Erickson, K. A., & Thomas, J. E. (2019). Rethinking post-tenure malaise: An interactional, pathways approach to understanding the post-tenure period. *The Journal of Higher Education*, *90*(4), 644–664. https://doi.org/10.1080/00221546.2018.1554397

Case, K. (Ed.). (2013). *Deconstructing privilege: Teaching and learning as allies in the classroom*. Routledge.

Eaton, A. A., Grzanka, P. R., Schlehofer, M. M., & Silka, L. (2021). Public psychology: Introduction to the special issue. *American Psychologist, 76*(8), 1209–1216. http://dx.doi.org/10.1037/amp0000933

Grzanka, P. R. (2018). Intersectionality and feminist psychology: Power, knowledge, and process. In C. B. Travis, J. W. White, A. Rutherford, W. S. Williams, S. L. Cook, & K. F. Wyche (Eds.), *APA handbook of the psychology of women: History, theory, and battlegrounds* (pp. 585–602). American Psychological Association. https://doi.org/10.1037/0000059-030

Hill, J., Bond, M. A., Mulvey, A., & Terenzio, M. (2000). Methodological issues and challenges for a feminist community psychology: An introduction to a special issue. *American Journal of Community Psychology*, *28*(6), 759–772. https://doi.org/10.1023/A:1005120632029

Hill Collins, P. (1990). *Black feminist thought: Knowledge, consciousness, and the politics of empowerment*. Unwin Hyman.

Moss-Racusin, C. A., & Rudman, L. A. (2010). Disruptions in women's self-promotion: The backlash avoidance model. *Psychology of Women Quarterly, 34*, 186–202. https://doi.org/10.1111/j.1471-6402.2010.01561.x

Mountz, A., Bonds, A., Mansfield, B., Loyd, J., Hyndman, J., Walton-Roberts, M., Basu, R., Whitson, R., Hawkins, R., Hamilton, T., & Curran, W. (2015). For slow scholarship: A feminist politics of resistance through collective action in the neoliberal university. *ACME: An International Journal for Critical Geographies, 14*(4), 1235–1259. https://www.acme-journal.org/index.php/acme/article/view/1058

Ozer, E. J., Langhout, R. D., & Weinstein, R. S. (2021). Promoting institutional change to support public psychology: Innovations and challenges at the University of California. *American Psychologist, 76*(8), 1293–1306. https://doi.org/10.1037/amp0000877

Rios, D., & Case, K.A. (2020). Unlikely alliances from Appalachia to East L.A.: Insider without and outsider within. In Y. Flores Niemann, G. Gutierrez y Muhs, & C. G. Gonzalez (Eds.), *Presumed Incompetent Volume 2* (pp. 131–142). Utah State University Press.

Signorella, M. L. (2020). Toward a more just feminism. *Psychology of Women Quarterly, 44*(2), 256–265. https://doi.org/10.1177/0361684320908320

Smith, J. L., & Huntoon, M. (2013). Women's bragging rights: Overcoming modesty norms to facilitate women's self-promotion. *Psychology of Women Quarterly, 38*(4), 447–459. https://doi.org/10.1177/0361684313515840

Stengers, I. (2018). *Another science is possible: A manifesto for slow science*. Polity Press.

Williams, J. W., & Case, K. (2019). Filling a gap in professional development: Midcareer faculty peer mentoring. In V. L. Baker (Ed.), *Success after tenure: Supporting mid-career faculty* (pp. 249–262). Stylus.

CHAPTER 17

Conclusion
Your Success Is a Feminist Project

- Isis H. Settles, Stephanie A. Shields, and Kate Richmond

So you have tenure? Why should you have to think about *another* promotion? This first promotion was exhausting enough! In this, our last chapter of *Road to Tenure*, we want to encourage you to consider why thinking beyond the significant achievement of tenure is important to your continued success and advancement as a feminist scholar.

First, take some time to recenter and take stock (Chapter 16, this volume). And then appreciate that the often difficult road from graduate school to earning tenure is just the beginning of your career, wherever it takes you. After tenure, you will probably have another 30-plus years of professional life ahead of you. So, as you take stock and think about the future, you can take the long view—to really envision and plan for the career you want. And know that the next steps to professor in 6 to 10 years (or so) are much more under your control and less fraught than the publish-or-perish days pre-tenure.

Our advice here is shaped by our experiences moving through the academic ranks. Isis was promoted to professor in 2016 at two institutions (Michigan State University [MSU] and the University of Michigan [U-M]), because in the middle of the promotion process at MSU, she was offered a position at U-M, which required its own promotion process as part of the hire. Kate was promoted to professor in 2020 at Muhlenberg College, a liberal arts college. Stephanie was promoted to professor at University of California, Davis in 1990 and then moved as professor to Pennsylvania State University in 1996, both research-intensive institutions. We have worked together for over 10 years, and through that work, we have learned from each other and grown together. We attribute our individual success to our shared collective goal of feminism and also our shared commitment toward working collaboratively with one another. Friendship is a powerful antidote to patriarchy.

Academic Life After Tenure

There are many wonderful ways in which your academic life changes post-tenure. You can now pursue projects that you had put on the back burner pre-tenure, perhaps because they didn't align with your department's tenure requirements. Post-tenure is also a time when you can scale up and think big about the projects you've already been doing. Do you want to develop and test an intervention to address the problem you've been studying? You now have the opportunity to take risks in your research, teaching, and service. Perhaps you've imagined a creative, untested study design, but thought it might not work. Now you can apply for a grant to make that possible. Maybe you've wanted to redesign a course and try out novel teaching strategies. Or perhaps you've wanted to get involved in service outside of your department—at the university level, in the community, or with one of your professional societies. With the security of tenure, you can pursue your academic goals, push the field toward greater innovation, and afford to fail.

At the same time, be prepared to have bids for your service to intensify once you have tenure. Because others (hopefully) wanted you to get tenure, they (hopefully) supported you by keeping service requests to a minimum. But once you have tenure, the floodgates will likely open up as people seek to make good use of your skills and expertise. If you are someone in a marginalized group (e.g., woman of color), know that the demands for your service will be even greater (and that you may not even have been protected pre-tenure). The advice offered in Chapter 13 on value-driven service is just as useful now as it was pre-tenure. The increase in service requests is a double-edged sword: On the one hand, you will have many options for different types of service and can pick what aligns best with your values and goals; on the other hand, you will have to master the ability to say no!

Pre-tenure you began to develop your invisible college (Chapter 4, this volume); with tenure you can devote your time to deepening those relationships and bringing the next generation of feminist scholars into your community. You may find that your invisible college not only supports you in your academic work, but brings you joy, as colleagues become friends you can't wait to reconnect with at conferences. Hopefully, you will also come into your own as a mentor and learn how to amplify and support junior colleagues.

Post-tenure you can think expansively about impact (Chapter 16, this volume). Pre-tenure, chances are that the main type of impact you sought to have was through publishing and presenting in academic outlets. After all, this is what you were evaluated on. After tenure, leverage your invisible college. At the core of feminist work is attention to relationships, so be sure to stay connected. Reach out to colleagues, go to professional conferences, and organize panels and social hours. Having strong professional friendships will see you through challenging times and will also help you to have courage to lead and move the field forward. For example, through these relationships, you might consider organizing and facilitating webinars, coediting a special edition, or leading a study-abroad trip with students.

At a personal level, you might decide that you want your influence to extend to the communities you study. For example, you might expand your influence through publishing op-eds or writing for other nonacademic audiences, by giving community talks or by developing a new program or intervention informed by your work. You might want your impact to shape your institution and work toward this aim by chairing important committees, serving on promotion and tenure committees, or taking on leadership roles. Perhaps you want to direct your efforts toward changing your field; you might serve as a journal editor, volunteer or run for office in your professional organization, or even direct your academic writing toward this aim. In all cases, it is important to know the criteria for promotion to professor so that you can balance what you *need* to do for the promotion with what you *want* to do. It is not unlike your pre-tenure decision-making, but without the do-or-die pressure of the tenure clock. It is important to remember at every step that, once you have tenure, you have much greater control over your career's direction and timetable.

How Is Life as Professor Different From Life as Associate Professor?

With the promotion to professor, professional opportunities expand. You won't have more time than you did pre-tenure or as associate professor, as much as we would all like that to happen. But you will have more autonomy and control over that time and where you invest it. And although your stress will not magically melt away, the knowledge that you have some security in your position makes a world of difference once you get to that next level. As professors the stress is more about having more projects we want to do than time to do them!

Then, once you are professor, you have even greater freedom to speak as a scholar in the profession and as a member of your institution. Stephanie recalls that when she and a feminist friend in the German department were promoted to professor at UC Davis, they realized, "Yikes!! *We* are now the senior women!" and they needed to think through the advantages and disadvantages of this new position and how these were discernibly different than what they experienced as tenured associate professors. One outcome—with the efforts of other new "senior women"—was that they pressed for and obtained a salary equity initiative.

We want to emphasize that achieving the rank of professor is not simply about power and status, but about realizing your feminist values in the most meaningful way you can. With that final promotion, you are able to be more nourishing to yourself and to your students, colleagues, and other stakeholders. It is a feminist position of power *to*, not power *over*. Tenure certainly gives one a similar freedom, but one's impact as researcher, administrator, and mover and shaker will be even greater when you are professor.

How Is Working Toward Professor Different From Working Toward Tenure?

Even though there is no equivalent to the "tenure clock," striving for promotion in 6 to 10 years after tenure is reasonable. After 10 years, the expectations of deans and promotion committees grow exponentially. The anxieties surrounding this timetable might be a headache, but they are not nearly as anxiety provoking as the pre-job, pre-tenure years. It isn't up or out. You have tenure! In addition, you have more knowledge of the institution than before, more space to get support or information, more control over the process, a wider professional network, and so on. You can take advantage of everything you learned pre-tenure about how your discipline and your institution work so that you can operate from a much more informed position than before.

In many ways, the criteria for professor are similar to those for tenure—just bigger, with more options and opportunities! At most universities, promotion to full requires that you have built a national reputation, which means that scholars outside your institution are familiar with you and your work. Some ways to build a national reputation are to present at national or international conferences, accept speaking invitations at other universities, organize symposia or focused conferences, and take on leadership roles in your professional organizations (e.g., membership chair). For example, Kate (then just up for tenure at a teaching-oriented liberal arts college) and Isis (newly promoted associate professor at a research-oriented Midwestern research university) were invited by Stephanie (then 20 years into being professor) to organize her brain child, the Institute for Academic Feminist Psychology in 2011. Since then, we have run three institutes and edited this book! And our work together has created important connections not only with one another, but also in our respective invisible colleges, giving each of us a better position to connect with and advocate for junior colleagues across North America.

Often, promotion committees want to see you developing into a leader, but "leader" is broadly defined. You might take on formal leadership roles (e.g., university committee, professional organization executive committee), and those roles might be at your university, within your professional organization, or in your community. Know that formal leadership can mean being on an important committee; it doesn't require you to chair the committee. In fact, you may want to wait to be professor before you chair committees or take on leadership with high visibility (e.g., department chair). Leadership can also be informal, such as organizing a reading group or journal club for your department. The key is to be able to communicate the ways in which you contribute through your leadership.

Also, remember to be an advocate of your work, and the work of others in your invisible college. Often, we are surprised by how many of our highly qualified colleagues are not formally recognized with national awards. This is a gendered phenomenon, and we encourage you to boldly reject it! After you put together a promotion file, you have also written most of the narrative for an award application. Now is not the time to be shy! Seek out awards through your university, local communities, and national organizations *and* apply. Nominate your colleagues and don't be afraid to self-nominate. This recognition is another way to demonstrate national reputation.

Just as for tenure, one critical aspect of promotion to professor is learning what it takes at *your* institution. If you are at a research-intensive institution do you need to have *submitted* grants? Do you need to have *funded* grants? Do you need to demonstrate you have international standing in your field? If you are at a teaching-oriented institution, what type of research and publication efforts are most valued? Those that include undergraduate collaborators? Those that relate to the scholarship of teaching? Textbooks? Or peer-reviewed research publications?

As full professors, we have served on many promotion and tenure committees at our institutions and written many promotion letters over the years. From these experiences, we know that each institution has its own criteria they provide to evaluators they ask to write a promotion letter. As promotion letter writers, we take care to provide our evaluation in the context of the university's specific promotion criteria. Make sure you have a copy of those criteria early on and consult frequently with the people you trust to help you make good decisions about how best to work toward promotion.

Your Success Is a Feminist Project

Promotion to professor is the *last* promotion you will have to worry about if you continue in academia. Even if you leave to pursue another profession, promotion is valuable because your resume indicates that in your last academic position, you achieved the highest rank before opting for another career path. And if you would like to stay an academic, but as an administrator rather than researcher and teacher, the promotion will open doors for you that are not open to associate professors. Unfortunately, the reality is that you may not be competitive for advancement in administrative positions if you remain "only" an associate professor.

Promotion to professor opens doors and gives you a position of authority to speak from that few have in other industries. Not only can you determine the course of your research and content of your teaching, you can also develop a perspective and action plan to help shape the academy in a way that fosters feminist values of inclusivity, rigorous inquiry, and expansive scholarship. As we write, many of the values we hold as feminists, scientists and scholars, educators, and informed citizens are not as secure as we had believed even just a decade ago. We do not know what the future holds for the academic landscape—many aspects of conventional academic life are in flux, and we have no clear view of what the near or longer term prospects are for our junior colleagues. As a professor, you are in a position to influence, lead, and reimagine a future in academia that centers feminist values and ensures access, amplifies voices, and sets all community members up for success.

Not-So Final Words

Your success and the success of other feminist scholars is a feminist project in every aspect of our work. As academics, we contribute to the knowledge base, and specifically as feminist scholars our contribution to the knowledge base ensures that issues of social justice and equity will be included. The knowledge we create through our research influences social norms and culture, public policy, and even notions of citizenship, weaving gender equity and other forms of inclusion into them. Our relationships with our students and the time we share with them are powerful and transformative. As bell hooks (1994) said, "The classroom remains the most radical space of possibility in the academy. ... Urging all of us to open our minds and hearts so that we can know beyond the boundaries of what is acceptable, so that we can think and rethink, so that we can create new visions" (p. 12). We want feminism to be part of how our students understand social problems and systems of inequality. As feminist leaders, we can shape the academy toward a space of greater access, inclusion, and equity.

You have chosen to pursue a career in academe because you believe a profession focused on creating new knowledge is of value to society. Our goal in this book is to provide you with information you need to make your way to tenure. We are also committed to helping you see beyond that looming goal toward what you can aspire to by achieving tenure and what lies beyond it. We encourage you to take the long view on your career. As many of our contributors emphasize, identifying your values and goals will help you shape not only your next steps in the path to tenure, but guide you toward the meaningful and rewarding career that set you on this path originally and will sustain you as you achieve your goals.

Reference

hooks, b. (1994). *Teaching to transgress: Education as the practice of freedom*. Routledge.

Index

A
academic life after tenure, 225–227
activist, challenging, badass feminist scholarship, 2
Adair, Z. R., 27
advocate, 218
Ahmed, S., 94
American Psychological Foundation, 113
amplify, 218
Annamma, S., 140
Antecol, H., 31
APA publication manual, 56–57
article tracking, 71–72
Association for Women in Psychology, 17
authors' rights and responsibilities, 58

B
Beauboeuf-Lafontant, T., 220
Bem, S., 157
Bible Belt, 82
bibliometrics, 38
Black feminist
  consciousness, 12
  pedagogy, 27
  scholarship, 19
  thought, 13
Black, Indigenous, and people of color (BIPOC), 92, 146–147, 158, 169–170
Black women, 12–13
  Black womanhood, 170
  gendered racial identity, 14, 16, 170
  identity development and formation of, 113
  mental health of, 12
  narratives from, 172–175
  phenomenological experiences of, 18
Boler, M., 136
boundaried generosity, 147
Boyle, R., 38
Bozeman, B., 40
Buchanan, N., 219

C
career-related decisions, 6–7
Case, K. A., 127, 212
celebrate and relax, 215–216
Centers for Disease Control and Prevention (CDC), 113
centrality, 43
classroom without borders, 164–165
collective goals, 2
collegiality, 102–104
communities, 137–138
  and collaboration, 7
  building, 187
  cultivating, 185–197
community-based participatory action research (CBPAR), 113
community-based work/research, 156–167
  context, 159–163
  (im)practical outcomes, 163–165
  last chance becomes first chance, 159–160
  learning from elders, 157
  movidas, 157–159, 165–166
  overview, 156–157
  rage, 157–159
  (re)socialization, 162–163
  structural barriers, 157–159
  trusting relationship, 160–162
Cooper, B., 152, 159
Council of Undergraduate Research, 85
creating meaning and value, 188
critical reflexivity, 15
cultivate feminist research ethics, 15
cultivating communities, 185–197
  maintain momentum, 195–196
  overview, 185–187
  reassess target spaces, 190–195
  reconceptualize networking meanings, 187–188
  restructuring networking strategies, 188–190

D
Deconstructing Privilege (Case), 221
Deep Work: Rules for Focused Success in a Distracted World (Newport), 108
Department of Justice (DOJ), 113
Dickens, D., 113
DOI (digital object identifier), 57
dysfunctional education ecologies, 140–153
  challenges and strategies, 149–151
  challenging oppressive structures, 151–152
  coping with, 141–149
  overview, 140
  positionality, 141

E
Eaton, A., 32
editorial process, 55–64
  importance of reviewing, 62–64
  review process, 56–60
  revising a paper, 60–62
editors' rights and responsibilities, 58
Edwards, K., 113
eloquent rage, 159
Erchull, M., 82
Espinoza, D., 158

231

F

Faculty of Color, 28
Feminism & Psychology, 63
feminist academics/scholars, 126–127
  awareness of field and state of higher education, 5–6
  defined, 3
  path to tenure, 5–8
  research and scholarship requirements, 26–27
  tenure as, 1–9
feminist and sustainable approach to productivity, 94–110
  mentoring students within lab, 98–101
  overview, 94–95
  promoting, 101–106
  shape within constraints of institution, 96
  sustainability, 106–110
  vision for research program, 95–96
feminist lab, 94. *See also* feminist and sustainable approach to productivity
feminist lab environment, 101–106
  collaborations, 104–106
  collegiality, 102–104
feminist mentorship network, 16–17
feminist pedagogy, 141
feminist research
  challenges, 16–21
  critical reflexivity, 15
  critical reflexivity statements, 12–13
  empowerment, 15–16
  ethics, 15
  feminist mentorship network, 16–17
  in structural and multilevel analysis, 14
  intersectional questions, 13–14
  mixed methods and methodological flexibility, 14
  promise and perils of, 11–21
  public scholarship, 20–21
  push back against dominant research paradigms, 18–20
  resist sexism, 18–20
  sister circle of support, 17–18
  social justice, 15–16
  strategies, 13–16
Few, A. L., 25, 29
Fine, M., 157, 165
flipped paper, 57

G

Global Feminisms Project, 9
Grammarly or the Belcher Editing Diagnostic Test, 68
grants. *See also* securing grants
  aims/project summary, 117
  budget, 118–119
  components of, 117–120
  feedback, 122–123
  management, 124
  project narrative, 118
  review criteria, 121–122
  reviewers, 120–121
  study funded, 115
  timeline, 119–120

H

healthy boundaries, 147–148
heterophily, 42
Hispanic-serving institution, 129
homophily, 41
hooks, b., 157, 159, 164, 230

I

identity safety cues, 143
(im)practical outcomes, 163–165
independent journalist, 20
individualized goals, 2
Institutes for Academic Feminist Psychologists, 3–5, 17
institution
  recommendations for, 32–34
  tenure process, 24–26
interdisciplinarity, 200–212
  dividends of interdisciplinary travel, 212
  job, 204–205
  job work, 206–212
  overview, 200–203
  strengths-based approach, 203–204
interdisciplinary careers, 201
  strengths-based approach to, 203–204
interdisciplinary women, gender, and sexuality (WGS) studies program, 202
international students, 92
interpreting decision letters, 72–73
intersectional and antiracist pedagogy, 125–138
  community, 137–138
  critical pedagogies, 132–133
  feminist pedagogy means, 130
  feminist scholar, 126–127
  impact on teaching, 127–128
  inclusive practices and, 132
  intersectional identities, 127–128
  journeys, 128–130
  skills, 130–132
  strengthening case for promotion and tenure, 134–137
  teaching as soul's work, 125–126
intersectional feminist research questions, 13–14
intersectional social locations, 215
intimate, collaborative relationship, 25
invisible college, 2, 37–47, 190
  approaches and strategies in, 39–44
  issues and challenges in, 45–46
  maintaining, 44–45
  need to build, 38–39
  origin and conceptualization of, 38
  overview, 37

J

Journal/Author Name Estimator (JANE), 69
justice, 217
justice, equity, diversity, and inclusion (JEDI), 169–171, 174

K

Kite, M., 212

L

lab. *See also* feminist lab environment
  boundaries, 98–99

identity, 97
maintenance, 98
mentoring students within, 98–101
processes, 99–100
team, 97
Laszloffy, T., 126
Lewis, J. A., 13, 27
Lievrouw, L. A., 38
Living a Feminist Life (Ahmed), 94
Lorde, A., 20, 32

M

mainstream researchers, 66
Manchester, C. F., 31
manuscript preparation, 52–55
  targeting specific journal, 55
  tips for successful writing, 52–55
Martínez, R., 25, 29
McBride, H., 109
members of the invisible college (MIC), 44–45
mentoring processes, 99–100
mentorship network, 16–17
Michigan State University (MSU), 225
microaggressions, 144–147
minority-serving institution (MSI), 170
Morrison, D., 140
movidas, 157–159, 165–166
mythical norm, 125

N

National Center for Faculty Development and Diversity (NCFDD), 100
National Institute of Health (NIH), 113, 188
National Institute on Alcohol Abuse and Alcoholism (NIAAA), 115
National Science Foundation (NSF), 113
negative emotions during peer review, 73–76
networking
  concept of, 185
  framing, 185
  reconceptualize meanings, 187–188
  reframe capital, 189
  restructuring strategies, 188–190
  social media, 193

network of coauthorship, 38
Neville, H. A., 17
Newport, C., 108
The New York Times, 205
"no" committee, 182
no-cost extension, 119

O

Office of Sponsored Programs (OSP), 115–116
open educational resources (OER), 143
organize, 218

P

pacing and work–life balance, 30–32
Pang, A. S-K., 110
peer review process, 66–80
  interpreting decision letters, 72–73
  manuscripts moving along the pathway, 77–80
  negative emotions during, 73–76
  overview, 66–67
  revising and resubmitting manuscripts, 76–77
  submitting high-quality paper, 67–71
  tracking article after submission, 71–72
Personality and Social Psychology Bulletin, 70
power, 216–220
predominantly white institution (PWI), 129, 169
principal investigator (PI), 117
professor and associate professor, 227–228
Professor Watchlist (PW) website, 150
project narrative, 118
propinquity, 40
Psychology of Gender, 27
Psychology of Women Quarterly (PWQ), 51–52, 56, 63–64, 70, 192
public scholarship, 20–21
publishing, 51–64, 66–80
  editorial process, 55–64
  manuscript preparation, 52–55
  overview, 51–52
pursuit of passions, 188

R

rage, 157–159. *See also* eloquent rage
Rate My Professors website, 149
recalibrate and refocus, 220–222
redefine (or shift) tasks, 182
replicability crisis, 47
research lab/team, 88–90. *See also* lab
research program, 81–92
  overview, 81
  parting advice, 92
  requirements, 85–87
  sufficient research, 83–85
  tenure requirements, 82–83
  vision for, 95–96
  working with students, 87–88
research time protection, 91–92
(re)socialization, 162–163
Rest: Why You Get More Done When You Work Less (Pang), 110
revise-and-resubmit decision (R&R), 74
revising and resubmitting manuscripts, 76–77
Richmond, K., 4
Rios, D., 127
Rockquemore, K., 126
Royal Society, 2

S

scholar squad, 190
securing grants, 112–124. *See also* grants
  components of grants, 117–120
  grants management, 124
  positionality, 113
  reason, 112
  rejection management, 123–124
  staying motivated, 123–124
  writing first grant, 114–117
  writing strong grant proposal, 120–123
See, S. E., 24
self-care, 32
service efforts, 219–220
Settles, I., 4
Sex Roles, 52, 70
Shields, S., 3–4, 7–8
Sifaki, A., 30
sister circle of support, 17–18

social justice, 7–8, 15–16
social locations, 127–128, 215
social media, 193
Society for the Psychology of Women, 3, 17
solidarity, 170
Sooho, L., 40
speak up, 217–218
sponsor, 218
Stewart, A. J., 27, 29
stop-the-clock policies, 31
strategies and tools to support career advancement, 8
student dissatisfaction, 136
student evaluations of teaching (SETs), 143–144
study funded grants, 115
success, 229–230
sufficient research, 83–85
supportive networks, 150–151
sustainability, 106–110
sustainable life–work integration, 109–110

T

teaching as soul's work, 125–126
Teaching Community (hooks), 157, 164
tenure
  academic life after, 225–227
  as feminist academics, 1–9
  requirements, 82–83
tenure clock, 23–34, 228
  institutions process, 24–26
  overview, 23–24
  pacing and work–life balance, 30–32
  recommendations for institutions, 32–34
  research and scholarship requirements, 26–27
  service requirements, 28–30
  strategies and tactics, 24–32
  teaching requirements, 27–28
tenured feminist scholar, 217
tips and tricks for saying no, 180–182

U

Underrepresented Perspectives (UP) Lab, 97
United Negro College Fund, 113
University of Michigan (U-M), 225
University of North Carolina (UNC), 152
unmask radical professors, 150

V

Valian, V., 27
value-congruent decisions, 176–177
value-driven service, 169–182
  author's values and positionality, 169–170
  identify and clarify values, 176
  narratives from Black women faculty, 172–175
  prioritizing and enacting tips, 175–180
  risk, 171–172
  service and raced-gendered context, 170–171
  tips and tricks for saying no, 180–182

W

Weisstein, N., 2
Williams, J., 221
Williams, M. G., 13–15, 27
Williams, W., 212
The Wisdom of Your Body (McBride), 109
Workshop Activity for Gender Equity Simulation-Academic (WAGES-Academic), 33
writing first grant, 114–117
writing strong grant proposal, 120–123

About the Editors

Kate Richmond, PhD, is Professor of Psychology and Director of Women & Gender Studies at Muhlenberg College. She is widely published in the areas of multicultural psychology, gender ideology, masculinity, and trauma. Her co-authored undergraduate textbook, entitled *Psychology of Women & Gender*, was awarded the 2020 Distinguished Publication Award by the Association of Women in Psychology. Dr. Richmond has been nationally recognized on several occasions for excellence in teaching, facilitation, and mentorship, including receiving the Florence Denmark Distinguished Mentoring Award and the Paul C. Empie Memorial Award for Excellence in Teaching. She is passionate about community-based organizing and most recently, has worked within the Lehigh County Corrections facility and is a former member of the SCI-Graterford Prison Think Tank. Dr. Richmond is also a licensed psychologist and maintains a private practice in Philadelphia, PA. She is also a consultant for Kaleel Jamison Consulting Group, a firm that specializes in organization development.

Isis H. Settles, PhD, is Professor of Psychology and Associate Dean for Diversity, Equity, and Inclusion in the College of Literature, Science, and the Arts at the University of Michigan, where she also earned her PhD in psychology. Using an interdisciplinary, intersectional framework, her research focuses on two related processes: the experiences, perceptions, and consequences of unfair treatment directed at devalued social group members, especially Black people and women; and protective factors and coping strategies used by members of devalued social groups to counteract experiences of mistreatment, especially those protective factors related to group identity (e.g., racial identity). Dr. Settles is a fellow of the Society for the Psychology of Women, Society for the Psychological Study of Social Issues, and Society for the Psychological Study of Culture, Ethnicity, and Race. She has received national awards for her research and service, and her research has been funded by the National Institute of Mental Health and the National Science Foundation.

Stephanie A. Shields', PhD, research is at the intersection of human emotion, gender, and feminist psychology. *Speaking from the Heart: Gender and the Social Meaning of Emotion* (2002) received the Association for Women in Psychology's Distinguished Publication Award, as did her special issue of *Sex Roles* on intersectionality of social identities (2008). Her experiential learning tool WAGES (wages.la.psu.edu) illustrates the cumulative effect of unconscious bias in the workplace. She served as the director of women's studies at Penn State and the University of California, Davis, and was founding director of the UC Davis Consortium for Research on Women and Gender, and is a past president of the Society for the Psychology of Women (SPW; APA Division 35). Notable awards include SPW's Carolyn Sherif Award, recognizing sustained and substantial contributions to the field of the psychology of women and gender; and the Society for General Psychology's (APA Division 1) Ernest Hilgard Lifetime Achievement Award, recognizing significant and long-lasting contributions across topical areas in psychology.

Alexandra I. Zelin, PhD, is Associate Professor of Psychology at the University of Tennessee at Chattanooga. She received her PhD in industrial-organizational psychology from the University of Akron. Her research centers around women's experiences both in and outside of the workplace, including sexual harassment, sexual assault, and sexism, and how various intersecting identities impact those experiences. Dr. Zelin is the director of the Intersectional Sexism, Workplace, and Gender (ISWAG) lab, where she actively encourages undergraduate student-led research projects. She is the winner of the 2020 Mary Roth Walsh Teaching the Psychology of Women award from the Society for the Psychology of Women (SPW). She has also served as the Women's Inclusion Network chair for the Society of Industrial and Organizational Psychology and as the Violence Against Women chair for SPW. Dr. Zelin attended the 2018 Academic Feminist Institute.

About the Contributors

NiCole T. Buchanan, PhD, is professor at Michigan State University. Buchanan researches the interplay of race, gender, and victimization and how they impact the nature of harassment, its impact, and organizational best practices. She also studies faculty of color and ways in which their research is marginalized (i.e., epistemic exclusion). She has been highlighted in hundreds of media outlets, is a featured speaker (including TEDx and National Public Radio [NPR]) and provides bias and diversity-related training and consultation (e.g., medical professionals, faculty, clinicians, human resource managers, and police departments). Buchanan is a fellow of the Association for Psychological Science, four divisions of the American Psychological Association (Society of Clinical Psychology, Society for the Psychological Study of Social Issues, Society for the Psychological Study of Ethnic Minority Issues, and Society for the Psychology of Women), and has received national and international awards for her research, teaching, and professional service.

Kim Case, PhD, is a tenured professor and director of faculty success in the Office of the Provost at Virginia Commonwealth University. As director, she oversees the Center for Teaching and Learning Excellence, develops programs to advance faculty career development, and implements strategies to support faculty writing and scholarship goals. Case is a social psychologist by training and applies critical race theory, feminist theory, queer theory, and intersectional theory to her teaching, research, and service to the profession, on campus, and in the surrounding community. Her mixed-methods research currently examines teaching and workplace interventions to support equity and inclusion for student and faculty success. Her scholarship and three books on teaching address inclusive, antiracist, and social justice pedagogies. Her consulting work (www.drkimcase.com) includes talks and workshops, an online course on White antiracism, and group coaching for social justice academics.

Elizabeth R. Cole, PhD, is professor of psychology, women's and gender studies, and Afro-American and African studies at the University of Michigan (U-M). She taught at Northeastern University before joining U-M in 2000. Her research has appeared in journals including *American Psychologist*,

Cultural Diversity and Ethnic Minority Psychology, and *Psychology of Women Quarterly*. She is a past president and a fellow of the Society for the Psychological Study of Social Issues. She has received the Committee on Women in Psychology Leadership Award from the American Psychological Association and the Harold R. Johnson Diversity Service Award. Cole has served as the associate dean for social sciences and the interim dean of the College of Literature, Science, and the Arts, and is currently director of the National Center for Institutional Diversity. Her scholarship applies feminist theory on intersectionality to social science research on race, gender, and social justice.

Sarah Cronin, PhD, LP (she/they), is an assistant professor of psychology at Bemidji State University. At the time their book chapter was written, Sarah had submitted their tenure and promotion application and was patiently waiting the university's decision. Sarah is a codirector of the Indigenous Students in Psychology Training (InPsyT) program, which supports Indigenous undergraduate psychology majors on their paths to graduate school and serving their communities. Sarah values cocreating research and classroom experiences with her students. Their approach in the classroom is collaborative and encourages self-exploration and identity formation. Sarah also takes this collaborative approach in mentoring staff and faculty. Having published in journals such as *Journal of Prevention and Health Promotion*, Sarah is passionate about publishing research with implications that benefit communities and helping professionals. A graduate of the University of Minnesota's Counseling and Student Personnel Psychology (CSPP) program, she works to integrate her lens as a scientist-practitioner into all professional settings.

Danielle Dickens, PhD, is an associate professor in the Department of Psychology at Spelman College. Dickens earned her BA in psychology from Spelman College and her MS and PhD from Colorado State University in applied social and health psychology. Her program of research focuses on Black womanhood and their implications for health behaviors, academic performance, experiences of discrimination, coping strategies, and psychological well-being. In all, her teaching and research aims to contextually position and understand the lived experiences of Black women in the United States, to identify effective strategies to reduce inequalities, and to improve their career development and mental and behavioral health outcomes. Due to her productivity and innovations in teaching and research, she often serves as an expert scholar and invited speaker on issues affecting underserved and underrepresented individuals in education and in the workplace.

Asia Eaton, PhD, is a feminist social psychologist and associate professor of psychology at Florida International University. She is the is the director of the new psychology PhD track in Applied Social and Cultural Psychology, as well as a core faculty member in the Developmental Psychology and I-O Psychology tracks. She is the PI of the Power, Women, and Relationships (PWR) Lab, which explores how gender intersects with identities such as race, sexual orientation, age, and class to affect individuals' access to and experience with power. In our quantitative, qualitative, and mixed-methods work, we engage social and cultural psychological theories and methods to address real-world social problems in collaboration with local, state, and national organizations and institutions. For example, since 2016 Asia has also served as head of research for Cyber Civil Rights Initiative (CCRI), which is working to understand and end the epidemic of image-based sexual abuse in the United States.

Katie Edwards, PhD, is an associate professor at the University of Nebraska–Lincoln where she directs the Interpersonal Violence Research Laboratory. Using community-based participatory action research, Edwards seeks to answer two questions in her work: (1) *How do we prevent sexual and related forms of violence?* and (2) *How do we most effectively support survivors in the aftermath of violent victimization?* Much of Edwards's work focuses on minoritized populations, specifically Native American/Indigenous youth and families as well as LGBTQIA2S+ youth and emerging adults. Edwards highly values community leadership in developing and evaluating strengths-focused, affirming, culturally grounded initiatives to prevent and respond to sexual and related forms of violence. To date, she has published more than 185 peer-reviewed journal articles and over the past 10 years has accrued over $12 million in federal funding from the Centers for Disease Control, National Institutes of Health, National Institute of Justice, Office on Violence against Women, and National Science Foundation.

Jillian Fish, PhD, LP, is from the Tuscarora Nation of the Haudenosaunee Confederacy of Western New York. She is a counseling psychologist by training and earned her PhD from the University of Minnesota in 2020. Jill uses innovative story-based strategies, traditional medicines, and cultural modalities of healing to empower Native American and Indigenous peoples in her research, teaching, and clinical practice. She considers herself a public scholar and disseminates her work at the community level as often as she can. Her TEDxTalk, "Honoring Indigenous Cultures and Histories," has been viewed over 30,000 times.

Sarah Gervais, PhD (she/her/hers), is a professor of psychology at the University of Nebraska–Lincoln. Her research focuses on sexual objectification, dehumanization, and violence and lies at the intersections between gender, social psychology, the law, and public health. Her work is funded by the National Institute of Health and National Science Foundation. She has been the recipient of the Georgia Babladelis Best Paper Award from *Psychology of Women Quarterly* as well as the Gordon Allport Intergroup Relations Prize from the Society for the Psychological Study of Social Issues. She is past associate editor of *Psychology of Women Quarterly*, *Journal of Experimental Social Psychology*, and *British Journal of Social Psychology*.

Patrick R. Grzanka, PhD, is an applied social issues researcher who studies the complex ways that institutions such as health care, science, and education reproduce harm at the intersections of race, gender, and sexuality. He is a professor in the Department of Psychology at the University of Tennessee, where he is also chair of the interdisciplinary program in women, gender, and sexuality. He is the 2018 winner of the Michele Alexander Early Career Award from the Society for the Psychological Study of Social Issues (SPSSI) and is a fellow of American Psychological Association's Divisions 9 (SPSSI), 17 (Society for Counseling Psychology), and 44 (Society for the Psychology of Sexual Orientation and Gender Diversity). Terminally undisciplined, he holds a PhD in American studies and BA in journalism, both from the University of Maryland.

Kathryn Holland, PhD (she/her), is an assistant professor of psychology and women's and gender studies at the University of Nebraska–Lincoln. She received her MS and PhD in psychology and women's studies from the University of Michigan, and her BA in applied psychology from the University of Illinois at Chicago. Her work focuses on understanding people's experiences of sexual assault and sexual health, particularly those who are marginalized by gender and/or sexuality. She received the 2019 Distinguished Publication Award from the Association for Women in Psychology and an NSF CAREER Award for her research examining mandatory reporting policies for sexual assault in higher education.

Martinque "Marti" Jones, PhD, is a licensed psychologist and assistant professor in the Department of Psychology's Counseling Psychology Program at the University of North Texas. She earned her PhD in counseling psychology at the University of Houston and completed an APA-accredited internship at the University of Florida Counseling & Wellness Center. She also completed research postdoctoral fellowships at the University of Michigan and Teachers College, Columbia University. Jones has expertise in racial and gender identity and counseling processes specific to Black women. Her research specifically examines how Black women self-define their Black womanhood (referred to as gendered racial identity), how Black women's gendered racial identity and stereotypical portrayals of their race-gender group impacts their mental health, and best clinical practices in working with Black women.

Kat Klement, PhD, is an assistant professor of psychology at Bemidji State University, teaching courses primarily related to sexuality and gender. They received their PhD in Psychology from Northern Illinois University and their MA in psychology and BA in psychology and political science from Concordia University Chicago. Their major lines of research examine attributions of sexual assault blame, how transphobia relates to other systems of oppression, and transgender patients' health care experiences. They have also published work related to consensual BDSM, sexual consent, and sexual entitlement and are a member of the *Journal of Positive Sexuality*'s editorial board. They are cofounder and codirector of the Northwoods Queer Outreach, which provides training and resources for organizational staff, educators, and health care providers to better serve 2SLGBTQ+ people. They were a 2018 fellow in the Institute for Academic Feminist Psychologists and received the BSU Shared Fundamental Values Award for Diversity, Equity, and Inclusion in 2021.

Jioni A. Lewis, PhD, is an associate professor of counseling psychology in the Department of Counseling, Higher Education, and Special Education at the University of Maryland, College Park. She received her PhD in counseling psychology from the University of Illinois at Urbana-Champaign. Lewis is a leading expert on the impact of systemic racism and sexism (i.e., gendered racism) on the health of women of color. Her primary research applies intersectionality theory to investigate the influence of gendered racism on Black women's health and well-being. She also examines protective factors that buffer individuals against the negative effects of discrimination, such as radical healing, collective coping, and resistance strategies. Lewis has received several national awards for her research, teaching, mentoring, and social justice advocacy. She is past president of the Psychology of Black Women (Section I: Society for the Psychology of Women, 2020–2021), where she served as lead coordinator of the Inaugural Psychology of Black Women Conference.

Jes Matsick, PhD, holds a joint appointment as assistant professor of psychology and women's, gender, and sexuality studies at Penn State. She received a dual-title PhD in psychology and women's studies from the University of Michigan in 2016. In her research, she incorporates feminist perspectives into the psychological study of stigma and prejudice. Much of her research focuses on the link between stigma and social disparities experienced by LGBTQ+ people. She directs the Underrepresented Perspectives Laboratory, which provides a collaborative, intellectually stimulating space for graduate and undergraduate students who learn to engage feminist theory and methods in social psychological research. She has been recognized with Penn State's Graduate Faculty Mentoring Award, Outstanding Teaching Award for Tenure-Line Faculty, and Academic Achievement award from the Center for Sexual and Gender Diversity. She has received funding from various sources, including the NSF, NIH's Clinical and Translational Science Institute, and American Institute of Bisexuality.

Sahana Mukherjee, PhD, assistant professor of psychology at Gettysburg College, is a social and cultural psychologist. She received her PhD in social psychology from the University of Kansas. Her research interests lie in the bidirectional relationship between psychological experiences (e.g., national identity) and cultural practices and products (e.g., history museums). Professor Mukherjee uses a variety of research methods (e.g., laboratory research, interviews, field research) to conduct research in the United States, Canada, and India. A common thread connecting all her projects is the focus on social justice, and she strives toward conducting research that can be used to understand and alleviate social inequalities.

Desdamona Rios, PhD, is an associate professor of social psychology and director of the Latinx and Latin American Studies program at the University of Houston-Clear Lake (UHCL). She has published on intersectionality in the academy, including pedagogical practices and faculty and student experiences. She is the recipient of three national teaching awards from the American Psychological Association's Society for the Teaching of Psychology, the Society for the Psychological Study of Social Issues, and the Association for Women in Psychology. She is also the recipient of UHCL's Hayes diversity award for her work with underrepresented groups in academia. She currently serves as consulting editor for *Psychology of Women Quarterly*, executive council for the Society for the Psychological Study of Social Issues, and is on the advisory board for Magnolia Park Arts Center in Houston. Her current research focuses on examining collaborative practices among nonprofit organizations serving Houston's East End.

Natalie J. Sabik, PhD, is an associate professor at the University of Rhode Island. Sabik received a joint PhD in psychology and women's studies from the University of Michigan and completed a postdoctoral fellowship in health psychology at Brandeis University. Her work spans the fields of psychology, gender studies, and public health, and she examines how health and well-being are shaped by a variety of social and identity factors, such as body perceptions, stress, social interactions, gender roles, and aging. Her work integrates an intersectional perspective that examines these factors in the context of different demographic and identity categories. She is a consulting editor for *Psychology of Women Quarterly*, and her work has been recognized by the American Public Health Association, the Society for the Psychological Study of Social Issues, and the American Psychological Association, and she is a fellow of the Institute for Academic Feminist Psychology.

Dionne Stephens, PhD, a Black womanist scholar, is professor of psychology at Florida International University in Miami. Her program of research addressing examines social determinants of health and the ways meanings about health inequalities are informed by marginalized populations' intersectional identities. For her work, Stephens has received numerous research, teaching, and mentorship recognitions. Stephens purposefully links her professional efforts to her personal community social justice commitments. She is also the founding codirector of Level UP, a community collaborative that provides community members with research training to ensure their equitable roles in the creation of knowledge and access to resources that benefit surrounding low-resource communities. Stephens also implements collaborative projects with Girl Power—a multisite afterschool program in Miami's low-resource communities—and the Public Health Research Institute of India, a women's health clinic in Mysore, India, to increase capacity building opportunities.

Ying Tang, PhD, is an associate professor in psychology at Youngstown State University (YSU). Her research interests center around the self and social perception, particularly on topics such as attribution and stigma. An avid educator, she teaches a wide range of undergraduate courses, including Social Psychology and Psychology of Women. She has served as the cochair of the Committee on Academic Feminist Psychology (APA, Division 35) from 2017–2021 and currently holds a leadership role on the board of YWCA Mahoning Valley. She has been the recipient of the YSU Distinguished Professorship Awards in Service (2021)/Scholarship (2022), Teaching Resources Award (2021) from SPSSI (APA, Division 9), and Mahoning Valley Young Professionals 25 Under 35 MVP Award (2020). Originally from Chengdu, China, she received her BA in psychology and sociological studies from Wesleyan College and her master's and PhD in social psychology from Syracuse University.

S. Brooke Vick, PhD, is the associate provost for faculty and diversity initiatives and associate professor of psychology at Muhlenberg College. She comes to diversity, equity, inclusion, and antiracist leadership through her work as a social psychologist specializing in prejudice, discrimination, intergroup relations, and marginalized social identities. Vick's writing in the areas of prejudice and social stigma, as well as inclusion and equity in higher education, has been published in journals of psychology and higher education, including *Inside Higher Ed*, *Liberal Education*, and *Perspectives in Psychological Science*. Vick has been recognized for excellence in teaching and scholarship with The Robert Fluno Award for Distinguished Teaching in the Social Sciences and the Paul Garrett Fellow award. Vick regularly works with faculty and staff at institutions across the country on inclusive and antiracist practices and currently serves as the president and cochair of the Liberal Arts Diversity Officers consortium.

Leah Warner, PhD, is a professor of psychology at Ramapo College of New Jersey. She received her BA from Vassar College and PhD in social psychology and women's studies from The Pennsylvania State University. Her interdisciplinary scholarship concerns intersectionality, having written widely on the challenges and transformative potential of integrating intersectionality into psychological research. In addition, she engages in scholarship on social justice pedagogy, providing teaching strategies for addressing controversial social issues within U.S. sociopolitical contexts, efforts that led her to receive the Society for the Psychological Study of Social Issues Teaching Innovation Award, a SPSSI Action Teaching grant, and an Association for Psychological Science Teaching grant. She is currently on the editorial board for *Sex Roles* and *Psychology of Women Quarterly*. Finally, she has held numerous positions at her institution to promote diversity and inclusion, including faculty fellow for equity and diversity programs.

Marlene Williams, PhD, is an assistant professor and licensed psychologist in Texas. She currently serves as faculty in the graduate Counseling Psychology program at Texas Woman's University. Her research applies an intersectional feminist framework on exploring the impact of gendered racism on mental health outcomes among Black women. Marlene has a passionate commitment to social justice advocacy and identity-based equity, which is exemplified in her research, teaching, and practice. In addition to teaching, she is actively engaged in private practice, serving predominantly BIPOC and LGBTQIA+ individuals.

Janice D. Yoder, PhD, was editor of *Psychology of Women Quarterly* (2010–2015) and *Sex Roles* (2016–2020) after years of service to both journals' editorial boards and authoring published articles. She served as president of the Society for the Psychology of Women (2000–2001) and was the recipient of SPW's Carolyn Sherif Award (2016), the Distinguished Leader for Women in Psychology Award from APA's Committee on Women in Psychology

(2012), SPSSI's (APA, Division 9) Outstanding Teaching and Mentoring Award (2015), and the Denmark-Grunewald Award for Feminist Research and Service from the International Council of Psychologists (2015). Jan retired from the University of Akron as professor emerita in 2015 and moved to Kent State University as a research professor throughout her term as editor of *Sex Roles*. She now stays active professionally as an academic affiliate professor of psychology and women's, gender, and sexuality studies at Penn State and active personally with her granddaughter.

CPSIA information can be obtained
at www.ICGtesting.com
Printed in the USA
BVHW020935170323
660662BV00008B/1141